In Love with Paper Crafts

LEISURE ARTS
the art of everyday living
www.leisurearts.com

PAPER CRAFTS

Find us on
Facebook

Follow us on
twitter

www.PaperCraftsMag.com
www.PaperCraftsConnection.com

Editorial

Editor-in-Chief Jennifer Schaerer

Managing Editor Kerri Miller

Online Editor P. Kelly Smith

Creative Editor Susan Opel

Trends Editor Cath Edvalson

Editorial Assistant Ahtanya Johnson

Design

Art Director Matt Anderson

Graphic Designer Holly Mills

Photography bpd Studios, American Color

Offices

Editorial
Paper Crafts magazine
14850 Pony Express Rd., Suite 200
Bluffdale, UT 84065-4801

Phone 801-816-8300

Fax 801-816-8302

E-mail *editor@PaperCraftsMag.com*

Web site *www.PaperCraftsMag.com*

Published by Leisure Arts, Inc., 5701 Ranch Drive, Little Rock, Arkansas 72223-9633. 501-868-8800. *www.leisurearts.com*

Library of Congress Control Number: 2011920219
ISBN-13/EAN: 978-1-60900-245-9

Leisure Arts Staff

Editor-in-Chief Susan White Sullivan

Quilt and Craft Publications Director Cheryl Johnson

Special Projects Director Susan Frantz Wiles

Senior Prepress Director Mark Hawkins

Publishing Systems Administrator Becky Riddle

Publishing Systems Assistant Robert Young

Chief Executive Officer Rick Barton

Vice President and Chief Operating Officer Tom Siebenmorgen

Director of Finance and Administration Laticia Mull Dittrich

National Sales Director Martha Adams

Information Technology Director Hermine Linz

Vice President, Operations Jim Dittrich

Retail Customer Service Manager Stan Raynor

Print Production Manager Fred F. Pruss

Creative Crafts Group, LLC

President and CEO: Stephen J. Kent

VP/Group Publisher: Tina Battock

Chief Financial Officer: Mark F. Arnett

Controller: Jordan Bohrer

VP/Publishing Director: Joel P. Toner

VP/Production & Technology: Derek W. Corson

Visit our web sites:

www.PaperCraftsMag.com
www.PaperCraftsConnection.com
www.MoxieFabWorld.com

PUBLICATION—*Paper Crafts*™ (ISSN 1548-5706) (USPS 506250) Vol. 33, is published 6 times per year in Jan/Feb, Mar/Apr, May/June, Jul/Aug, Sept/Oct and Nov/Dec, by Creative Crafts Group, LLC, 741 Corporate Circle, Suite A, Golden CO 80401. Periodicals postage paid at Salt Lake City, UT and additional mailing offices.

REPRINT PERMISSION—For information on obtaining reprints and excerpts, please contact Wright's Reprints at 877/652-5295. (Customers outside the U.S. and Canada should call 281/419-5725.)

TRADEMARKED NAMES mentioned in this book may not always be followed with a trademark symbol. The names are used only in an editorial fashion and to the benefit of the trademark owner, with no intention of infringement of the trademark.

PROJECTS—*Paper Crafts* magazine believes these projects are reliable when made, but none are guaranteed. Due to different climatic conditions and variations in materials, *Paper Crafts* disclaims any liability for untoward results in doing the projects represented. Use of the magazine does not guarantee successful results. We provide this information WITHOUT WARRANTY OF ANY KIND, EXPRESSED, IMPLIED, OR STATUTORY; AND WE SPECIFICALLY DISCLAIM ANY IMPLIED WARRANTIES OF MERCHANTABILITY OR FITNESS FOR A PARTICULAR PURPOSE. Also, we urge parents to supervise young children carefully in their participation in any of these projects.

Printed in China

Posted under Canadian Publication Agreement Number 0551724

For the Love of Paper

From marriage and anniversary to Valentines and sweet treat gifts, love is expressed in so many ways to so many people in our lives. To help keep you inspired over the years, we've shared hundreds of ideas in our magazines and special issues. Now, in this new and dynamic anthology of paper crafted inspiration, you have a go-to resource for design guidance in all the categories of love.

If you're interested in scrapbook layouts highlighting items or hobbies you love, don't miss *A Lot Like Love* starting on p. 243. Do you need ideas for Valentine treats and greetings? There are dozens of ideas in our features on pgs. 58, 84, and 96. And there are always weddings and anniversaries to celebrate, so be sure to take a look at *Here Comes the Bride* (p. 162), *All Dressed in White* (p. 172) and *Wedding Wishes* (p. 183).

We've even included a section on techniques that you'll love to learn how to do. Featuring clever ways to use basic tools and products and a variety of stamping techniques, this *Love & Learn* section has ideas that you'll want to use on your very next project!

Go ahead—find your crafty sweet spot, connect with your passion for paper, and share your creativity with those you love.

Jennifer

In Love with Paper Crafts

93

111

Contents

ultifaceted event

Forever

Chocolate and You, what a sweet treat

Love Notes

Love-ly Paper Crafting

Create a romantic keepsake.

I say "I love you" frequently, but I don't often go deeper than that. This love-note layout tells my husband the feelings of my heart in a permanent way. Photos aren't necessary—this one is all about the words. To finish, add a title and a few embellishments. I plan to do this every year so he'll always know of my love.

All My Love by Maggie Holmes. **Supplies** *Patterned paper:* Hambly Screen Prints (brown), Heidi Swapp for Advantus (hearts) and Making Memories (pink scallop); *Acrylic heart, chipboard bracket and rhinestones:* Making Memories; *Ribbon:* American Crafts (diagonal stripe) and Making Memories (pink eyelet and pink stripe); *Pin accent and rub-ons:* American Crafts; *Brads:* Hot Off The Press; *Playing card:* Heidi Swapp for Advantus; *Pens:* American Crafts and Sharpie, Newell Rubbermaid; *Other:* Staples.

*M*ake a visible reminder of your love language.

"I love you up to the sky and back" is part of our family love language. I turned it into a more lasting and visible love note by creating this home-decor piece. It will hang in our playroom, where my children will be reminded of my love every single day.

Up to the Sky and Back by Maggie Holmes. **Supplies** *Letter stickers:* American Crafts (light-pink felt) and Making Memories (chipboard, glitter and dark-pink felt); *Crystal flourish:* Prima; *Heart mirror:* Heidi Swapp for Advantus; *Epoxy hearts, rhinestones and paint:* Making Memories.

Idea: To achieve the pink "frame" look, simply tape off inside the canvas's edge (around 1" in) and paint directly on the canvas.

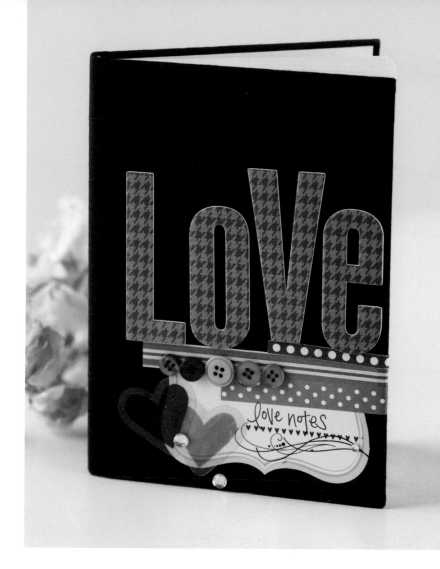

Write love letters to each other.

I'm a very lucky girl. My husband and children often leave me little notes expressing their love for me. But until now, I hadn't known what to do with them. This love-note journal allows us all to leave sentiments for one another in one cute book! We'll keep the journal out and available in our home all year long.

You could also use a journal to exchange love notes with distant family members. Imagine Grandma and Grandpa receiving a love-notes journal from you, adding their own messages and sending it back. This is a sure way to continue the spirit of love throughout the year.

Love Notes Journal by Maggie Holmes. **Supplies** *Journal:* Pottery Barn; *Rub-ons:* Heidi Grace Designs (swirls) and Luxe Designs (hearts and words); *Sticker tape:* Heidi Swapp for Advantus (pink dot and stripe) and Making Memories (gray dot); *Buttons and rhinestones:* Making Memories; *Acrylic and sticker hearts and chipboard letters:* Heidi Swapp for Advantus; *Journaling card:* Jenni Bowlin Studio; *Pen:* American Crafts.

INSIDE THE FRONT COVER

INTERIOR PAGES

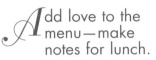dd love to the menu—make notes for lunch.

My sons go crazy for little notes in their school lunches. How cool will it be to have these all ready and on hand? My boys will be reminded of my love every day, not just on Valentine's Day.

Lunch Box Love Notes by *Maggie Holmes.* **Supplies** *Tin box:* Making Memories; *Rub-ons and stamps:* Luxe Designs; *Ink:* ColorBox, Clearsnap; *Corner-rounder punch:* Zutter Innovative Products; *Pen:* American Crafts; *Other:* Cardstock, ribbon and rhinestones.

Here's how easy it is to make little lunchtime love notes:

Note:

You can repurpose the cute packaging that scrapbook supplies come in. This silver tin originally held some Making Memories flowers.

1. Stamp image on paper.

2. Round the corners.

3. Draw a black border around the edge of each note.

4. Write notes and store in tin for everyday use.

$\mathcal{L}$ ist the things you love about someone.

I also wanted to document what I adore about each of my children. For Tyler's layout, I listed all his wonderful qualities. I included two small photos on my layout, but you don't have to include any. Just make sure the focus is on the things you love about that special someone. I know Tyler will love to read this page over and over.

16 Things *by Maggie Holmes.* **Supplies** *Cardstock:* Bazzill Basics Paper; *Patterned paper:* Heidi Swapp for Advantus; *Journaling shapes and rub-ons:* Luxe Designs; *Ticket:* Jenni Bowlin Studio; *Brads:* Hot Off The Press; *Corner-rounder punch:* Fiskars; *Chipboard, stickers, ribbon and pen:* American Crafts; *Other:* Staples.

My Romance

Editor: Nalalie Jackman

Give your creations a romantic feel by incorporating lace, buttons, and vintage patterns. It's remarkable how an old-fashioned key, hatpin, or antique ink finish can turn anything into a treasure.

Love Letters Box

Designer: Wendy Johnson

1. Cut patterned paper to fit around box; ink edges and adhere.
2. Cover lid with patterned paper; ink edges.
3. Ink edges of border strips; affix around lip of lid.
4. Adhere key and affix stickers to lid. *Note: Adhere flower, love, and alphabet stickers with foam tape.*
5. Print "Through the years" on cardstock. Trim, ink edges, and adhere.
6. Mat stickers with cardstock. Adhere keyhole and stickers to box front.

Finished size: 7½" x 7½" x 3"

SUPPLIES: *Cardstock:* (brown) *Patterned paper:* (Brown Paisley, Stripes from More To Adore collection) Close To My Heart *Dye ink:* (Close To Cocoa) Stampin' Up! *Accents:* (keyhole) Melissa Frances; (key) Westrim Crafts *Stickers:* (More To Adore alphabet, border strips, floral, love) Close To My Heart *Font:* (Pegasanna) Hallmark *Adhesive:* (foam tape) 3M *Other:* (box) The Craft Pedlars

Grow With Love Journal

Designer: Alisa Bangerter

❶ Adhere patterned paper, solid side up, to notebook cover. Ink edges.

❷ Stamp and emboss Bohemian Background.

❸ Ink ribbon and adhere around cover.

❹ Adhere rhinestones.

❺ Cut heart from pattern on p. 282. Ink edges and adhere.

❻ Stamp and emboss sentiment on solid side of patterned paper. Trim, round corners, and ink edges. Adhere with foam tape.

Finished size: 7½" x 9¾"

Je T'aime Card

Designer: Jessica Witty

❶ Make card from cardstock.

❷ Adhere patterned paper.

❸ Adhere heart.

❹ Ink ribbon; tie around front flap.

❺ Pin label to ribbon.

Finished size: 5½" square

SUPPLIES: *Cardstock:* (red) *Patterned paper:* (First Gift from Wonderland collection) Cosmo Cricket *Rubber stamps:* (All Things Grow With Love, Bohemian Background) Inkadinkado *Dye ink:* (black) Stewart Superior Corp. *Watermark ink:* Tsukineko *Embossing powder:* (black) Stampin' Up! *Accents:* (rhinestones) Westrim Crafts *Fibers:* (cream ribbon) Making Memories *Adhesive:* (foam tape) Making Memories *Tool:* (corner rounder punch) *Other:* (composition notebook)

SUPPLIES: *Cardstock:* (Basic Black) Stampin' Up! *Patterned paper:* (Cream Victorian Die Cut) Creative Imaginations *Chalk ink:* (Charcoal) Clearsnap *Accents:* (black safety pin) Making Memories; (fabric label) Me & My Big Ideas; (red wood heart) *Fibers:* (black gingham ribbon) Jo-Ann Stores

Romantic Monogrammed Journal

Designer: Nichole Heady

❶ Adhere patterned paper to binder covers.

❷ Cut cardstock to cover spine; stitch edges and adhere.

❸ Tie ribbon around binder.

❹ Punch tag from each cardstock. Stamp corner flourish on cream tag and ink edges; apply rub-on. Adhere lace trim to brown tag. Tie tags to ribbon around binder with ribbon.

❺ Stamp Le London Script on flowers; ink edges. Attach together with brad. Adhere to pin and insert in ribbon knot.

Finished size: 5¼" x 7½"

Treasures of Yesterday Box

Designer: Susan Neal

PREPARE

❶ Remove hinges and clasp.

❷ Cover box with patterned paper; sand and ink edges.

❸ Cut patterned paper to fit top of lid; sand edges. Cut slightly smaller piece of patterned paper; adhere to piece, solid side up. Stitch and ink edges; adhere.

❹ Replace hinges and clasp.

DECORATE

❶ Adhere ribbon to lid and box.

❷ Trim stickers; ink edges and mat with cardstock. Stitch edges. Attach brads and adhere with foam tape.

Finished size: 5¼" x 6" x 5¼"

SUPPLIES: *Cardstock:* (brown, cream) Bazzill Basics Paper *Patterned paper:* (Tranquility from Classical Garden collection) Webster's Pages *Rubber stamp:* (Le London Script) Stampabilities *Clear stamp:* (corner flourish from Vintage Labels set) Fontwerks *Specialty ink:* (Burnt Umber hybrid) Stewart Superior Corp. *Accents:* (stick pin) Around The Block; (decorative brad) The Paper Studio; (cream flowers) Making Memories *Rub-on:* (Fred alphabet) American Crafts *Fibers:* (cream organdy ribbon) Offray; (cream polka dot ribbon) American Crafts; (white lace trim) Making Memories *Tools:* (tag punches) McGill *Other:* (binder) Hot Off The Press

SUPPLIES: *Cardstock:* (Espresso) Provo Craft *Patterned paper:* (Circles/Blue Batik, Blue Tiles/Dark Brown Weave, Plaid/Dark Brown Batik from Timeless collection) Deja Views *Dye ink:* (Walnut Ink) Ranger Industries *Accents:* (antique gold brads) Imaginisce *Stickers:* (treasures of yesterday, we remember) Deja Views *Fibers:* (brown velvet ribbon) Deja Views *Adhesive:* (foam tape) 3M *Other:* (box) Jo-Ann Stores

Buttons & Lace Love Card

Designer: Kim Hughes

❶ Make card from solid side of patterned paper; sand and ink edges.

❷ Cut patterned paper pieces; sand edges and adhere.

❸ Stitch edges of card and paper pieces.

❹ Tie lace around front flap. Sand edges of label; adhere.

❺ Adhere heart.

❻ Thread floss through buttons; adhere.

Finished size: 4¼" x 5"

Belle Jardinière Frame

Designer: Cath Edvalson

❶ Cut patterned paper to fit frame and adhere; sand edges.

❷ Affix sticker.

❸ Trim die cut; adhere with foam tape.

❹ Insert photo.

Finished size: 8" x 8"

SUPPLIES: *Patterned paper:* (Worn Lined Background) Scenic Route; (Ivy from Samantha collection, Kelp from Crush collection) Crate Paper; (Ledger, Print from Vintage Red collection) Jenni Bowlin *Dye ink:* (brown) Around The Block *Accents:* (light green buttons) Autumn Leaves; (clear acrylic heart) Heidi Grace Designs; (love label) Daisy D's *Fibers:* (cream lace) Beaux Regards; (white floss) Scrapworks

SUPPLIES: All supplies from My Mind's Eye unless otherwise noted. *Patterned paper:* (Family Tree Peach Floral from Tres Bien collection) *Accents:* (vintage die cut) *Sticker:* (border strip) *Adhesive:* (decoupage) Michaels; (foam tape) *Other:* (wood frame) Provo Craft; (photo)

Gratitude Card

Designer: Laura Griffin

1. Make card from cardstock; trim bottom of front flap with decorative-edge scissors.
2. Cut patterned paper to fit card front; ink edges. Trim bottom with decorative-edge scissors. Adhere.
3. Stamp image.
4. Tie with lace trim.

Finished size: 5½" x 4"

SUPPLIES: *Cardstock:* (Celery) Stampin' Up! *Patterned paper:* (Floral) My Mind's Eye *Clear stamp:* (gratitude from G set) Hero Arts *Dye ink:* (Soft Leaf) Stewart Superior Corp. *Fibers:* (white lace trim) Making Memories *Tool:* (decorative-edge scissors)

Yours Truly Card

Designer: Melanie Douthit

1. Make card from cardstock.
2. Cut patterned paper in graduated sizes; mat together. Mat with cardstock. Ink and stitch edges. Tie with ribbon. Adhere.
3. Adhere lace trim.
4. Cover heart and tag with patterned paper.
5. Mat tag with patterned paper; trim with decorative-edge scissors. Adhere. Adhere flower and button; apply rub-on.
6. Sand edges of heart; adhere. Adhere buttons.

Finished size: 4¼" x 5½"

SUPPLIES: *Cardstock:* (Island Mist Light, Sugar Cream) Prism *Patterned paper:* (Enchantment, Glee, Joy from Delight collection) Dream Street Papers *Chalk ink:* (Chestnut Roan, Sapphire) Clearsnap *Accents:* (chipboard heart) The Paper Studio; (chipboard tag) Sarah Heidt Photo Craft; (light blue flower) Prima; (cream flat buttons) Autumn Leaves; (pearl button) *Rub-on:* (yours truly) Flair Designs *Fibers:* (cream organdy ribbon, lace trim) *Tool:* (decorative-edge scissors)

With Love Card

Designer: Dee Gallimore-Perry

❶ Make card from cardstock.

❷ Adhere lace trims to outside edge.

❸ Cut patterned paper to fit card front; sand edges and adhere.

❹ Cut patterned paper; sand edges and mat with patterned paper. Sand edges. Tie with ribbon and adhere. Add random zigzag stitches.

❺ Stitch card edges.

❻ Paint heart; sand edges and adhere with foam tape. Affix sticker. Tie string through button; adhere.

Finished size: 4½" x 8"

⁵ Friendship Card

Designer: Melissa Phillips

❶ Make card from cardstock.

❷ Ink edges of sticker; affix.

❸ Cut patterned paper pieces; ink edges and adhere. Stitch edges.

❹ Adhere buttons.

❺ Cut slit in card fold; thread ribbon snap through slit. Punch hole, place flower over hole, and snap in place.

Finished size: 3¾" x 5"

SUPPLIES: *Cardstock:* (white) Bazzill Basics Paper *Patterned paper:* (Blue & Green Bouquet, Blue Gingham, Blue Lace Column from Addison collection) K&Company *Paint:* (Wicker White) Plaid *Accents:* (blue button) Lasting Impressions for Paper; (chipboard heart) Heidi Swapp *Sticker:* (with love) K&Company *Fibers:* (gold organdy ribbon, cream crochet lace trim) Bo-Bunny Press; (cream lace trim, white string) *Adhesive:* (foam tape)

SUPPLIES: *Cardstock:* (cream shimmer) Bazzill Basics Paper *Patterned paper:* (Gracie, Sara) Melissa Frances; *Dye ink:* (Old Paper) Ranger Industries *Accents:* (cream ribbon snap, cream buttons) Melissa Frances; (cream flower) *Sticker:* (friendship) Melissa Frances

Birthday Flowers Card

Designer: Anabelle O'Malley

PREPARE

❶ Make card from cardstock.

❷ Cut cardstock block slightly smaller than card; ink edges.

❸ Punch border in patterned paper strip; ink edges and adhere.

❹ Cut pieces of remaining patterned paper; ink edges and adhere.

❺ Adhere trim.

❻ Adhere to card.

DECORATE

❶ Ink edges of tags; adhere.

❷ Adhere flowers, label, and rhinestones.

Finished size: 4¼" x 5½"

SUPPLIES: *Cardstock:* (aqua) Bazzill Basics Paper; (yellow) Paper Salon *Patterned paper:* (Polka Bursts from Sizzle collection) Paper Salon; (Worn Blue Grid Background) Scenic Route; (My North Star from Blue Cardigan collection) Imagination Project *Chalk ink:* (brown) Clearsnap *Accents:* (rhinestones) Darice; (cream flowers) My Mind's Eye; (patterned tags) *Sticker:* (happy birthday label) EK Success *Fibers:* (cream lace trim) May Arts *Tool:* (border punch) Fiskars

Sweet Heart Card

Designer: Kim Hughes

❶ Make card from solid side of patterned paper; ink edges.

❷ Cut patterned paper; ink and stitch edges. Adhere, solid side up. Affix sticker.

❸ Cut photo corner and heart from solid side of patterned paper; ink and stitch edges.

❹ Cut patterned paper; ink, stitch edges, and adhere. Adhere photo corner and heart.

❺ Apply rub-ons.

❻ Pin together flowers; adhere feather to back. Adhere.

❼ Cover flourish with solid side of patterned paper; ink edges and adhere.

Finished size: 6¼" x 4"

SUPPLIES: *Patterned paper:* (Snapdragon from Samantha collection) Crate Paper; (Dot/Rose from Darling collection) My Mind's Eye; (Salt from Infuse collection) BasicGrey *Chalk ink:* (Chestnut Roan) Clearsnap *Accents:* (chipboard flourish) Bo-Bunny Press; (cream flowers) Prima; (beaded pin) Making Memories; (white feather) *Rub-ons:* (arrow, sweet) American Crafts *Sticker:* (border strip) My Mind's Eye

✦5✦ Adore Card

Designer: Teri Anderson

❶ Make card from patterned paper.

❷ Adhere patterned paper piece.

❸ Adhere main die cut; adhere roses and bow die cuts with foam tape.

❹ Adhere beads.

❺ Spell "Adore" with stickers. Attach bookplate using brads.

Finished size: 5" x 6"

SUPPLIES: *Patterned paper:* (Pink Line Die Cut from Sweet Pea collection) Creative Imaginations; (Blue Floral from You're a Natural collection) My Mind's Eye *Accents:* (flower die cuts) Anna Griffin; (cream bookplate) Making Memories; (pearl beads) K&Company; (silver brads) Oriental Trading Co. *Stickers:* (Tiny alphabet) Making Memories *Adhesive:* (foam tape)

Lucky You're Mine Card

Designer: Sherry Wright

❶ Make card from patterned paper.

❷ Cut patterned paper pieces; ink edges and adhere.

❸ Punch hearts from cardstock; ink edges and adhere.

❹ Adhere lace trim and knotted ribbon.

❺ Attach brads to label; adhere.

❻ Adhere medallion to button; adhere.

❼ Affix sticker.

Finished size: 6" x 5"

SUPPLIES: *Cardstock:* (light blue) *Patterned paper:* (Blue Floral Die Cut from Blue Bell collection) Creative Imaginations *Chalk ink:* (French Blue) Clearsnap *Accents:* (chipboard label) Creative Imaginations; (light blue brads) Making Memories; (white button) *Stickers:* (flourish, medallion) Creative Imaginations *Fibers:* (blue velvet ribbon) Michaels; (cream lace trim) *Tool:* (heart punch) Marvy Uchida

new

love

Love doesn't make
the world go round.
Love is what makes
the ride worthwhile.

Robert and Stacy, 2008

Where is it written that love can only be represented by shades of red and pink?
Truly, the entire color palette is at our disposal when we're creating love-themed pages.
This year, celebrate your loved ones with layouts donned in unexpected color combinations
for a fresh, updated look.

DESIGN TIP

To keep the mood as tender as the
photo, follow Stacy Cohen's example.
Choose light colors and delicate patterns
and keep the design simple, adding
layers of cardstock and patterned paper
to give the layout more depth. There's
not a shred of red in sight, but isn't it
romantic?

PHOTO TIP

Instead of taking a photo of two people
looking directly into the camera, ask one
to give you eye contact while the other
looks at her partner or sneaks a little
peck on the cheek. The interaction is
sure to produce great expressions.

Love by Stacy Cohen. **Supplies** *Cardstock:* Bazzill Basics Paper; *Patterned paper:* Lily Bee; *Letter stickers:* American Crafts; *Chipboard heart:* Heidi Swapp for Advantus; *Pearls:* Kaisercraft; *Charm and pearl beads:* Darice; *Paint:* Ranger Industries; *Thread:* Gütermann; *Font:* Franklin Gothic; *Adhesive:* Fabri-tac, Beacon Adhesives; Scotch ATG, 3M; Tombow; *Other:* Buttons and ribbon.

I have been with him nearly every day for the past ten years and I still LOVE this man!

Sure, we have had rough patches. Sure, we fight. But getting married was still the best decision I ever made. Kelby is my soul mate. He is my best friend! Nobody knows me like he does, and yet he loves me too.

JOURNALING TIP

Pull a phrase from your journaling text to use as the page title. If you're stumped for what your title should be, sit down and write your journaling—something might just jump out at you, as it did for Pamela Young.

DESIGN TIP

Don't be afraid to let an embellishment trail off the bottom or side of the page.

IF YOU LIVE TO BE A HUNDRED, I WANT TO BE A HUNDRED MINUS ONE DAY SO I NEVER HAVE TO LIVE WITHOUT YOU."

—A. A. Milne

Love This Man by Pamela Young. **Supplies** Patterned paper and stickers: Pebbles Inc.; Stamps: Unity Stamp Company; Ink: Stampin' Up!; Glitter and paint: Scribbles; Lace trim: Webster's Pages; Embroidery floss: DMC; Adhesive: Tombow.

PHOTO TIP

Combine pictures of people (such as siblings) from a variety of different times and occasions. Your layout will showcase your subjects' relationship more thoroughly than if you used a single photograph.

All We Need Is Love by Stephanie Howell. **Supplies** *Cardstock:* Bazzill Basics Paper; *Patterned paper:* Creative Imaginations (orange scallop) and Making Memories (kraft); *Letter stickers:* American Crafts (medium black), Cosmo Cricket (large black) and Making Memories (mini); *Stick pins:* Making Memories; *Brads:* Creative Café, EK Success; *Transparencies:* Little Yellow Bicycle, *Rub-ons:* Glitz Design; *Pearls:* Kaisercraft; *Felt flowers and pen:* American Crafts; *Adhesive:* Glue Dots International and Scrapbook Adhesives by 3L.

TECHNIQUE TIP

Pull out your sewing machine (or you can hand-stitch) and create several hearts in various thread colors for a great background design.

In Love by Cindy Tobey. **Supplies** *Cardstock:* Bo-Bunny Press; *Patterned paper:* Bo-Bunny Press (yellow dot) and Cosmo Cricket (others); *Chipboard:* BasicGrey (letters) and Scenic Route (heart).

TECHNIQUE TIP

If you like the look of doodles but aren't comfortable going totally free-form on your page, try Andrea Friebus' solution: doodle on squares of cardstock and arrange them in a linear fashion on your layout. You'll end up with a fun, unique look that won't overwhelm your photos.

TITLE TIP

Can you take part of your name and highlight it to come up with a creative title? Andrea's title is a play on her last name. It's so clever! If your name doesn't lend itself to capitalization manipulation, consider trying a similar approach with a word that has smaller words inside it.

friebUS *by Andrea Friebus.* **Supplies** *Cardstock:* American Crafts; *Patterned paper:* Chatterbox (white flourish) and Creative Memories (black dot); *Border die cut:* Bazzill Basics Paper; *Tags:* Creative Imaginations; *Brads:* Making Memories; *Felt:* Queen & Co.; *Letter stickers:* me & my BIG ideas; *Die-cutting machine:* Slice, Making Memories; *Pen:* Sharpie, Newell Rubbermaid; *Adhesive:* Therm O Web.

Sensational Schemes

Try one of these great color palettes for your layouts this month.

Amber, Jetstream, Thunder
Bazzill Basics Paper
BazzillBasics.com

Papaya Puree Light, Crabapple Light, Wizard Medium
Prism Papers
PrismPapers.com

Bright Magenta, Re-Entry Red, Cocoa
Wausau Paper
WausauPaper.com **ck**

WHEN IT'S SUMMER TIME, the lovin' is easy. Maybe that's why so many weddings take place during the summer months. Chances are, you'll be scrapbooking the big event sometime soon; if not for yourself, for someone you love. But don't let the formality of the occasion restrict your scrapbooking style. You can still have fun with wedding pages. Our readers show you how to capture anything a wedding can throw at you—from the expected to the unexpected, the good to the bad, the solemn to the silly. Capture it all with style!

Some photos are must-haves, and a picture of your wedding rings is one of them. Remember to capture this special symbol of your love. **Piradee Talvanna** reinforced the symbolism represented in her photo by accenting it with heart patterned paper, a die-cut heart, and words of love.

Together by Piradee Talvanna. **Supplies:** *Cardstock:* Bazzill Basics Paper; *Patterned paper:* My Mind's Eye; *Chipboard accents:* American Crafts and Maya Road; *Brad and pen:* American Crafts; *Punches:* Martha Stewart Crafts; *Die cuts:* My Mind's Eye and Ellison; *Crackle paint:* Advantus; *Adhesive:* EK Success and Glue Dots International.

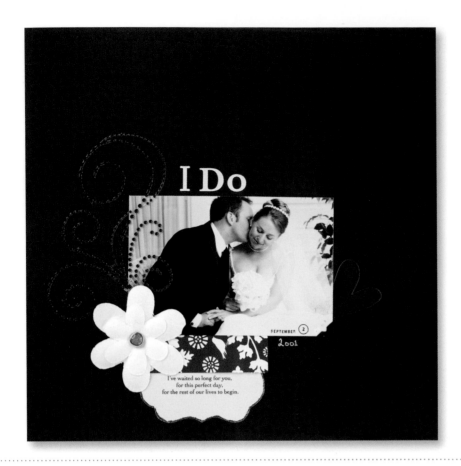

Julie Fairman took her very traditional layout and made it shine by adding a rhinestone flourish to her page. The look is elegant and classy.

DESIGN TIP:

Use a small amount of a vibrant color on your page to add interest without overwhelming your photo.

I Do by Julie Fairman. **Photo** by Eric Cable. **Supplies:** *Cardstock:* Die Cuts with a View and Prima; *Flower, jewel brad, and letter stickers:* Making Memories; *Journaling tag:* K&Company; *Rub-ons:* BasicGrey; *Acrylic heart:* Advantus; *Pen:* Sakura; *Glitter glue:* Ranger Industries.

The photos on **Stephanie Klauch's** page look wedding-typical, but don't let that little-boy charm fool you. This layout is about the lengths to which Stephanie had to go to get her little boy to pose with her sister, the bride. A game of I Spy to the rescue! What behind-the-scenes wedding stories can you share in your scrapbooks?

PHOTO TIP:

Distract non-posers (the young and the not-so-young alike), so their focus is not on the camera. The result will be more natural and relaxed photos.

I Spy by Stephanie Klauch. **Sketch** by Becky Higgins. **Supplies:** *Cardstock:* Bazzill Basics Paper; *Patterned paper:* Fancy Pants Designs and Making Memories; *Brads and flowers:* Heidi Grace Designs; *Letter stickers:* BasicGrey; *Rub-ons:* Fancy Pants Designs; *Pen:* Sakura; *Adhesive:* Tombow.

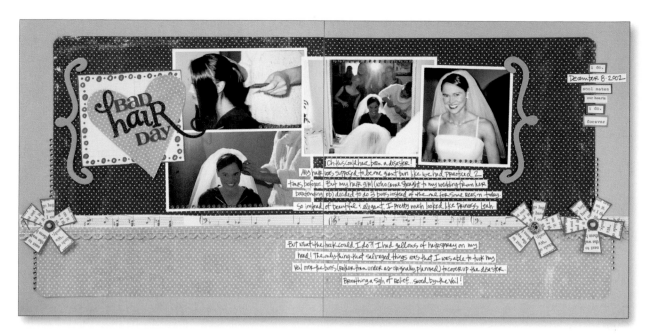

It's not a big event until something goes wrong, and weddings are no exception. Unfortunately for **Gretchen McElveen** that something was her hair style. Not a good time for a bad hair day! But she smiled through it (note the photo proof!), and used that something wrong to create a great scrapbook page. Don't be afraid to capture these moments. Someday you'll look back on them and laugh—we promise.

DESIGN TIP:

Add a little sparkle to your photos by adding strips of bling along their edges.

Bad Hair Day by Gretchen McElveen. **Supplies:** *Cardstock:* Prism Papers; *Patterned paper:* KI Memories and My Mind's Eye; *Brads:* BasicGrey; *Rhinestones:* Advantus; *Chipboard and pen:* American Crafts; *Stickers:* BasicGrey and Making Memories; *Punches:* Creative Memories and Fiskars Americas; *Adhesive:* Therm O Web.

Ah, cutting the cake . . . eating the cake . . . wearing the cake? For **Lisa Pate**, the cake was more than just good dessert; it became a moment that symbolized how much fun she and her husband always have together. To give her layout a playful feel, she highlighted her "wearing of the cake" photo, and added several whimsical touches (such as her choice of fonts, brackets, and a fun border) to her layout to enhance the playful mood. Take a cue from Lisa and capture the fun aspects of the big day and accentuate them with fun product.

PHOTO TIP:

Don't just rely on your photographer to document the big day. Ask family and friends to snap away and capture all of those behind-the-scenes moments.

Cutting the Cake by Lisa Pate. **Digital Supplies:** *Software:* Adobe; *Cardstock:* Michelle Martin, Andrea Victoria, and Rob and Bob Studios; *Letters:* Katie Pertiet and Pattie Knox; *Embellishments:* Anna Aspnes, Katie Pertiet, Lynn Grieveson, and Rob and Bob Studios; *Brushes:* Katie Pertiet, Ali Edwards, Art Warehouse, and Lynn Grieveson; *Font:* VT Portable Remington.

Neutrals Punch Pad
Martha Stewart Crafts
marthastewartcrafts.com

Mr. & Mrs. line
The Paper Company Studios
tpcstudios.com

Le' Romantique Collection
Graphic45
G45papers.com

Elegance line
K&Company
kandcompany.com

JOURNALING PROMPTS:

- The first time I wore my wedding ring I . . .

- I certainly didn't expect _____ to happen at the reception.

- I didn't think it was funny at the time, but now . . .

- The best part about picking out my dress was . . .

- The worst thing about finding the right cake was . . .

- I chose my wedding colors because . . .

- The funniest thing that happened on our wedding day was . . .

QUOTES TO USE ON YOUR PAGE:

- Love one another and you will be happy. It's as simple and as difficult as that.

  – MICHAEL LEUNIG

- When you meet someone who can cook and do housework—don't hesitate a minute—marry him.

  – UNKNOWN

- I love thee to the depth and breadth and height my soul can reach.

  – ELIZABETH BARRETT BROWNING

- A man in love is incomplete until he is married. Then he's finished.

  – ZSA ZSA GABOR **ck**

HAP·PI·NESS

[I found happiness and joy with you]

Playing together, giggling together, sharing secrets, and stealing sweet little kisses. It's these little glimpses of "everyday love" that make me smile from the inside out, and prove that at the end of the day, you genuinely do love one another after all... despite all the arguing.

sweet little moments

Focus on the love you share with the people dearest to you—say thanks for everything they do and to let them know how they make your life complete.

ACTIVITY #1:

Scrapbook the everyday activities your children enjoy together that have helped them grow close. For a fun twist, interview them about the activities they enjoy doing with their siblings. Incorporate their answers as the journaling on your page.

Sheri Reguly backed the holes in her chipboard heart with assorted scraps of colored cardstock to bring a lighthearted, playful energy to her page.

Sweet Little Moments by Sheri Reguly. **Supplies** *Software:* Picture It! Photo Premium 9, Microsoft; *Cardstock:* Bazzill Basics Paper; *Patterned paper:* Bo-Bunny Press (pink dot), Creative Imaginations (cream dot) and Heidi Grace Designs (birds); *Chipboard flower button, chipboard heart and metal clip:* Making Memories; *Buttons:* BasicGrey (pink) and Doodlebug Design (white); *Digital stamp:* Happiness by Paislee Press; *Journaling tag die cut:* Jenni Bowlin Studio; *Fonts:* Constantia (title) and Times New Roman (journaling); *Other:* Adhesive foam, embroidery floss and thread.

ACTIVITY #2:

Create an oversized card for your child to give to her dad for Valentine's Day. Simply create an 8½" x 11" layout, then mount it on the front of a folded 11" x 17" sheet of paper or cardstock (you can purchase individual sheets at a copy center). Have your child write a message to her father and voilà! An instant keepsake.

INSIDE OF CARD

ACTIVITY #3:

Spend the day on a photo scavenger hunt, taking 26 pictures of items you love—one starting with each letter of the alphabet.

Funny Valentine Card by Cindy Tobey. **Supplies**
Software: Adobe Photoshop Elements 6.0; *Cardstock:* Bazzill Basics Paper; *Patterned paper, buttons and rub-ons:* Fancy Pants Designs; *Letter stickers:* American Crafts; *Paint:* Making Memories; *Ink:* Clearsnap; *Thread:* Gutermann.

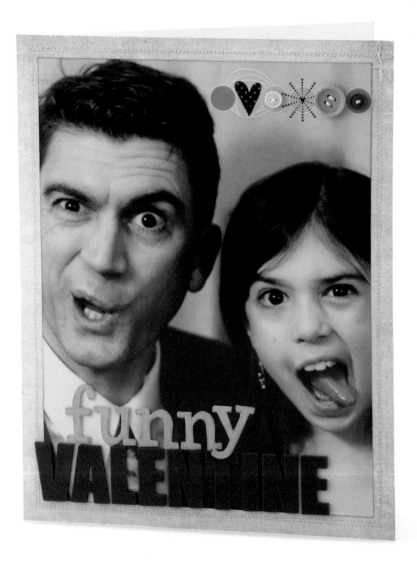

Valentine ABCs by Amanda Johnston. **Supplies** *Software:* Adobe Photoshop Elements 5.0; *Digital patterned paper:* Sande Krieger (red) and Shabby Princess (cream); *Letter stickers:* Jesse Edwards; *Template (altered):* Miss Mint; *Chipboard action:* Atomic Cupcake; *Corner rounder:* Amanda's own design; *Fonts:* Greer, Times New Roman and Turtle Club.

He Crazy in Love by Liana Suwandi. **Supplies** Software: Adobe Photoshop; Cardstock: Bazzill Basics Paper (white and red) and We R Memory Keepers (turquoise); Patterned paper: BasicGrey (red floral) and We R Memory Keepers (paisley and stripe); Rub-ons: 7gypsies ("Happily Ever After"), BasicGrey (flourish and "Happy Couple") and Die Cuts With a View ("Love"); Stamps: 7gypsies (round) and Stampin' Up! (heart); Ink: Stampin' Up!; Ribbon and chipboard: We R Memory Keepers; Letter stickers: EK Success; Brads: KI Memories (green) and SEI (red); Decorative paper strips: Doodlebug Design; Circle cutter: Making Memories; Font: CBX Leen.

ACTIVITY #4:

Create a heart-shaped photo collage with your favorite pictures. The photos don't have to be from weddings but could be a mix of favorite photos from everyday activities your family enjoys together.

Create A Heart Frame

① Find a heart-shaped paper or cut one from a 12" x 12" sheet.

② Use a craft knife to cut a smaller heart inside the heart-shaped paper (just eyeball it).

③ Cut apart the bottom edge of the heart frame and overlap the ends for a unique twist.

ACTIVITY #5:

Bake a heart-themed breakfast. Not only do I love Lisa Dorsey's incredible layout design, but I also loved the activity she scrapbooked—and I thought you would love it, too. (Check out the steps at right.)

ACTIVITY #6:

Make a "clothesline" for love notes or favorite photos to display somewhere in your home.

SERVE A "HEARTY" BREAKFAST

1. Make heart-shaped pancakes (Lisa also made cakes from a heart-shaped baking tin).

2. Punch or cut small hearts, journal on them, then place them on the breakfast plate with temporary adhesive. You could also arrange strawberries on the plate to form heart shapes.

3. Create heart-shaped placemats from 12" x 12" cardstock.

4. Apply punched, rub-on or sticker hearts to a glass for milk or juice.

5. Enjoy a delightful meal with your family—one that will always bring back happy memories.

My Sweet Cakes *by Lisa Dorsey.* **Supplies** *Cardstock:* Bazzill Basics Paper; *Patterned paper:* Chatterbox (stripe) and SEI (dot); *Rub-ons and letter stickers:* American Crafts; *Ribbon:* C.M. Offray & Son; *Epoxy heart:* Making Memories; *Font:* Century Gothic; *Other:* Buttons and thread.

Heart Clothesline *by Wilna Furstenberg*

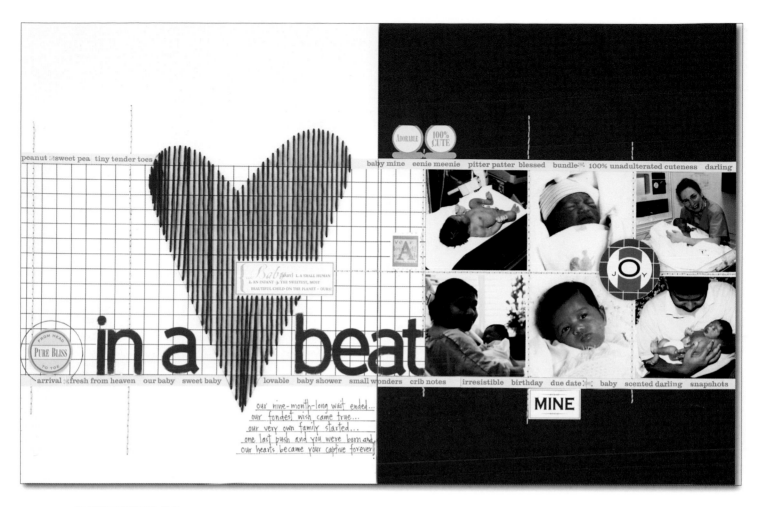

Create a layout about the most meaningful event in your life that you haven't scrapbooked yet—whatever the theme may be. Today is the perfect time to celebrate it and how the event changed your life.

In a {Heart}beat *by Mou Saha.* **Supplies** *Software:* Adobe Photoshop Elements 5.0; *Cardstock:* Frances Meyer; *Patterned paper and letter stickers:* Luxe Designs; *Cardstock stickers:* 7gypsies; *Embroidery floss:* DMC; *Circle punch:* Marvy Uchida; *Pen:* American Crafts.

Stitch A Heart Design

❶ Use pencil to lightly draw a heart outline.

❷ Punch holes around the edges of the traced heart.

❸ Thread embroidery floss vertically through the holes.

Heart You *by Wilna Furstenberg.* **Supplies** *Cardstock, patterned paper, chipboard letters and paint:* Making Memories; *Lace paper:* KI Memories; *Pen:* Sharpie, Newell Rubbermaid; *Other:* Miniature clothespins, watercolors, masking tape, string, foam squares and thread.

Nothing better for me than to hear Jadenn call for me early in the morning, to get his kisses and hugs during the day. Nothing better to see Anthony doing good at school, being more happy and to hear him laugh. Nothing better than a kiss from Raymond, a good conversation and a snuggle on the couch while watching a movie together. These things do not cost a thing, so it is really true, the best things in life are free.

ACTIVITY #8:

Write a love letter to your husband or boyfriend, letting him know all the "little things" he does that have captured your heart.

ACTIVITY #9:

Get out from behind the camera (yes, I know you live behind it) and take pictures of you with your loved ones. You take plenty of photos of them, so give them the gift of photos of you together! They'll be some of the most precious photos you take for them, and it can take as little as five minutes to capture great pictures of you hugging. Simply ask another family member or a friend to take some shots, use the self-timer mode or hold the camera at arm's length. It's easy—and worth it!

The Best Things in Life Are Free *by Corinne Delis.* **Supplies** *Cardstock:* Bazzill Basics Paper; *Letter stickers:* American Crafts (blue), Jenni Bowlin Studio (red) and Toga Scrapbooking (black); *Acrylic heart:* Heidi Swapp for Advantus; *Felt hearts:* American Crafts; *Pen:* Pentel; *Font:* Arial.

FILL UP YOUR HEART

The love a mother has for her child fills her heart to the brim. To reflect this indescribable emotion, Laura Vegas made the heart on her page burst at the seams with happy flowers and bright buttons. Here's how to create this look in two easy steps:

With All My Heart by Laura Vegas. **Supplies** *Cardstock:* Bazzill Basics Paper; *Patterned paper, buttons, die-cutting machine, heart dies, flowers and ribbon:* Making Memories; *Stamp:* Hero Arts; *Ink:* Tsukineko; *Embossing plate and embossing machine:* Cuttlebug, Provo Craft; *Silver accents:* Michaels; *Pens:* American Crafts; *Adhesive:* All Night Media, EK Success and Therm O Web.

❶ Die-cut a heart from a block of white cardstock, set the heart aside and affix dimensional adhesive to the back.

❷ Affix the white block to a block of red cardstock, and adhere buttons and flowers to the center of the heart.

Love & Learn

While you are creating pretty paper crafts for your loved ones, try some different techniques and turn the project into a learning experience.

DECORATIVE-EDGE SCISSORS TECHNIQUE

Make instant rickrack

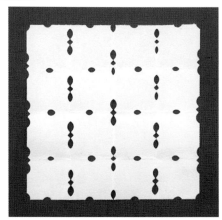
Fold and trim to create paper lace

Fashion faux postage stamps

Create a cardstock bookplate

Add texture by layering different edges

Trim quick and easy borders

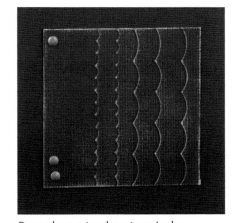
Dry emboss using the scissors' edge

Create clever frames

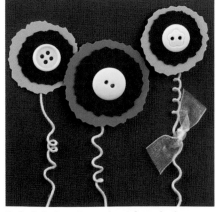
Embellish the edges of motifs and other focal points

Sending My Love Card

Designer: Alisa Bangerter

STAMP

1. Cut rectangle from transparency to create stencil. Place stencil on cardstock and sponge rectangle with ink. Remove transparency.

2. Stamp heart, flourish, love, and numbers.

3. Repeat steps 1-2 for remaining rectangles.

4. Pierce around stamped images and trim piece with decorative-edge scissors.

5. Adhere to cardstock with foam tape. Mat piece with cardstock.

CARD

1. Make card from cardstock. Adhere patterned paper.

2. Trim cardstock strip with decorative-edge scissors, mat with cardstock, and adhere.

3. Print "Sending my love" on cardstock, sponge with ink, and adhere with foam tape.

4. Adhere stamped piece.

Finished size: 5" x 7"

DESIGNER TIP

Create faux postage stamps by combining your decorative-edge scissors with stickers, stamps, or rubons. Change the colors and motifs to create postage-inspired projects for Christmas, birthdays, thank you, and much more.

SUPPLIES: *Cardstock:* (brown, pink, white) *Patterned paper:* (Patio Umbrella from Daydream collection) October Afternoon *Transparency:* Hammermill *Clear stamps:* (heart from Brushed Designs set) Fancy Pants Designs; (love from Just Between Friends set) Fiskars; (numbers, flourish from Wedding Day set) Papertrey Ink *Dye ink:* (Cool Caribbean, Creamy Caramel) Stampin' Up!; (Twilight) Close To My Heart; (pink) *Font:* (Script MT Bold) www.myfonts.com *Adhesive:* (foam tape) *Tools:* (decorative-edge scissors) Fiskars

Reveal background images with a punch out.

Create special effects with different mediums, such as watercolor crayons.

"Kiss" stamps with inked or un-inked background stamps to create new patterns.

Stamp a background image on different papers. Cut and assemble for a mosaic look.

Background stamps create consistent patterns over large elements like plain silk flowers.

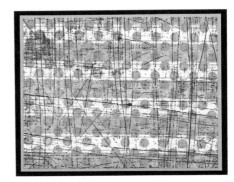

Create a completely new look by combining two or more background stamps and colors.

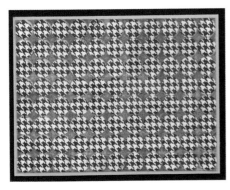

Stamp one background image and heat-emboss to create a mask. Stamp again with a different image and wipe ink from the embossed pattern.

Cut or punch part of the background image and layer for a focal point that really pops.

Spotlight part of a background image by inking that portion with a darker color than the rest of the image. After stamping, brighten the area with chalk.

Perfect Pair Card

Designer: Susan Neal

1. Make card from cardstock.
2. Die-cut two 3" pears from cardstock. Trim piece to 5" x 3½".
3. Type sentiment and print on paper. Adhere die cut piece with repositionable adhesive and print again.
4. Stamp Paisley twice on cardstock. Trim and adhere behind die cut piece with foam tape.
5. Mat piece with cardstock; adhere to card.

Finished size: 6" x 4½"

SUPPLIES: Cardstock: (Precious, Daisy, black, white) Bazzill Basics Paper Paper: (white) Rubber stamp: (Paisley) Stampin' Up! Pigment ink: (Onyx Black) Tsukineko Fonts: (Anglia Script) www.fontshop.com; (Arial) Microsoft Adhesive: (foam tape) 3L; (repositionable) Die: (pear) Provo Craft Tool: (die cut machine) Provo Craft

Love You Baby Tag

Designer: Tresa Black

1. Make tag from patterned paper.
2. Brush edges with paint.
3. Mat tag with cardstock; distress edges.
4. Stamp sentiment (see "Build a Sentiment Technique").
5. Attach flowers with brads.
6. Adhere square of cardstock to tag. Adhere hemp loop and button.

Finished size: 3¾" x 6"

DESIGNER TIPS

- Use fine-tip, sharp scissors to carefully cut clear stamps apart. After stamping the image, return the pieces back to their original sheets to use again.
- Mix and match clear sentiment stamps to maximize your options for sentiments. Mismatched fonts and differing sizes add to the charm of the design.

SUPPLIES: *Cardstock:* (cranberry, black) Close To My Heart *Patterned paper:* (Velvet Floral from Ooh La La collection) Bo-Bunny Press *Clear stamps:* (lips, love from Love & Kisses set; you from Happy Flowers set; baby from New Arrival Set) Adornit-Carolee's Creations *Dye ink:* (black, cranberry) Close To My Heart *Paint:* (Wicker White) Plaid *Accents:* (red button, white flowers, red brads) Close To My Heart *Fibers:* (hemp) Close to My Heart

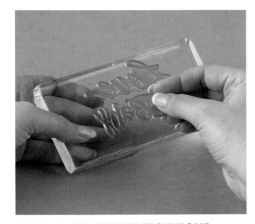

BUILD A SENTIMENT TECHNIQUE
Arrange stamps on acrylic block.

Ink and stamp sentiment.

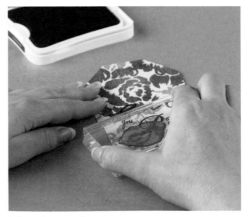

Ink and stamp lips image.

STAMP SHAPING TECHNIQUE
Adhere punched cardstock circle to acrylic block with removable adhesive.

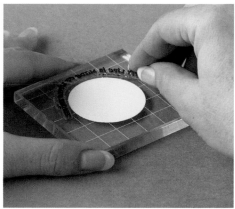

Adhere stamp, bending around circle.

Ink and stamp sentiment.

Little Things Card

Designer: Nichole Heady

1. Make card from cardstock.
2. Adhere patterned paper to card front.
3. Die-cut flower from cardstock; adhere chipboard flower.
4. Cut sentiment block from cardstock; double-mat with cardstock. Adhere flowers.
5. Attach brads. Punch circles from patterned paper; adhere to brads.
6. Stamp sentiment on cardstock (see "Stamp Shaping Technique"). Adhere with foam tape.

Finished size: 4¼" x 5½"

SUPPLIES: *Cardstock:* (Old Olive) Stampin' Up!; (white) Papertrey Ink *Patterned paper:* (Moonlight Meadow Paisley) Heidi Grace Designs *Clear stamp:* (sentiment from Little Lady set) Papertrey Ink *Dye ink:* (Night of Navy) Stampin' Up! *Accents:* (silver brads) Making Memories; (chipboard flower) *Adhesive:* (foam tape) The Paper Studio *Die:* (flower) QuicKutz *Tools:* (⅛" circle punch) Fiskars; (die cut machine) QuicKutz; (1¾" circle punch)

GLAZE AND GLITTER TECHNIQUE
Stamp image. Apply dimensional glaze.

Sprinkle with glitter. Let dry.

⑤ Two Birds Card

Designer: Lisa Strahl

❶ Make card from cardstock.

❷ Stamp images and embellish (see "Glaze and Glitter Technique"). Tap side of card to shake off excess glitter. Let dry.

❸ Apply dimensional paint to sentiment.

❹ Adhere rhinestone; tie on ribbon.

Finished size: 3¼" x 5¼"

SUPPLIES: *Cardstock:* (celery) *Rubber stamps:* (birds, swirl from Cute Curls set, sentiment from Pretty Birds set) Cornish Heritage Farms *Pigment ink:* (Dark Brown, Dark Moss) Clearsnap *Paint:* (Ruby Red dimensional) Ranger Industries *Accents:* (crystal glitter) Martha Stewart Crafts; (red rhinestone) *Fibers:* (red/pink satin ribbon) May Arts *Other:* (dimensional glaze) Ranger Industries

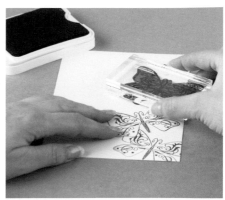

REPEATING AN IMAGE TECHNIQUE
Stamp image once on scrap paper and once on cardstock.

Cut image from scrap paper. Adhere over stamped image on cardstock using repositionable adhesive.

Stamp image additional times, moving mask as needed. *Note: Mask allows you to stamp butterflies without seeing overlap.*

For the Bride & Groom Card

Designer: Tresa Black

1. Make card from cardstock; ink edges.
2. Stamp design using mask (see "Repeating an Image Technique"). Color design with chalk.
3. Cut strips from patterned paper; adhere.
4. Stamp sentiment on patterned paper; trim and ink edges. Adhere to card.
5. Print "For the" on cardstock; trim and sand edges. Attach brad; adhere to card.

Finished size: 5" x 7"

DESIGNER TIPS

- To save time cutting, don't include small details in the mask, such as the antennae on the butterfly.
- You can reuse your masks. Store used masks with the stamp or stamp set so you can easily find them.

SUPPLIES: *Cardstock:* (Colonial White, Honey) Close To My Heart *Patterned paper:* (Fortune Teller Stripe from Gypsy Harvest collection) Daisy D's; (Earth Pattern from Far East collection) Die Cuts With a View *Clear stamps:* (butterfly from Boho Buzz set) Technique Tuesday; (Bride & Groom from Our Wedding Day set) Close To My Heart *Dye ink:* (Barn Red, Black, Chocolate) Close To My Heart *Color medium:* (brown, gold chalk) Close To My Heart *Font:* (Times New Roman) Microsoft

⁵ Velvet Valentine Card

Designer: Nichole Heady

1 Make card from cardstock; cut window in front.

2 Emboss velvet (see "Embossing Velvet Technique"); adhere to inside of card with packing tape. Cover inside with cardstock.

3 Draw frame around window with marker.

4 Spell "Be mine" with rub-ons. Insert brad in flower; adhere.

Finished size: 6¾" x 4"

DESIGNER TIP
When selecting velvet, look for one that is a rayon/acetate blend for best results.

SUPPLIES: *Cardstock:* (White Linen) Bazzill Basics Paper *Rubber stamp:* (On the Spot) Stampin' Up! *Color medium:* (Chocolate Chip marker) Stampin' Up! *Accents:* (purple brad) Making Memories; (brown flower) Maya Road *Rub-ons:* (Fred alphabet) American Crafts *Adhesive:* (packing tape) *Tool:* (iron) *Other:* (plum velvet fabric)

EMBOSSING VELVET TECHNIQUE
Place stamp face up. Place velvet right side down on stamp.

Cover with damp cloth; iron with hot, dry iron for 3-4 seconds. Repeat until all stamp areas are ironed.

Remove velvet from stamp; trim.

Psychedelic Thank You Bag

Designer: Linda Beeson

1. Ink and stamp images (see "Kissing an Un-Inked Stamp Technique").
2. Trim, ink edges, and mat with cardstock. Adhere to bag.
3. Trim bag top with decorative-edge scissors.
4. Stamp thank you on cardstock and punch into tag.
5. Punch holes in bag and tag. Tie tag to bag with ribbon.

Finished size: 3½" x 5¾"

SUPPLIES: *Cardstock:* (Pure White, Purple Grape) WorldWin *Rubber stamps:* (Just for Fun, Shape 10) Rubber Soul; (thank you from Cute Curls set) Cornish Heritage Farms *Dye ink:* (Berry Blaze, black) Tsukineko *Fibers:* (white grosgrain ribbon) May Arts *Tools:* (tag punch) McGill; (decorative-edge scissors) *Other:* (pink bag)

KISSING AN UN-INKED STAMP TECHNIQUE
Ink stamp. Press un-inked stamp into inked stamp.

Press inked image on paper.

DOILY KISSING TECHNIQUE
Ink stamp thoroughly.

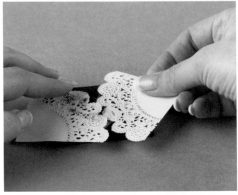

Press edges of doily on inked stamp.

Remove doily and stamp image on paper.

DESIGNER TIP

Create a similar effect by kissing your stamp with a kitchen sponge, lace, or any other textured item you have around the house.

⁵⁵ᵗᵉᵖˢ Lacey Love Card

Designer: Alisa Bangerter

Sand all patterned paper edges.

❶ Make card from cardstock. Adhere and stitch patterned paper.

❷ Mat reverse side of patterned paper with reverse side of patterned paper and apply rub-on. Attach with brads.

❸ Create stamped image (see "Doily Kissing Technique"). Trim with decorative-edge scissors.

❹ Adhere heart to reverse side of patterned paper with foam tape. Trim, and adhere.

❺ Apply rub-ons to reverse side of patterned paper. Trim, and adhere with foam tape.

Finished size: 7" x 5"

SUPPLIES: *Cardstock:* (white) Prism *Patterned paper:* (Cummerbund, Tux from The Goods collection) American Crafts *Foam stamp:* (heart from Love set) Making Memories *Dye ink:* (Coffee) Plaid *Accents:* (white brads) Making Memories *Rub-ons:* (congratulations) Scrapworks; (love, love border) Cloud 9 Design *Adhesive:* (foam tape) *Tool:* (decorative-edge scissors) *Other:* (doily)

Elegant Miss You Card

Designer: Anabelle O'Malley

❶ Make card from cardstock. Adhere slightly smaller piece of patterned paper.

❷ Trim cardstock with decorative-edge scissors; adhere. Ink edges of patterned paper strip; adhere.

❸ Apply rub-on; stitch edges.

❹ Cover chipboard with patterned paper; sand edges and adhere.

❺ Stamp and emboss image on glossy cardstock (see "Resisting with Walnut Ink Technique").

❻ Stamp sentiment and punch image into oval; adhere.

❼ Punch flowers from patterned paper; adhere. Thread buttons and adhere.

Finished size: 5" square

SUPPLIES: *Cardstock:* (brown, white) Prism; (white glossy) Stampin' Up! *Patterned paper:* (silhouettes, plaid, tiles, circles, stripe from Timeless collection) Deja Views *Clear stamps:* (Flower Trio) Autumn Leaves; (I miss you) My Sentiments Exactly! *Watermark ink; Walnut ink:* Tsukineko *Embossing powder:* (Frosted Crystal) Ranger Industries *Accents:* (blue buttons) Autumn Leaves; (chipboard rectangle) *Rub-on:* (corner flourish) Deja Views *Tools:* (flower punch) EK Success; (oval punch, decorative-edge scissors)

RESISTING WITH WALNUT INK TECHNIQUE
Stamp and heat set image.

Spritz with walnut ink.

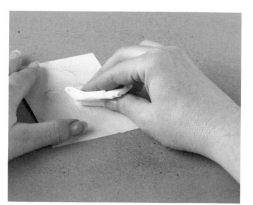

Remove excess ink with paper towel.

MASKING A SHAPE TECHNIQUE
Punch shape from scrap paper.

Adhere punched paper (mask) to cardstock with removable adhesive. Stamp design, moving stamp as needed.

Color design; remove mask.

⟨5 STEPS⟩ Treasure the Moments Box

Designer: Nichole Heady

1. Stamp flower design on cardstock (see "Masking a Shape Technique"). Before removing mask, stamp script. Punch with scalloped punch. Repeat to create three designs.

2. Cut squares from patterned paper; adhere solid side up to cardstock. Adhere to top of box.

3. Adhere designs to squares, using foam tape for two designs. Affix stickers.

4. Adhere ribbon to lip of box lid.

Finished size: 5" x 5" x 2"

DESIGNER TIP

To color the designs, use a sponge and apply ink in a circular motion around the inside edge of the mask.

SUPPLIES: *Cardstock:* (white) Papertrey Ink *Patterned paper:* (Sincere, Pure from True collection) Fancy Pants Designs *Clear stamps:* (circle flower flourish, script from Bella Brush set) Fancy Pants Designs *Dye inks:* (Old Olive, Buckaroo Blue) Stampin' Up! *Stickers:* (treasure, the, moments) Making Memories *Fibers:* (blue stitched ribbon) Fancy Pants Designs *Adhesive:* (foam tape) *Tools:* (2" circle punch) EK Success; (2" scalloped circle punch) Marvy Uchida *Other:* (paper mache box) Expo International

⁵Forever Tag

Designer: Anabelle O'Malley

1. Make tag from reverse side of patterned paper; stitch edges.

2. Wrap trim around tag; adhere to back. Adhere buttons.

3. Create design with thick embossing powder (see "Thick Embossing Powder Technique"); rub with pigment powder. Tear around design; adhere to tag.

4. Punch hole in tag; adhere reinforcer and tie with ribbon.

5. Affix sticker.

Finished size: 2¾" x 5¼"

Designer Tips

- Completely ink the cardstock before sprinkling it with thick embossing powder. You may want to use the edge of the ink pad to apply extra to the center of the cardstock to ensure even coverage.

- Use bold stamp designs for the best results.

SUPPLIES: *Cardstock:* (Antique White) WorldWin *Patterned paper:* (Words from Snowday collection) Paper Salon *Clear stamp:* (flourish from Fall Frolic set) Paper Salon *Watermark ink:* Tsukineko *Embossing powder:* (clear ultra thick) Ranger Industries *Color medium:* (green, yellow pigment powder) Jacquard Products *Accents:* (hole reinforcer) Target; (cream buttons) *Sticker:* (forever) 7gypsies *Fibers:* (crotchet lace trim) May Arts; (cream organza ribbon)

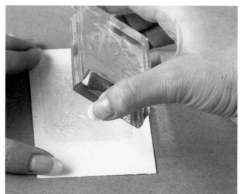

THICK EMBOSSING POWDER TECHNIQUE

Ink cardstock with watermark ink; sprinkle with thick embossing powder. Heat. Repeat inking, applying powder, and heating three more times.

Press stamp into thick embossing powder while it is still warm.

Remove stamp once thick embossing powder has hardened.

Key to My ♥ Heart

From large chipboard keys to decorative key stamps to keys made of rhinestones, this handy tool has become a hot motif in the world of paper crafting. Take a look at the wonderful ways designers have put keys and keyholes to work on these projects.

DESIGNER TIP

Use a paper piercer and a ruler to make holes before stitching with floss. This makes the process go faster and look smooth and straight.

Lovely Card

Designer: Melissa Phillips

1. Make gatefold card from cardstock.

2. Cover bottom flap with patterned paper; stitch bottom edge.

3. Cover top flap with patterned paper; stitch edges. Ink card edges.

4. Adhere die cuts. Fold flower in half; adhere. Tie with ribbon.

5. Tie chipboard key and button to ribbon with twine.

6. Apply rub-on and adhere pearls.

Finished size: 4½" x 5¼"

Key to My Heart Card

Designer: Ashley Harris

1. Make card from cardstock.

2. Adhere patterned paper; stitch edges with floss.

3. Adhere patterned paper. Affix stickers to create sentiment; adhere trim.

4. Cut heart from cardstock; stitch edges with floss and adhere.

5. Adhere button to flower; adhere to card. Tie key with floss; adhere.

Finished size: 5½" x 4¼"

SUPPLIES: *Cardstock:* (Apple Green) Bazzill Basics Paper *Patterned paper:* (Patterns from Simplicity collection) Fancy Pants Designs; (Ella Scallop Circle from Animal Crackers collection) Making Memories *Dye ink:* (Old Paper) Ranger Industries *Accents:* (flower die cuts) Making Memories; (pink/white flower) Prima; (pink pearls) Kaisercraft; (white button) Melissa Frances; (chipboard key) Tattered Angels *Rub-on:* (lovely) Crate Paper *Fibers:* (scalloped green ribbon) Making Memories; (hemp twine) Darice

SUPPLIES: *Cardstock:* (Chiffon) Bazzill Basics Paper *Patterned paper:* (Unchained Melody from Baby 2 Bride collection) Graphic45 *Accents:* (cream flower) Bazzill Basics Paper; (pink button) Autumn Leaves; (antique brass key) *Stickers:* (Tiny alphabet) Making Memories *Fibers:* (cream lace trim) Melissa Frances; (cream floss) DMC

Heart 2 Drive Card

Designer: Ana Wohlfahrt

ACCENT

❶ Die-cut circle from cardstock. Stamp circle congrats; die-cut scalloped circle from cardstock and mat.

❷ Die-cut two circles from cardstock; double-mat stamped piece.

❸ Emboss cardstock square; mat with cardstock. Adhere circle piece.

❹ Stamp car on cardstock; cut out. Color with marker, accent with dimensional glaze, and adhere with foam tape.

❺ Attach charms to piece with brad.

CARD

❶ Make card from cardstock.

❷ Cut patterned paper, mat with cardstock, and adhere.

❸ Cut cardstock strip, mat with cardstock, and adhere. Stamp celebrate; tie with ribbon.

❹ Adhere accent with foam tape.

Finished size: 4¼" x 5½"

With All My Heart Card

Designer: Melissa Phillips

❶ Make card from cardstock; round bottom front corners.

❷ Cut patterned paper slightly smaller than card front; round bottom corners. Ink edges and adhere.

❸ Cut patterned paper; round bottom corners, ink edges, and adhere.

❹ Adhere borders.

❺ Ink edges of heart circle die cut and stitch around heart with floss. Punch hole, tie with ribbon, and adhere with foam tape.

❻ Adhere keyhole and pearls.

Finished size: 5½" x 3¾"

SUPPLIES: *Cardstock:* (Bayou Blue, Real Red, kraft, Going Gray, Sky Blue, Whisper White) Stampin' Up! *Patterned paper:* (Port Holes from Hampton collection) Crate Paper *Clear stamps:* (circle congrats, celebrate, car from Congrats All Around set) My Favorite Things *Dye ink:* (Sahara Sand) Stampin' Up! *Pigment ink:* (Onyx Black) Tsukineko *Color medium:* (blue marker) Copic Marker *Accents:* (pewter key, drive tag charms) Karen Foster Design; (black glitter brad) Making Memories *Fibers:* (red ribbon) Stampin' Up! *Adhesive:* (foam tape) *Template:* (Swiss dots embossing) Provo Craft *Dies:* (circle, scalloped circle) Spellbinders *Tools:* (die cut machine) Spellbinders; (embossing machine) Provo Craft *Other:* (dimensional glaze)

SUPPLIES: *Cardstock:* (brown) Bazzill Basics Paper *Patterned paper:* (Be Mine from Kiss & Tell collection, Tiny Dots from Out & About No. 1 collection) My Mind's Eye *Dye ink:* (Cocoa) Clearsnap *Accents:* (heart circle die cut; scalloped, heart borders) My Mind's Eye; (key hole) Melissa Frances; (flat pearls) K&Company *Adhesive:* (foam tape) *Fibers:* (red gingham ribbon, red floss) *Tool:* (corner rounder punch)

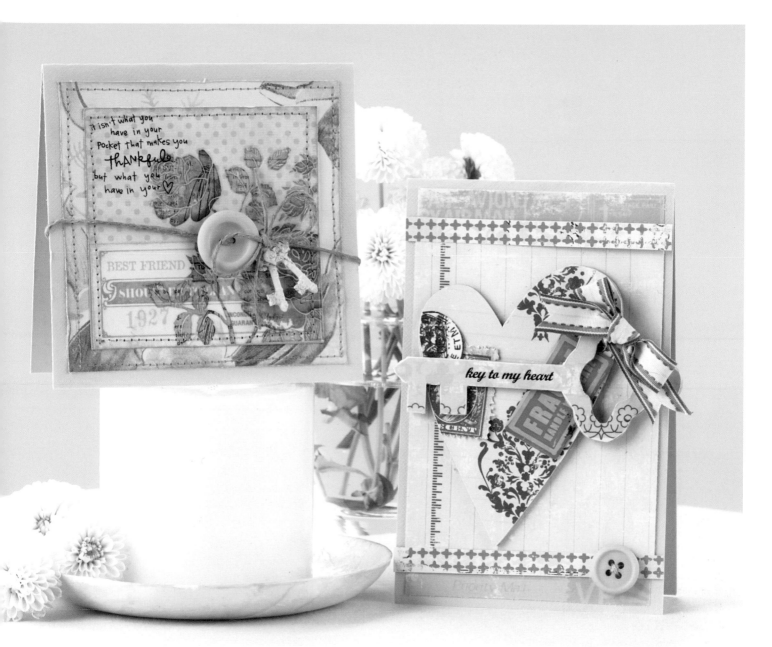

⑤ What You Have in Your Heart Card

Designer: Melissa Phillips

❶ Make card from cardstock.

❷ Cut patterned paper slightly smaller than card front; stitch, ink edges, and adhere.

❸ Cut patterned paper; adhere ticket die cut. Stitch, ink edges, and adhere.

❹ Apply rub-ons.

❺ Thread twine through button and keys; tie around card front.

Finished size: 4½" square

SUPPLIES: *Cardstock:* (Powder Blue) Bazzill Basics Paper *Patterned paper:* (Laura, Paige) Melissa Frances *Dye ink:* (Old Paper) Ranger Industries *Accents:* (ticket die cut, white keys) Melissa Frances; (white button) *Rub-ons:* (roses) Fancy Pants Designs; (sentiment) Melissa Frances *Fibers:* (hemp twine) Darice

⑤ Key to My Heart Collage Card

Designer: Charity Hassel

❶ Make card from cardstock.

❷ Adhere patterned paper. Adhere patterned paper strips.

❸ Cover chipboard heart with patterned paper. Cut stamp and postmark from patterned paper; adhere. Affix sticker.

❹ Cover chipboard key with patterned paper. Apply rub-on, tie with ribbon, and adhere to heart.

❺ Adhere heart to card. Thread button with floss; adhere.

Finished size: 4" x 6"

SUPPLIES: *Cardstock:* (blue) Bazzill Basics Paper *Patterned paper:* (Stripe, Ledger Teal, Ledger Stamp, Folded Map, Postcard from Passport collection) Making Memories *Accents:* (chipboard key) Fancy Pants Designs; (chipboard heart) Cosmo Cricket; (pink button) My Mind's Eye *Rub-on:* (key to my heart) Maya Road *Sticker:* (fragile epoxy label) Making Memories *Fibers:* (striped ribbon) Making Memories; (pink floss)

Your Help Was Key Card
Designer: Teri Anderson

1. Make card from cardstock.
2. Print "Thanks, your help was" on cardstock; trim and adhere.
3. Stamp key randomly on patterned paper strip; adhere.
4. Adhere ribbon. Attach brads.
5. Spell "Key" with chipboard alphabet.

Finished size: 6" x 3¼"

DESIGNER TIP

Clean your stamp before inking and stamping. Small fibers stuck to your stamp can prevent a clear, sharp image.

BONUS IDEA

Change the sentiment to "You are the key to our success."

Home Is Wall Hanging
Designer: Kalyn Kepner

1. Trim cardstock rectangle with decorative-edge scissors; ink edges.
2. Cut cardstock smaller than base; stamp swirls. Mat with cardstock, stitch edges with floss, and adhere.
3. Cut triangle of patterned paper and square of cardstock; ink edges. Adhere together to form house. Trim rectangle from cardstock; adhere. Wrap with twine.
4. Mat piece with cardstock. Affix heart sticker and adhere key. Adhere piece with foam tape.
5. Spell "Home" with stickers and stamp sentiment.
6. Adhere ribbon to create hanger.

Finished size: 7¾" x 8¼"

SUPPLIES: *Cardstock:* (cream) Provo Craft *Patterned paper:* (Arithmetic from Recess collection) BasicGrey *Rubber stamp:* (key from Keys set) Art Declassified *Dye ink:* (Chocolate) Close To My Heart *Accents:* (Lemonade Stand chipboard alphabet) Heidi Swapp; (tan brads) Oriental Trading Co. *Fibers:* (pink, striped ribbon) Making Memories *Font:* (CK Holiday Spirit) Creating Keepsakes

SUPPLIES: *Cardstock:* (cream, pink, kraft, black) Wausau *Patterned paper:* (Harvest Chestnut Plaid) Scenic Route *Clear stamps:* (Small Variety alphabet) Hero Arts; (swirl from Swirls v.1 set) Autumn Leaves *Chalk ink:* (Chestnut Roan, Creamy Brown) Clearsnap *Accents:* (pewter key) Making Memories *Stickers:* (Pajamas alphabet) American Crafts; (pink/red felt heart) Provo Craft *Fibers:* (red floss) DMC; (jute twine, pink/brown ribbon) *Adhesive:* (foam tape) *Tool:* (decorative-edge scissors)

Love is the Master Key Card

Designer: Cari Fennell

❶ Make card from cardstock.

❷ Adhere patterned paper pieces.

❸ Print quote on transparency sheet; trim and adhere to chipboard circle. Adhere to card.

❹ Adhere rhinestones. Tie with rickrack.

Finished size: 4¼" x 5½"

BONUS IDEA

Look for the versatility in your favorite quotes. Here, both designers used the same quote but created two very different projects.

SUPPLIES: *Cardstock:* (Khaki) Bazzill Basics Paper *Patterned paper:* (Diagoji, Katsura from Tea & Silk collection) Prima *Transparency sheet:* 3L *Accents:* (chipboard circle) Prima; (clear rhinestone hearts) Imaginisce; (rhinestone love key) Prima *Fibers:* (white velvet rickrack) May Arts *Font:* (Verdana) www.fonts.com

Love Is Mini Album

Designer: Susan Neal

❶ Cover album covers with patterned paper; ink edges.

❷ Die-cut 4" heart from patterned paper; ink edges. Stamp quote and emboss. Cut slits above and below author's name.

❸ Stamp Antique Heart Key on cardstock; emboss. Paint image, mixing colors as desired, and let dry. Cut out, insert key through slits in heart, and adhere. Attach brad.

❹ Mount heart on chipboard; adhere to cover with foam tape.

❺ Thread ribbon under heart; tie around album.

Finished size: 7" x 5"

SUPPLIES: *Cardstock:* (Natural) Bazzill Basics Paper *Patterned paper:* (Addie Brocade Dot, Addie Pattern Stripe from Noteworthy collection) Making Memories *Rubber stamp:* (Antique Heart Key) Impression Obsession *Clear stamp:* (quote from Simple Thoughts-Love set) Cloud 9 Design *Pigment ink:* (Vintage Sepia) Tsukineko *Embossing powder:* (clear) Ranger Industries *Paint:* (Nutmeg, Pink Grapefruit, Golden Sand, Yellow Rose) LuminArte *Accent:* (pewter brad) Making Memories *Fibers:* (white ribbon) *Adhesive:* (foam tape) 3L *Die:* (heart) Provo Craft *Tool:* (die cut machine) Provo Craft *Other:* (gatefold album) 7gypsies; (chipboard)

Welcome Home Tag

Designer: Beatriz Jennings

❶ Make tag from cardstock; cover with patterned paper. Trim bottom edge with punch.

❷ Stitch and ink edges. Punch hole, affix hole reinforcer, and tie with ribbon.

❸ Paint chipboard house roof; let dry. Adhere patterned paper and stitch edges.

❹ Adhere ribbon and trim. Adhere house to tag.

❺ Adhere flowers. Thread button with floss; adhere. Tie twine around tag.

❻ Tie key to twine with floss. Spell sentiment with stickers.

Finished size: 2½" x 5¼"

DESIGNER TIP

Save your paper scraps—they make great tags!

⁵⁵ₜₑₚ Listen to Your Heart Card

Designer: Daniela Dobson

❶ Make card from cardstock; trim right edge with decorative-edge scissors.

❷ Adhere patterned paper pieces; stitch edges.

❸ Adhere acrylic label and label die cut. Trim floral spray from patterned paper; adhere.

❹ Layer butterflies; adhere. Adhere key and buttons.

Finished size: 4" x 6"

SUPPLIES: *Cardstock:* (white) DMD, Inc. *Patterned paper:* (Flutterby from Feather Nest collection) Webster's Pages; (pink polka dot from Small Wonders Girl collection) K&Company *Dye ink:* (Antique Linen) Ranger Industries *Paint:* (white) *Accents:* (chipboard house, silver key) Maya Road; (white button) Creative Café; (white/pink flowers) *Stickers:* (Tiny alphabet) Making Memories; (white hole reinforcer) *Fibers:* (red velvet ribbon) Making Memories; (cream twill ribbon, hemp twine, pink trim, mauve floss) *Tool:* (scalloped edge punch) Fiskars

SUPPLIES: *Cardstock:* (white) Bazzill Basics Paper *Patterned paper:* (Love Song, Floral from Tangerine Dream collection) Jenni Bowlin Studio *Accents:* (label die cut, felt butterfly) Jenni Bowlin Studio; (chipboard butterfly) American Crafts; (brass key) 7gypsies; (acrylic sentiment label) Making Memories; (blue buttons) *Tool:* (decorative-edge scissors) Provo Craft

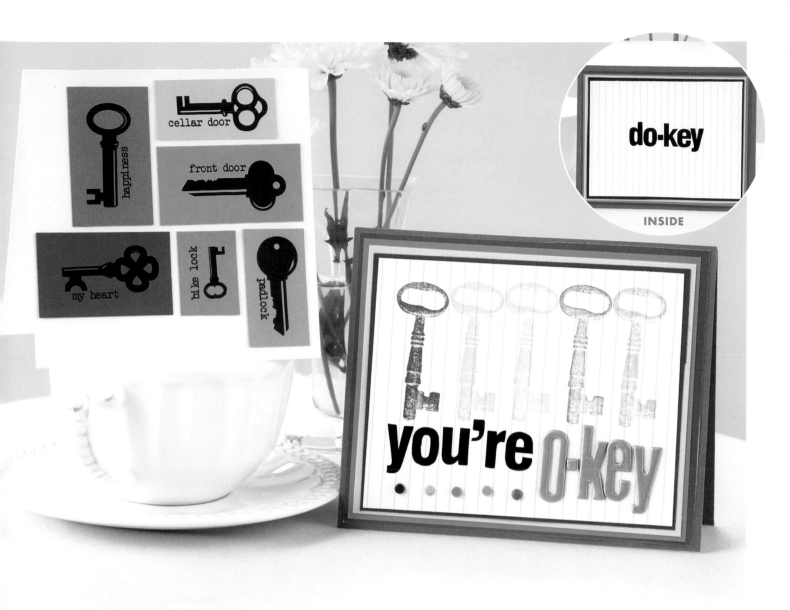

INSIGHT

You Hold Them All Card

Designer: Kim Kesti

❶ Make card from cardstock.

❷ Print names of keys on cardstock; trim. Apply rub-ons and adhere.

❸ Print sentiment on cardstock; adhere inside card.

Finished size: 5" square

SIMPLE SENTIMENT

The inside of the card says, "You hold them all."

BONUS IDEA

Leave the inside of the card blank and create the entire sentiment on the card cover.

O-Key Card

Designer: Teri Anderson

OUTSIDE

❶ Make card from cardstock. Cover with cardstock.

❷ Stamp key repeatedly on patterned paper; trim.

❸ Spell sentiment with stickers and chipboard alphabet. Attach brads.

❹ Quadruple-mat piece with cardstock; adhere.

INSIDE

❶ Cover card inside with cardstock.

❷ Cut patterned paper. Spell "Do-key" with stickers.

❸ Quadruple-mat piece with cardstock; adhere.

Finished size: 6¼" x 5¼"

SUPPLIES: *Cardstock:* (Brilliant White, Ruby Red, Pacific, Green Tea, Parakeet, Swimming Pool, Festive, Cheddar) Bazzill Basics Paper *Rub-ons:* (keys) Maya Road *Font:* (Another Typewriter) www.dafont.com

SUPPLIES: *Cardstock:* (yellow) Bazzill Basics Paper; (red, green, blue, purple, white) WorldWin *Patterned paper:* (White Line Background) Scenic Route *Rubber stamp:* (key from Keys set) Art Declassified *Dye ink:* (Cherry, Deep Lilac, Yellow) Marvy Uchida; (Sweet Leaf, Twilight) Close To My Heart *Accents:* (assorted brads) Creative Impressions; (silver chipboard alphabet) Heidi Swapp *Stickers:* (JFK alphabet) American Crafts

Valentines
FOR EVERYONE ON YOUR LIST

Looking for a way to show someone how much you care? There are so many people that are important to us, from family and friends to coworkers and neighbors. Check out these trendy valentine cards, and treat containers for all stages of life and for all kinds of recipients!

DESIGNER TIPS

Sending this card in the mail? Use a padded envelope to keep the wiggle eyes from getting smashed.

BONUS IDEAS

Rather than using a traditional card as your base, try two panels of cardstock. Use a paper clip to hold the panels together.

Happiness Is Card

Designer: Juliana Michaels

1 Make card from cardstock. Trim patterned paper, ink edges, and adhere.
2 Punch patterned paper strip, crimp, and adhere.
3 Trim happiness section from patterned paper, tie on twine, and adhere with foam tape.
4 Insert stick pin.
5 Paint chipboard people, let dry, and adhere.
6 Trim flower and flower center from patterned paper. Adhere each piece with foam tape.

Finished size: 4¼" square

SUPPLIES: *Cardstock:* (kraft) DMD, Inc. *Patterned paper:* (Cannellini Beans, Olive Oil, Elbow Macaroni from Minestrone collection) Jillibean Soup *Dye ink:* (Vintage Photo) Ranger Industries *Paint:* (Tapioca) Plaid *Accents:* (chipboard people) Magistical Memories; (white pearl stick pin) Fibers: (twine) *Tools:* (crimper, border punch) Fiskars

Whooo Loves You Card

Designer: Teri Anderson

1 Make card from cardstock. Trim cardstock, round bottom right corner, and adhere.
2 Stamp branch on cardstock piece. Round two opposite corners, and adhere.
3 Stamp owl on different colors of cardstock. Trim pieces and adhere.
4 Trim heart from cardstock and adhere. Adhere wiggle eyes.
5 Stamp sentiment on cardstock, trim, and adhere. Staple.
6 Attach paper clip.

Finished size: 4¼" x 5"

SUPPLIES: *Cardstock:* (brown, kraft) Neenah Paper; (yellow, red, white) Worldwin; (light tan) Provo Craft *Rubber stamp:* (Big Owl) Hero Arts *Clear stamps:* (sentiment, branch from Whooo Loves You set) Close To My Heart *Dye ink:* (Chocolate) Close To My Heart; (black) Marvy Uchida *Accents:* (wiggle eyes) Darice; (red paper clip) Dollar Tree Stores; (silver staple) *Tool:* (corner rounder punch) Zutter

⑸ P.S. I Heart U Card

Designer: Emeline Seet

① Make card from cardstock. Round bottom corners.

② Round bottom corners of patterned paper; adhere.

③ Affix letters and heart to spell sentiment on cardstock. Trim, round corner, and adhere.

④ Punch edge of cardstock strip and adhere.

⑤ Cut circles from cardstock and patterned paper; layer and adhere with foam tape.

Finished size: 5" x 6"

⑸ Hey Buddy Robot Card

Designer: Betsy Veldman

① Make card from cardstock. Trim patterned paper, ink edges, and adhere.

② Adhere patterned paper and zigzag-stitch.

③ Ink edges of die cut and adhere. Attach brad to spiral clip and adhere.

④ Affix alphabet stickers to spell sentiment. Affix heart sticker.

⑤ Trim robot and adhere with foam tape.

Finished size: 5½" x 4¼"

SUPPLIES: *Cardstock:* (Classic Orange) Prism; (white) *Patterned paper:* (Sweet Nothings from Sweet Cakes collection) Pink Paislee *Stickers:* (Roosevelt Jr. alphabet) American Crafts; (heart, Just My Type alphabet) Doodlebug Design *Tools:* (corner rounder punch) Zutter; (circle cutter) Fiskars; (border punch)

SUPPLIES: *Cardstock:* (Grenadine) Bazzill Basics Paper *Patterned paper:* (Xtron from K-Bots collection) Kaisercraft; (Love Lines from Hugs-n-Kisses collection) Dream Street Papers *Chalk ink:* (Creamy Brown) Clearsnap *Accents:* (heart brad) BasicGrey; (silver spiral clip) Creative Impressions; (journaling square die cut) My Mind's Eye *Stickers:* (heart, Lime Rickey alphabet) BasicGrey

DESIGNER TIP

Choose your favorite color scheme and make it shine with a myriad of colorful accents all in one place!

Love You This Much Card

Designer: Susan Stringfellow

Draw borders with pen around all patterned paper.

1. Make card from cardstock. Round bottom corners.
2. Trim patterned paper, round bottom corners, and adhere.
3. Cut patterned paper strip and adhere.
4. Cut heart from patterned paper and adhere.
5. Thread ribbon through slide and adhere. Adhere bear.
6. Spell "You" with stickers.
7. Print "Love this much!" on cardstock, trim, and adhere.

Finished size: 5½" x 4¼"

5 steps XO Smooch Card

Designer: Susan R. Opel

1. Make card from cardstock. Affix packing tape.
2. Adhere chipboard frame. Attach brad to paper flower and adhere.
3. Adhere tile to badge, affix badge to flower, and adhere.
4. Tie ribbon through button and adhere. Tie ribbon on frame.
5. Adhere XO rhinestones.

Finished size: 4¼" x 5½"

SUPPLIES: *Cardstock:* (white) Die Cuts With a View *Patterned paper:* (blue medallions, red, striped from The Green Stack pad) Die Cuts With a View *Color medium:* (black marker) Faber-Castell USA *Accents:* (chipboard bear, ribbon slide) Die Cuts With a View *Stickers:* (Daiquiri alphabet) American Crafts *Fibers:* (green stitched ribbon) Die Cuts With a View *Font:* (Pharmacy) www.dafont.com *Tool:* (corner rounder punch) Creative Memories

SUPPLIES: *Cardstock:* (gray) Bazzill Basics Paper *Accents:* (red polka dot chipboard frame, smooch tile) KI Memories; (red felt flower) American Crafts; (red paper flower) Prima; (XO rhinestones) Me & My Big Ideas; (red/silver starburst brad) Karen Foster Design; (red button) *Stickers:* (red polka dot badge) American Crafts; (red decorative packing tape) Fancy That! *Fibers:* (red dotted ribbon, red striped ribbon)

Crush on You Card

Designer: Betsy Veldman

1. Make card from cardstock. Adhere patterned paper.
2. Adhere strip of patterned paper. Die-cut thought bubble from cardstock; ink edges and stamp small heart randomly. Adhere and zig-zag stitch.
3. Die-cut tag from cardstock, attach brad, and adhere. Stitch.
4. Affix crush sticker to cardstock, trim with decorative-edge scissors, and mat with cardstock using foam tape. Adhere to card.
5. Affix heart stickers.
6. Stamp "I have a" and "On you".

Finished size: 5 ½" x 4¼"

Birdie Love Card

Designer: Betsy Veldman

1. Make card from cardstock.
2. Trim journaling block; adhere. Adhere patterned paper piece and strip; ink edges and stitch.
3. Affix love sticker to cardstock, trim into circle, and adhere.
4. Tie ribbon on chipboard frame. Thread button with twine, tie on frame, and adhere frame with foam tape.
5. Adhere felt flower, chipboard flower, and rhinestone.
6. Affix bird sticker and adhere pearl.

Finished size: 5" x 3¾"

SUPPLIES: *Cardstock:* (Grenadine, Pistachio) Bazzill Basics Paper; (Hibiscus Burst, white) Papertrey Ink; (Honey) Core'dinations *Patterned paper:* (Monroe from Tiffany's collection, Flirt from Heart Attack collection) We R Memory Keepers *Clear stamps:* (small heart from Heart Prints set, Simple Alphabet set, Fresh Alphabet set) Papertrey Ink *Chalk ink:* (light brown) *Specialty ink:* (Aqua Mist, Pure Poppy hybrid) Papertrey Ink *Accent:* (red brad) Bazzill Basics Paper *Stickers:* (crush, epoxy hearts) Fiskars; (chipboard heart) We R Memory Keepers *Dies:* (tag, thought bubble) Provo Craft *Tool:* (decorative-edge scissors) Provo Craft

SUPPLIES: *Cardstock:* (Vintage Cream, kraft) Papertrey Ink *Patterned paper:* (Green Floral, Pink Tulip from Zinnia collection) Little Yellow Bicycle *Chalk ink:* (Creamy Brown) Clearsnap *Accents:* (green scalloped journaling block, pink button, green felt flower, purple rhinestone, purple pearl, chipboard glitter frame, chipboard flower) Little Yellow Bicycle *Stickers:* (bird, love square) Little Yellow Bicycle *Fibers:* (cream ribbon) Papertrey Ink; (twine) The Beadery

5 Sweet Lovin' Candy Dishes

Designer: Marla Kress

1. Cut patterned paper circle to fit inside petri dish lid. Cut circle from center and adhere.
2. Apply rub-on to lid.
3. Trim circle from patterned paper, punch hole, and affix badge.
4. Fill dishes with candy.
5. Stack dishes, thread circle with ribbon, and tie all together.

Finished size: 3½" diameter x 2" height

5 XOXO Heart Card

Designer: Kalyn Kepner

1. Make card from cardstock; stitch borders.
2. Trim cardstock strips with decorative-edge scissors; adhere.
3. Die-cut letters from cardstock to spell "XOXO" and adhere.
4. Die-cut hearts from patterned paper and cardstock, ink edges of some hearts, and adhere all using foam tape.
5. Thread buttons with floss and adhere.

Finished size: 6¼" x 5"

SUPPLIES: All supplies from American Crafts unless otherwise noted. *Patterned paper:* (First Love, Love Bug from Romance collection) *Rub-on:* (smooch label) *Sticker:* (sweet lovin' badge) *Fibers:* (cream/brown/pink striped ribbon) *Tool:* (circle cutter) Close To My Heart *Other:* (plastic petri dishes, candy) no source

SUPPLIES: *Cardstock:* (Vanilla, pink) Bazzill Basics Paper; (burgundy) *Patterned paper:* (First Love from Romance collection) American Crafts; (Mousse from Bittersweet collection) BasicGrey *Chalk ink:* (Creamy Brown) Clearsnap *Accents:* (pink buttons) *Fibers:* (white floss) *Dies:* (Nutmeg alphabet, heart) QuicKutz *Tool:* (decorative-edge scissors)

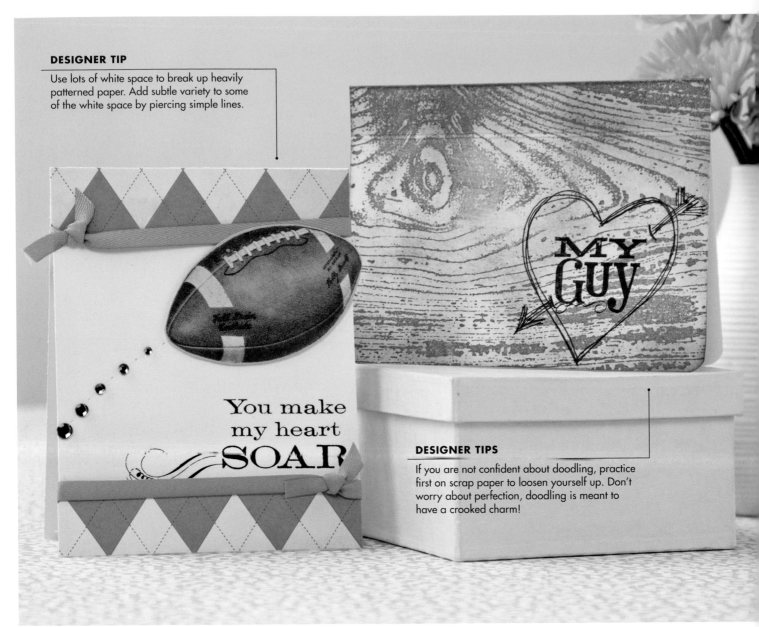

Soaring Football Card

Designer: Maren Benedict

1. Make card from cardstock. Adhere strips of patterned paper.
2. Apply rub-on. Tie on ribbon.
3. Trim football from patterned paper and adhere with foam tape.
4. Pierce football trail. Adhere rhinestones.

Finished size: 4¼" x 5½"

My Guy Card

Designer: Joanne Allison

1. Make card from cardstock. Round bottom corners.
2. Stamp Wood Grain Backgrounder. Lightly sponge ink over entire card.
3. Score card ¾" down from fold, front and back. Adhere to create flat hinge.
4. Stamp sentiment.
5. Doodle heart and arrow around sentiment.

Finished size: 5½" x 4¼"

SUPPLIES: *Cardstock:* (Vintage Cream) Papertrey Ink *Patterned paper:* (Dapper Dan, Elements from Lil' Man collection) Cosmo Cricket *Accents:* (blue rhinestones) Me & My Big Ideas *Rub-on:* (sentiment) Cosmo Cricket *Fibers:* (olive twill) Stampin' Up!

SUPPLIES: *Cardstock:* (white) *Rubber stamps:* (Wood Grain Backgrounder, sentiment from For the Men set) Cornish Heritage Farms *Dye ink:* (Vintage Photo) Ranger Industries *Solvent ink:* (Jet Black) Tsukineko *Color medium:* (black pen) Copic *Tools:* (corner rounder punch, scoring tool)

DESIGNER TIP

Use a paper piercer to mark each button hole before stitching. This will make it easier to stitch the buttons on exactly where you want them.

Heart Go Boom Card

Designer: Latisha Yoast

1. Make card from acrylic sheet. Adhere cardstock inside back cover.
2. Adhere patterned paper strip to front cover.
3. Tie on ribbon. Tie twine around ribbon.
4. Die-cut and emboss circle from cardstock. Stamp image and color. Adhere.
5. Spell "Love u" with stickers.

Finished size: 5½" x 4¼"

Be Mine Lace Card

Designer: Niki Estes

1. Make card from cardstock.
2. Cut patterned paper, adhere, and zigzag-stitch edges.
3. Adhere lace strips. Tie button with floss and adhere.
4. Stamp heart. Stamp and emboss sentiment; punch. Stitch on buttons with floss and adhere with foam tape.

Finished size: 4¼" x 5½"

SUPPLIES: *Cardstock:* (white) Papertrey Ink *Patterned paper:* (Wednesday from Girl Friday collection) Cosmo Cricket *Rubber stamp:* (Boom Goes My {Heart}) Unity Stamp Co. *Dye ink:* (Tuxedo Black) Tsukineko *Color medium:* (cream, pink, green markers) Copic *Stickers:* (Tiny Alpha alphabet) Making Memories *Fibers:* (pink ribbon) Offray; (white twine) May Arts *Die:* (3" circle) Spellbinders *Other:* (frosted acrylic sheet) SheetLoad ShortCuts

SUPPLIES: *Cardstock:* (white, kraft) Papertrey Ink *Patterned paper:* (pink floral from Just Perfect collection) My Mind's Eye *Clear stamps:* (heart, sentiment from Heart Prints set) Papertrey Ink *Dye ink:* (Hollyhock) Close To My Heart *Watermark ink:* Tsukineko *Embossing powder:* (white) Stewart Superior Corp. *Accents:* (white buttons) *Fibers:* (pink crocheted lace) My Mind's Eye, (white crocheted lace, pink floss) *Tool:* (heart punch) EK Success

DESIGNER TIP

Dampen cardboard to make it easier to separate.

Love You Card

Designer: Jo Kill

1. Make card from cardstock; ink edges.
2. Cut patterned paper slightly smaller than card front; distress and ink edges. Adhere.
3. Tear top layer from cardboard square, ink, and adhere. Adhere photo hanger.
4. Punch edge of patterned paper strip; ink edges. Thread ribbon through chipboard label and tie around strip. Adhere.
5. Thread string through buttons, tie bow, and adhere.
6. Attach flowers with brad; adhere. Spell "You" with stickers, affix love sticker, and adhere pearls.

Finished size: 5¼" square

SUPPLIES: *Cardstock:* (white) *Patterned paper:* (Raspberry Cream from Bittersweet collection) BasicGrey; (vintage notebook) *Pigment ink:* (Bark, white) Tsukineko *Accents:* (brown metal photo hanger) Creative Impressions; (brown button) BasicGrey; (red glitter brad) Doodlebug Design; (pink, cream flowers) Prima; (white pearls) K&Company; (red/white button) *Stickers:* (love, chipboard journaling label, Hip Mini alphabet) BasicGrey *Fibers:* (brown gingham ribbon) May Arts; (white string) *Tool:* (border punch) Martha Stewart Crafts *Other:* (corrugated cardboard)

Sweet Card

Designer: Danielle Flanders

1. Make card from cardstock.
2. Punch edge of patterned paper piece; adhere.
3. Apply butterfly and border rub-ons. Trim striped border and affix.
4. Affix letters to spell "Sweet" and apply butterfly rub-on.
5. Apply frame rub-on to chipboard frame, paint edges, and affix.
6. Paint flower stem edges and affix.
7. Adhere pearls.

Finished size: 4" x 4¾"

SUPPLIES: All supplies from Pink Paislee unless otherwise noted. *Cardstock:* (white) no source *Patterned paper:* (Pleasant from Enchanting collection) *Paint:* (off white) Delta *Accents:* (white pearls) Melissa Frances *Rub-ons:* (butterflies, border, frame) *Stickers:* (chipboard flower, frame; striped border, Enchanting alphabet) *Tool:* (border punch) Fiskars

Sweet Thoughts of You Card

Designer: Charity Hassel

1. Make card from acrylic sheet.
2. Tear edge of tag and adhere. Affix heart strip.
3. Trim bingo card to fit behind heart die cut; adhere. Adhere to card.
4. Adhere chipboard sweet and button.

Finished size: 5½" x 4¼"

All Yours Card

Designer: Beatriz Jennings

1. Make card from cardstock. Punch border.
2. Ink patterned paper edges and adhere.
3. Zigzag-stitch border around heart, ink edges, and adhere.
4. Apply rub-on.
5. Adhere buttons. Tie ribbon bow and adhere.

Finished size: 4" x 5½"

SUPPLIES: Accents: (XOXO bingo card) Jenni Bowlin Studio; (pink button) Chatterbox; (chipboard sweet) K&Company; (thinking of you tag) 7gypsies; (heart die cut) Sticker: (pink paper heart strip) K&Company Other: (frosted acrylic sheet) SheetLoad ShortCuts

SUPPLIES: Cardstock: (cream) DMD, Inc. Patterned paper: (Cupids from Crush collection) Teresa Collins Designs; (heart from Love Notes collection notebook) Making Memories Dye ink: (Antique Linen) Ranger Industries Accents: (assorted buttons) Rub-on: (sentiment) Making Memories Fibers: (red checkered ribbon) Tool: (border punch) March Stewart Crafts

DESIGNER TIP

If you don't have a love stamp that will work, change the font and color in your computer program to achieve the same effect.

BONUS IDEA

Use a soft sky blue cardstock and add a couple of white cardstock clouds instead of the cloud patterned paper.

Smooches Card

Designer: Dawn McVey

1. Make card from cardstock. Stamp polka dots.
2. Stamp damask and flourish on cardstock panel.
3. Punch border on cardstock strip; adhere to panel.
4. Tie on ribbon. Thread button with twine and tie around ribbon.
5. Adhere panel using foam tape.
6. Stamp sentiment.

Finished size: 5½" x 4¼"

When You Are in Love Card

Designer: Danni Reid

1. Make card from cardstock.
2. Print quote on cardstock. Note: Leave room for stamp. Stamp love, trim, and adhere.
3. Adhere patterned paper. Trim strip of patterned paper; adhere.
4. Stamp heart and adhere pearl.

Finished size: 4" x 6"

SUPPLIES: All supplies from Papertrey Ink unless otherwise noted. *Cardstock:* (kraft, Berry Sorbet, Pure Poppy) *Clear stamps:* (polka dots from Polka Dot Basics set, damask from Damask Designs set, flourish from Fancy Flourishes set, sentiment from Handwritten Notes set) *Pigment ink:* (Vintage Cream) *Specialty ink:* (Pure Poppy, Dark Chocolate hybrid) *Accent:* (red button) BasicGrey *Fibers:* (red stitched ribbon); (twine) no source *Tools:* (border, corner rounder punches) Stampin' Up!

SUPPLIES: *Cardstock:* (kraft) Papertrey Ink; (white) *Patterned paper:* (clouds from Actopus to Zelephant pad) K&Company; (olive scalloped stripes) *Clear stamps:* (heart from Fun Loving set) Hampton Art; (love from Tags & Words set) Heidi Grace Designs *Specialty ink:* (Pure Poppy hybrid) Papertrey Ink *Accent:* (white pearl) Martha Stewart Crafts *Font:* (Bookman Old Style) www.fonts.com

DESIGNER TIP

When working with dimensional glaze, apply a small amount in the center and then carefully push it to the edge of the image using the applicator tip or a paper piercing tool.

DESIGNER TIP

Ink the edges of white cardstock pieces to make them stand out on a busy card.

I Heart U Card

Designer: Kimber McGray

1. Make card from patterned paper; ink edges.
2. Stamp alphabet block on cardstock piece. Draw border.
3. Punch bottom edge of cardstock piece, color heart, and tie on ribbon. Adhere with foam tape.
4. Color only I, O, and U on alphabet block and stamp on cardstock. Trim, ink edges, adhere rhinestone, and adhere with foam tape.

Finished size: 4¼" x 4½"

Wanna Stay In Card

Designer: Julie Masse

1. Make card from cardstock.
2. Trim patterned paper strip and adhere.
3. Stamp chopsticks on cardstock strip, color, and apply dimensional glaze. Adhere.
4. Stamp sentiment and pierce line.
5. Tie cord around card.

Finished size: 4¼" x 5½"

SUPPLIES: *Cardstock:* (Snowflake) Core'dinations *Patterned paper:* (Chopped Tomatoes from Minestrone collection) Jillibean Soup *Rubber stamp:* (alphabet block from Confession: I {Luv} Unity set) Unity Stamp Co. *Dye ink:* (black) Ranger Industries *Color medium:* (red, black markers) Stampin' Up! *Accent:* (red heart rhinestone) *Fibers:* (red stitched ribbon) May Arts *Tool:* (border punch) Stampin' Up!

SUPPLIES: *Cardstock:* (white) Georgia-Pacific; (Real Red) Stampin' Up! *Patterned paper:* (Skyline from Metropolitan collection) American Crafts *Rubber stamps:* (chopsticks, sentiment from Flirty Fortunes set) Paper Pretties *Dye ink:* (Tuxedo Black) Tsukineko *Color medium:* (gold, red, gray markers) Copic *Fibers:* (gold cord) *Other:* (dimensional glaze) Stampin' Up!

Be Mine Candy Necklace Box

Designer: Betsy Veldman

1. Print template on patterned paper. Assemble box according to manufacturer instructions.
2. Stamp heart on cardstock, punch, and adhere.
3. Die-cut tag from cardstock. Stamp sentiment and adhere. Adhere epoxy dot.
4. Place candy necklace inside glassine bag, fold top, and punch holes. Tie string on bag.
5. Punch holes in box top; tie ribbon.
6. Place candy bag in box; adhere.

Finished size: 3¼" x 1" x 3¼"

Sweetest Card

Designer: Beatriz Jennings

1. Make card from cardstock.
2. Trim patterned paper, round top corners, ink edges, and adhere.
3. Punch edge of patterned paper, pierce sides, and adhere.
4. Apply rub-on.
5. Die-cut flowers from patterned paper, turn up edges, and adhere.
6. Adhere flowers. Tie ribbon bow and adhere.

Finished size: 3¼" x 6"

SUPPLIES: *Cardstock:* (white) Papertrey Ink *Patterned paper:* (Word from Everyday collection) American Crafts *Clear stamps:* (polka dot heart, sentiment from Heart Prints set) Papertrey Ink *Specialty ink:* (Spring Rain, Hibiscus Burst hybrid) Papertrey Ink *Accent:* (yellow epoxy dot) The Robin's Nest *Fibers:* (yellow ribbon) Papertrey Ink; (white twine) The Beadery *Template:* (desktop organizer) Papertrey Ink *Die:* (tag) Provo Craft *Tool:* (heart punch) EK Success *Other:* (glassine bag) Papertrey Ink; (candy necklace)

SUPPLIES: *Cardstock:* (red) Bazzill Basics Paper *Patterned paper:* (Bright Silk from Bright Skies collection, Pixy Stix from Eye Candy collection, Small Dots from Chianti collection) GCD Studios *Dye ink:* (Antique Linen) Ranger Industries *Accents:* (cream flowers) *Rub-on:* (sweetest) GCD Studios *Fibers:* (blue stitched ribbon) *Die:* (flower) Provo Craft *Tools:* (border, corner rounder punches) Fiskars

5 Hello Honey Card

Designer: Teri Anderson

1. Make card from cardstock. Cover with patterned paper.
2. Adhere square of patterned paper.
3. Adhere rhinestone circle. Tie on ribbon.
4. Stamp sentiment on cardstock, color, and punch into circle. Mat with punched cardstock circles; adhere to card.
5. Stamp bees on cardstock. Color and apply glitter glue. Trim and adhere.

Finished size: 4¼" square

Love Bug Cookie Bucket

Designer: Erin Madsen, courtesy of Die Cuts With a View

BUCKET

1. Make tag from cardstock; mat with cardstock.
2. Punch circles from cardstock to make ladybug body. Adhere cardstock strips for antennae.
3. Punch circle from patterned paper; cut in half. Adhere to ladybug. Adhere punched cardstock circles.
4. Cover cardstock head, body, and spots with dimensional glaze. Adhere with foam tape.
5. Stamp "Love bug" and hearts on cardstock. Punch out letters and hearts and ink edges. Adhere.
6. Punch slot, thread ribbon, and tie on bucket.

COOKIE TAG

1. Print love bug directions on cardstock. Trim into tag and mat with cardstock.
2. Spell "Love bug" with stickers.
3. Punch circles from cardstock, adhere, and cover with dimensional glaze.
4. Fill bag with cookies and tie closed with ribbon. Tie on tag.
5. Place cookie package in bucket.

Finished size: 5½" diameter x 5" height

SUPPLIES: *Cardstock:* (white, black) WorldWin *Patterned paper:* (Wednesday from Girl Friday collection) Cosmo Cricket; (black polka dot from Sabrina collection) Making Memories *Rubber stamps:* (sentiment, bees from The Birds and the Bees set) Cornish Heritage Farms *Dye ink:* (black) Marvy Uchida *Color medium:* (yellow, red markers) Copic *Accents:* (clear rhinestone circle) Zva Creative; (clear glitter glue) Ranger Industries *Fibers:* (red ribbon) May Arts *Tools:* (2" circle punch) Fiskars; (1¾" circle punch) EK Success

SUPPLIES: *Cardstock:* (white, black) Die Cuts With a View *Patterned paper:* (red polka dot from Summer Glitter pad) Die Cuts With a View *Rubber stamps:* (Simple Serif Mini Alphabet set) Stampin' Up! *Dye ink:* (Riding Hood Red, Basic Black) Stampin' Up! *Stickers:* (Flocked Red alphabet) Die Cuts With a View *Fibers:* (black stitched ribbon) Die Cuts With a View, (black, black gingham ribbon) Offray *Font:* (Benguiat Frisky) www. fonts.com *Tools:* (1¾", ¾" circle punches) EK Success, (horizontal slot punch) Stampin' Up *Other:* (dimensional glaze) Ranger Industries; (red bucket, cellophane bag) Wal-Mart; (cookies)

Dramatic Love Card

Designer: Rae Barthel

1. Make card from cardstock. Cover with patterned paper and ink edges.
2. Punch edges of patterned paper panel. Adhere patterned paper, ink edges, and tie on ribbon.
3. Adhere panel with foam tape.
4. Affix stickers to spell "Love" on tag. Adhere rhinestones.
5. Adhere tag with foam tape.

Finished size: 4" x 7¼"

Lucky in Love Card

Designer: Julie Campbell

1. Make card from cardstock.
2. Trim cardstock panels, ink edges, and adhere.
3. Adhere black pearls.
4. Affix stickers to spell "Lucky" and stamp "In love".
5. Tie on ribbon and tie black twine.
6. Adhere playing card using foam tape.

Finished size: 4¼" x 5½"

SUPPLIES: *Cardstock:* (kraft) *Patterned paper:* (Alluring from Fascinating collection, Rugged from Fetching collection) Pink Paislee; (Palace Blue from Marrakech collection) BasicGrey *Chalk ink:* (Warm Red) Clearsnap *Accents:* (scalloped oval tag) Jenni Bowlin Studio; (turquoise rhinestones) Michaels *Stickers:* (black glitter alphabet) Making Memories *Fibers:* (red ribbon) Offray *Tool:* (border punch) Martha Stewart Crafts

SUPPLIES: *Cardstock:* (black, kraft) Papertrey Ink *Clear stamps:* (Fresh Alphabet set) Papertrey Ink *Dye ink:* (Tuxedo Black) Tsukineko *Pigment ink:* (Vintage Cream) Papertrey Ink *Stickers:* (Red Rhinestone ABC Epoxy alphabet) Creative Imaginations *Accent:* (black pearls) Kaisercraft; (vintage playing card) *Fibers:* (red/cream striped ribbon, black twine) May Arts

You Warm My Heart Card

Designer: Jeanne Streiff

❶ Make card from cardstock.

❷ Cut strips of cardstock; punch border, adhere strips together, and stitch. Adhere to card.

❸ Wrap ribbon around card front; tie knot.

❹ Die-cut scalloped circle from cardstock; ink edges and adhere with foam tape.

❺ Stamp coffee cup on cardstock; color with markers, cut out, attach nail head, and adhere with foam tape.

❻ Stamp sentiment.

Finished size: 4¼" x 5½"

Key to My Heart Card

Designer: Kimber McGray

❶ Make card from patterned paper; ink edges.

❷ Stamp key and sentiment on cardstock; color with markers. Draw lines and border.

❸ Trim stamped piece; punch border. Mat with cardstock.
Note: Tear bottom edge of mat.

❹ Wrap ribbon around stamped piece; tie knot. Adhere piece with foam tape.

❺ Adhere pearls.

Finished size: 4" x 5¾"

SUPPLIES: *Cardstock:* (white, red, Tawny Medium) Prism *Clear stamps:* (coffee cup, sentiment from Cool Beans set) Elzybells Art Stamps *Dye ink:* (Black Soot, Vintage Photo) Ranger Industries *Color medium:* (beige, tan, red markers) Copic *Accent:* (gold nail head) *Fibers:* (brown gingham ribbon) May Arts *Die:* (scalloped circle) Spellbinders *Tool:* (border punch) Martha Stewart Crafts

SUPPLIES: *Cardstock:* (red, white) Core'dinations *Patterned paper:* (Fortitude from Prudence collection) Crate Paper *Rubber stamps:* (key, sentiment from Everyday Adorable set) Unity Stamp Co. *Dye ink:* (black) Ranger Industries *Color media:* (mustard, black, red markers) Stampin' Up!; (black fine-tip pen) *Accents:* (white pearls) Zva Creative *Fibers:* (black striped ribbon) May Arts *Tool:* (border punch) EK Success

Quotable You

Nothing says "I love you" like a beautiful poem or sentiment, but sometimes it's difficult to come up with just the right words—especially for Valentine's Day. Join us as we bring you romantic projects that incorporate quotes from your favorite songs, movies, books, and poems—quotes filled with all the right words.

Editor: Susan Hart

You Spin Me Card

Designer: Julie Campbell

❶ Make card from cardstock.

❷ Round corners of cardstock; adhere to card.

❸ Mat patterned paper with cardstock; adhere.

❹ Die-cut circles from cardstock. Punch hole in smallest circle. Adhere circles together; adhere to card.

❺ Stamp "Dead or alive" and "1985" on record. Stamp sentiment, baby, and hearts.

❻ Make "Right" label; affix.

❼ Apply glitter glue.

Finished size: 6" square

In the Name of Love Card

Designer: Wendy Price

❶ Make card from cardstock.

❷ Cut patterned paper; ink edges. Mat with cardstock and adhere to card.

❸ Punch circles from cardstock. Adhere cardstock strip and circles to card.

❹ Stamp Monica on cardstock. Cut out and adhere, stamp side down, to card with foam tape.

❺ Cut out octagon from cardstock; mat with cardstock. Apply rub-ons. Adhere cardstock strip and octagon with foam tape.

❻ Print "The Supremes" on cardstock; trim and adhere.

❼ Affix stickers, some with foam tape. Apply foil to patterned paper.

Finished size: 7" x 4"

SUPPLIES: *Cardstock:* (black) Prism; (white) Papertrey Ink *Patterned paper:* (Sugary Love from Sunshine Lollipop collection) Sassafras Lass *Rubber stamps:* (sentiment from Round & Round We Go set, baby from Baby Love set, hearts from Hugs and Kisses set) Cornish Heritage Farms *Clear stamps:* (Simple Alphabet) Papertrey Ink *Dye ink:* (Watermelon, Pitch Black) Ranger Industries *Accent:* (red glitter glue) Ranger Industries *Sticker:* (black label tape) Dymo *Dies:* (embossed circles) Spellbinders *Tools:* (corner rounder punch) EK Success; (label maker) Dymo; (die cut/embossing machine) Spellbinders; (¹/₈" circle punch)

SUPPLIES: *Cardstock:* (white, black, red, yellow, green) *Patterned paper:* (Black & White Mini Bangles) KI Memories *Rubber stamp:* (Monica) Rubbernecker Stamp Co. *Dye ink:* (black) *Rub-ons:* (Charleston alphabet) October Afternoon *Stickers:* (foam alphabet) Target; (Bookworks Mini alphabet) EK Success *Font:* (Times New Roman) Microsoft *Adhesive:* (foam tape) *Tools:* (1", 1¼" circle punches) EK Success *Other:* (silver foil) 7gypsies

Nothing So Sweet Card

Designer: Beatriz Jennings

❶ Make card from cardstock.

❷ Cover card with patterned paper; ink and stitch.

❸ Adhere patterned paper rectangle; zigzag-stitch top and bottom edges.

❹ Affix sticker. Thread button with floss; adhere.

❺ Die-cut butterflies from patterned paper. Layer, bend wings of top butterflies up slightly, and adhere.

❻ Tie with cord.

Finished size: 5" x 6"

Above All Pillow Box

Designer: Sherry Wright

❶ Cut patterned paper to fit box; distress and ink edges. Adhere.

❷ Tie on ribbon.

❸ Distress and ink edges of quote die cut; adhere.

❹ Adhere rhinestone and felt flowers.

Finished size: 7" x 4¼" x 1½"

SUPPLIES: *Cardstock:* (gray) DMD, Inc. *Patterned paper:* (red stripe, red brocade, blue swirl, cream starburst from Bailey collection) K&Company *Dye ink:* (Tea Dye) Ranger Industries *Accent:* (cream button) *Sticker:* (quote) Rusty Pickle *Fibers:* (hemp cord, white floss) *Die:* (butterfly) Provo Craft *Tool:* (die cut machine) Provo Craft

SUPPLIES: *Patterned paper:* (Velvet Floral from Ooh La La collection) Bo-Bunny Press *Chalk ink:* (Chestnut Roan) Clearsnap *Accents:* (green rhinestone, green felt flowers) Queen & Co.; (quote die cut) Hot Off The Press *Fibers:* (cream ribbon) Offray *Other:* (pillow box) Emma's Paperie

Love Looks Not Card

Designer: Shanna Vineyard

❶ Make card from cardstock; adhere patterned paper strips.

❷ Sand and stitch across top.

❸ Adhere trim.

❹ Cut heart from cardstock; stitch edges and adhere to card.

❺ Sand chipboard heart edges; adhere heart and wings.

❻ Print quote on cardstock; trim and adhere.

Finished size: 8" x 4¼"

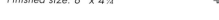

⑤ Love Is Card

Designer: Kalyn Kepner

❶ Make card from patterned paper; ink edges.

❷ Trim quote tag, ink edges, and adhere.

❸ Affix sticker.

❹ Adhere rhinestones.

Finished size: 3½" x 5 ¼"

SUPPLIES: *Cardstock:* (white) *Patterned paper:* (Twigs, Flutterby from Feather Your Nest collection) Webster's Pages; (Wish from Holiday Magic collection) Bo-Bunny Press *Accents:* (red chipboard heart) Heidi Swapp; (chipboard wings) Tattered Angels *Fibers:* (brown pompom trim) Jo-Ann Stores *Font:* (CK Cute) Creating Keepsakes

SUPPLIES: *Patterned paper:* (Cupid from Hey Sugar collection) Cosmo Cricket *Dye ink:* (orange) Clearsnap *Chalk ink:* (Chestnut Roan) Clearsnap *Accents:* (red rhinestones) K&Company; (love quote tag) My Mind's Eye *Stickers:* (dragonfly) K&Company

Youer Than You Candy Bouquet

Designer: Wendy Johnson

❶ Cut patterned paper strip; mat with cardstock. Trim with decorative-edge scissors. Adhere to container.

❷ Print "Love you!" on cardstock; trim and mat with cardstock. Adhere to container.

❸ Cut heart circle from patterned paper; adhere to container.

❹ Cut heart circles from patterned paper and adhere to lollipop sticks.

❺ Print quote on cardstock; trim and adhere to heart circle.

❻ Tie ribbon on lollipop.

❼ Fill container with candy; insert lollipops.

Finished size: 2¼" diameter x 8" height

Love is a Canvas Card

Designer: Stefanie Hamilton

❶ Make card from cardstock.

❷ Create finished size project in software; open digital elements.

❸ Drag cardstock to project. Place tree and sentiment.

❹ Resize stitching; drop in.

❺ Color flourishes; drag to project.

❻ Print card on photo paper; trim and adhere to card.

Finished size: 6" x 4"

SUPPLIES: *Cardstock:* (pink) Cloud 9 Design; (white) *Patterned paper:* (Sparkle Circles of Love, Be Loved Stripes from Be Loved collection) Cloud 9 Design *Fibers:* (green stitched ribbon) Michaels *Font:* (Century Gothic) www.myfonts.com *Tool:* (decorative-edge scissors) Fiskars *Other:* (acrylic container) American Crafts; (lollipop sticks, candy, heart lollipops)

SUPPLIES: *Cardstock:* (white) *Specialty paper:* (photo) *Digital elements:* (natural cardstock from Lisa kit) www.jenwilsondesigns.com; (tree brush from Love Grows kit; sentiment from Love WordART No. 02 kit) www.designerdigitals.com; (flourishes from Love Letters kit) www.scraporchard.com; (stitches from Splendid kit) www.shabbyprincess.com *Software:* (photo editing) Creative Memories

Heart Balloon Card

Designer: Wendy Johnson

❶ Make card from cardstock; adhere patterned paper.

❷ Print quote on cardstock; trim, mat with cardstock, and adhere.

❸ Print "Happy Valentine's day" on cardstock; trim and adhere with foam tape.

❹ Punch heart from cardstock and adhere with foam tape.

❺ Cut heart balloon shape from cardstock; adhere string. Adhere with foam tape.

❻ Affix alligator.

Finished size: 4¼" x 5½"

Love Mailbox

Designer: Heather Dewaelsche

❶ Remove flag from mailbox. Cover mailbox with patterned paper; spray with sealer.

❷ Trace flag on patterned paper. Cut out and adhere. Affix glitter heart sticker and attach flag to mailbox. Adhere button.

❸ Adhere cardstock strip and ribbon to mailbox.

❹ Affix love border, glitter heart, and love u stickers to mailbox door. Tie on ribbon.

❺ Adhere flowers and affix love circle sticker.

❻ Print heart stamp, cancellation marks and quote on photo paper; trim and adhere to cardstock. Punch hole and tie to ribbon with floss.

❼ Affix remaining stickers to cardstock; trim and insert into envelopes. Place in mailbox.

Finished size: 3" x 3½" x 5"

SUPPLIES: *Cardstock:* (Red Devil scalloped) Bazzill Basics Paper; (red, white) *Patterned paper:* (Spring Dot) Doodlebug Design *Sticker:* (alligator) EK Success *Fibers:* (white waxed string) Close To My Heart *Fonts:* (Century Gothic) www.myfonts.com; (First Grader) www.flyerstarter.com *Adhesive:* (foam tape) *Tool:* (heart punch) Fiskars

SUPPLIES: *Cardstock:* (white) The Paper Company; (white scalloped) Bazzill Basics Paper *Patterned paper:* (Unicorn Dreams, My Puppy from Girly Girl collection; From the Heart from The Love 2007 collection; Disco Love, Love Actually from The Love collection) Reminisce *Specialty paper:* (photo) *Finish:* (sealer) Krylon *Accents:* (white fabric glitter flowers) Heidi Swapp; (red button) Making Memories *Digital elements:* (heart stamp, cancellation marks) Reminisce *Stickers:* (love circle, love border, be mine, love u, glitter hearts, file folder, coupon) Reminisce *Fibers:* (pink, red gingham ribbon) Offray; (red stitched ribbon) Michaels; (hugs & kisses ribbon) Target; (red floss) DMC *Fonts:* (Cheri, Apple Garamond Light) www.dafont.com *Software:* (word processing) *Other:* (paper mache mailbox) Oriental Trading Co.; (vellum envelopes) Jo-Ann Stores

INSIDE

You & Me Card

Designer: Tanis Giesbrecht

OUTSIDE

❶ Make card from cardstock.

❷ Trim cardstock squares. Pierce around edges; faux stitch with marker and adhere to card..

❸ Punch scalloped circles from cardstock. Pierce around edges; adhere to squares.

❹ Punch circles from patterned paper; adhere. Spell "You" and "Me" with rub-ons.

❺ Stamp ampersand on cardstock. Cut out and mat with cardstock. Adhere to card with foam tape.

INSIDE

❶ Punch scalloped circle from cardstock. Pierce around edges and adhere.

❷ Punch circle from patterned paper. Mat with circle punched from cardstock; adhere.

❸ Apply rub-ons; write band and year with marker.

Finished size: 5" square

Just the Way You Are Gift Bag

Designer: Linda Harrison

❶ Cut patterned paper slightly smaller than bag front. Stamp stitched border, distress edges, and adhere.

❷ Stamp dotted heart on patterned paper and apply glitter; cut out and adhere to bag with foam tape.

❸ Stamp quote on cardstock; apply glitter. Cut out and adhere to bag with foam tape; insert stick pin.

❹ Adhere rhinestones.

Finished size: 4" x 5¼"

SUPPLIES: *Cardstock:* (Ruby Red, Blue Bayou, Wild Wasabi, Blush Blossom) Stampin' Up!; (Java) Bazzill Basics Paper *Patterned paper:* (Sparkle Circles of Love from Be Loved collection) Cloud 9 Design *Rubber stamp:* (ampersand from Jazzy Punctuation set) Inque Boutique *Pigment ink:* (Ruby Red) Stampin' Up! *Color medium:* (brown marker) Stampin' Up!; (black marker) *Rub-ons:* (Betty alphabet) KI Memories *Adhesive:* (foam tape) EK Success *Tools:* (1³/₈" circle punch, 1¾" scalloped circle punch) Stampin' Up!; (2½" scalloped circle punch) Marvy Uchida; (2 ¹/₈" circle punch) McGill

SUPPLIES: *Cardstock:* (pink) Bazzill Basics Paper *Patterned paper:* (Scallop Square from Love Story collection) Making Memories; (Floral from Magnolia Dream collection) My Mind's Eye *Rubber stamps:* (dotted heart from Stephanie Barnard Starter set, quote from Quotopia set, stitched border from In Stitches set) Inque Boutique *Dye ink:* (black) Inque Boutique *Accents:* (red rhinestones) Me & My Big Ideas; (tan heart stick pin) Heidi Grace Designs; (red glitter) Martha Stewart Crafts; (black glitter) Making Memories *Adhesive:* (foam tape) *Other:* (kraft gift bag)

INSIDE

Count the Ways Card

Designer: Kalyn Kepner

1. Make card from cardstock. Cut patterned paper block to fit card front.

2. Trim patterned paper strips with decorative-edge scissors; adhere behind block.

3. Cut patterned paper slightly smaller than block; adhere. Stitch corners with floss.

4. Adhere block to card. Adhere patterned paper strip.

5. Affix stickers. Write quote with pen.

6. Cut numbers from patterned paper; adhere with foam tape.

Finished size: 7½" x 4¾"

5 STEPS There is Only One Happiness Card

Designer: Angie Tieman

OUTSIDE

1. Make card from patterned paper.

2. Apply glitter to medallion die cut; adhere to card with foam tape.

3. Tie on ribbon. Attach brads to quote die cut. Adhere label and quote die cuts with foam tape.

INSIDE

1. Adhere cardstock panel.

2. Adhere chipboard flower. Tie ribbon on heart die cut; adhere to card.

Finished size: 5¼" square

SUPPLIES: *Cardstock:* (black) *Patterned paper:* (Uncle Dig's Auto from Main Street collection) Treehouse Memories; (Oh My! from Daydream collection) Sassafras Lass *Color medium:* (white gel pen) Sakura *Stickers:* (Cream Soda alphabet) American Crafts *Fibers:* (white floss) DMC *Adhesive:* (foam tape) *Tool:* (decorative-edge scissors)

SUPPLIES: *Cardstock:* (Basic Gray) Stampin' Up! *Patterned paper:* (Lacework from Lotus Faded China collection) K&Company *Accents:* (iridescent glitter, blue rhinestone brads) Stampin' Up!; (cream label, medallion, quote, heart die cuts; chipboard flower) K&Company *Fibers:* (gray ribbon) Michaels *Adhesive:* (foam tape)

INSIDE

Golden Thread Card
Designer: Melissa Phillips

❶ Make card from cardstock; round right front corners.

❷ Cut edge of patterned paper with decorative-edge scissors; punch holes and ink edges.

❸ Adhere trim to patterned paper piece.

❹ Ink edges of patterned paper rectangle and adhere to piece; stitch rectangle edges. Zigzag-stitch piece edge.

❺ Adhere piece to card. Adhere chipboard tag with foam tape; adhere tag die cut. Affix quote sticker.

❻ Apply rub-ons, adhere flowers, and affix stickers.

Finished size: 4" x 5¼"

Ever at Your Service Card
Designer: Melissa Phillips

OUTSIDE

❶ Make card from cardstock; paint edges.

❷ Ink edges of patterned paper pieces and adhere to card.

❸ Zigzag-stitch bottom and top edges; stitch around patterned paper rectangle.

❹ Adhere cupid die cut with foam tape. Affix stickers.

INSIDE

❶ Ink edges of patterned paper pieces and adhere.

❷ Adhere chipboard heart and affix stickers.

❸ Write "Shakespeare" with pen.

❹ Tie ribbon around card; tie on button with string.

Finished size: 3¾" x 5¼"

SUPPLIES: *Cardstock:* (Posie Pink) Bazzill Basics Paper *Patterned paper:* (Malta Spring from Margot collection) Collage Press *Dye ink:* (Old Paper) Ranger Industries *Accents:* (tag die cut) Collage Press; (chipboard tag) Autumn Leaves; (ivory, green polka dot flowers) Making Memories; (pearls) Kaisercraft *Rub-ons:* (flourishes) Crate Paper *Stickers:* (flowers, quote) Heidi Grace Designs *Fibers:* (white trim) Melissa Frances *Adhesive:* (foam tape) *Tools:* (decorative-edge scissors) Provo Craft; (¹⁄₈" circle, corner rounder punches)

SUPPLIES: *Cardstock:* (Creamy Cocoa) WorldWin *Patterned paper:* (Delectable from Sugared collection, Polished from Sultry collection, Be Mine from Blush collection) BasicGrey *Dye ink:* (Old Paper) Ranger Industries *Color medium:* (black pen) *Paint:* (Light Ivory) Delta *Accents:* (white glitter chipboard heart) Melissa Frances; (green button) Making Memories; (cupid die cut) My Mind's Eye *Stickers:* (Tiny alphabet) Making Memories *Fibers:* (white string) Darice; (pink ribbon) Martha Stewart Crafts *Adhesive:* (foam tape)

⦿5⦿ Rules for Happiness Gift Box

Designer: Sherry Wright

❶ Distress edges of patterned paper; adhere to box.

❷ Tie on ribbon.

❸ Affix sticker to patterned paper; trim. Distress edges and adhere.

❹ Cut berry stem from patterned paper and adhere.

Finished size: 4¼" x 5½" x 2½"

Beautiful Dream Card

Designer: Anabelle O'Malley

❶ Make card from cardstock.

❷ Trim patterned paper, cutting along flower petals. Adhere patterned paper strips to card.

❸ Double-stitch and ink edges of card.

❹ Cut quote from patterned paper; adhere to card, tucking under cut flower petals.

❺ Cut butterfly from patterned paper; adhere to acrylic butterfly. Fold and adhere to card.

❻ Adhere rhinestones.

Finished size: 5¼" x 4"

SUPPLIES: *Patterned paper:* (Elizabeth Berry Double-Stripe from 5th Avenue collection) Making Memories *Sticker:* (quote) 7gypsies *Fibers:* (cream ribbon) Offray *Other:* (white gable box) Emma's Paperie

SUPPLIES: *Cardstock:* (white) The Paper Company *Patterned paper:* (Cream, Drizzle from Raspberry Truffle collection) Webster's Pages *Pigment ink:* (Dune) Clearsnap *Accents:* (pink rhinestones) Prima; (acrylic butterfly) Heidi Swapp

Valentine's Day has never been so sweet.

We've packed our pages with fun ways to celebrate the holiday with friends and loved ones.

Indulge in our exciting ideas for cards, wrap, décor, and, of course, candy containers!

DESIGNER TIP

Use candy or chipboard hearts for BINGO chips.

Cutie Pie Classroom Party

Designer: Wendy Johnson

BINGO GAME CARD

❶ Print game card on cardstock (download at www.Paper-CraftsMag.com/mag). Mat with cardstock.

❷ Adhere patterned paper strip.

❸ Adhere rickrack and hearts.

TEACHER GIFT BUCKET

❶ Adhere patterned paper.

❷ Print teacher's name on cardstock; adhere.

❸ Adhere rickrack and hearts.

CANDY WRAPPER

❶ Wrap patterned paper around candy box.

❷ Print student's name on cardstock; trim and adhere.

❸ Adhere rickrack and hearts.

Dress up cupcakes or other valentine treats with heart food picks.

Finished sizes: BINGO card 7" x 8", teacher gift bucket 4¼" diameter x 4" height, candy wrapper 5" x 2" x ½"

SUPPLIES: *Cardstock:* (Petunia) Bazzill Basics Paper; (white) *Patterned paper:* (Décor Stripe from Oh So Loved collection) Heidi Grace Designs *Accents:* (chipboard hearts) Heidi Grace Designs *Fibers:* (light green rickrack) Colorbok; (white grosgrain, yellow ribbon) Offray *Font:* (CK Handprint) Creating Keepsakes *Other:* (pink bucket) Target; (box of candy)

REVEAL
SENTIMENT

Wild About You Card

Designer: Wendy Johnson

1. Print "I'm" and "about you!" on paper. Trim.

2. Cut cardstock strip. Spell sentiment with sticker and printed words.

3. Mat lion sticker with patterned paper. Adhere hearts punched from cardstock. Adhere to end of strip with foam tape.

4. Cut patterned paper square; cut slit slightly wider than sentiment strip. Attach brads to corners. Tuck strip in slit.

5. Affix foam tape to corners of square; adhere to slightly larger piece of cardstock.

Finished size: 5" square

SUPPLIES: *Cardstock:* (Pomegranate, Splash) Bazzill Basics Paper *Paper:* (white) *Patterned paper:* (Dots from Oh So Loved collection) Heidi Grace Designs *Accents:* (gold brads) Making Memories *Stickers:* (lion, wild) Pebbles Inc. *Font:* (TS Napoli) www.myfonts.com *Adhesive:* (foam tape) 3M *Tool:* (heart punch) EK Success

Babe Card

Designer: Maria Burke

1. Make card from cardstock.

2. Cut patterned paper; stitch edges and adhere.

3. Apply damask rub-on to tag. Adhere ribbon loop. Stitch button and adhere.

4. Paint heart. Apply rub-on and outline edges. Print "My heart is yours" on cardstock; cut out and adhere.

5. Adhere tag and heart to card.

Finished size: 5¼" x 4¼"

SUPPLIES: *Cardstock:* (Chalk) SEI *Patterned paper:* (Juicy Jellies from Cupid's Candy Shop collection) SEI *Paint:* (brick red) DecoArt *Color medium:* (white pen) American Crafts *Accents:* (be mine tag) SEI; (chipboard heart) Deluxe Designs; (cream button) *Rub-ons:* (babe) SEI; (damask) Imaginisce *Fibers:* (green polka dot ribbon) SEI *Font:* (SP You've Got Mail) Scrap Supply

For Keeps Card

Designer: Wendy Johnson

1. Make card from cardstock; cover with patterned paper.
2. Cut patterned paper piece; punch edge. Adhere.
3. Attach brad to label; affix.
4. Cut heart from patterned paper; affix stickers. Adhere with foam tape.

Finished size: 4" square

Be Mine Card

Designer: Amy Duff

1. Make card from cardstock.
2. Adhere patterned paper strip.
3. Staple ribbon over seam.
4. Apply rub-on to patterned paper; trim and adhere. Adhere lace trim.
5. Cut heart from patterned paper; mat with patterned paper. Stitch button in center. Adhere with foam tape.

Finished size: 6" x 4¼"

SUPPLIES: *Cardstock:* (white) *Patterned paper:* (Dancing Hearts from Pets collection) Around The Block; (Red Notebook, Weathered Dot) Creative Imaginations *Accent:* (black velvet brad) Creative Imaginations *Stickers:* (label, sentiment strips) Creative Imaginations *Adhesive:* (foam tape) *Tool:* (spiral binding punch) Stampin' Up!

SUPPLIES: *Cardstock:* (white) *Patterned paper:* (Anna, Audrey, Klara, Lena & Hans from Dutch Girl collection) Cosmo Cricket *Accents:* (red button) Jesse James & Co.; (red staples) *Rub-on:* (be mine) Royal & Langnickel *Fibers:* (red satin ribbon) Nicole Crafts; (white lace trim, string) *Adhesive:* (foam tape)

Authentic Card

Designer: Chris Cronin

Ink edges of paper pieces.

1. Make card from patterned paper.
2. Cut heart, following pattern on p. 282; adhere.
3. Punch holes and add stitches.
4. Stamp patterned paper; trim and adhere.
5. Tie floss through buttons; adhere.
6. Detail with pen.

Finished size: 5" x 6"

All Yours Card

Designer: Rachel Grieg

1. Make card from cardstock.
2. Adhere cardstock strip.
3. Adhere ribbon.
4. Cut rose from patterned paper; mat with cardstock. Adhere.
5. Affix sticker.

Finished size: 6" x 4"

SUPPLIES: *Patterned paper:* (Charmed, Romance from Blush collection) BasicGrey; (Dreamer from Wildheart collection) Fancy Pants Designs *Rubber stamp:* (authentic from Stamp of Authenticity set) Stampin' Up! *Pigment ink:* (black) *Color medium:* (black pen) American Crafts *Accents:* (red buttons) Making Memories *Fibers:* (turquoise floss) DMC *Tool:* (⅛" circle punch)

SUPPLIES: *Cardstock:* (Cameo, Pomegranate, Rosey) Bazzill Basics Paper *Patterned paper:* (Roses 9Up) Stamp It! Australia *Sticker:* (all yours) Making Memories *Fibers:* (striped ribbon) American Crafts

Pair of Hearts Card

Designer: Kim Frantz

1. Make card from cardstock.
2. Cut patterned paper; ink edges and adhere.
3. Cover hearts with patterned paper; sand edges. Adhere, overlapping, to card. *Note: Adhere small heart with foam tape.*
4. Adhere buttons.

Finished size: 4" square

SUPPLIES: *Cardstock:* (brown) Michaels *Patterned paper:* (Lace, Saturate, Suffuse from Infuse collection) BasicGrey *Pigment ink:* (brown) Tsukineko *Accents:* (chipboard hearts) Making Memories; (brown, pink buttons) Jesse James & Co. *Adhesive:* (foam tape) Plaid

Key to My Heart Card

Designer: Stefanie Hamilton

1. Make card from patterned paper; adhere chipboard behind front flap.
2. Print sentiment on patterned paper. Trim, mat with cardstock, and adhere.
3. Tie ribbon to charm; adhere.
4. Adhere door knob.

Finished size: 4" x 7"

SUPPLIES: *Cardstock:* (brown) *Patterned paper:* (Purify, Suffuse from Infuse collection) BasicGrey *Accents:* (door knob) 7gypsies; (key charm) Westrim Crafts *Fibers:* (brown ribbon) Offray *Font:* (Santa's Sleigh) www.dafont.com *Other:* (chipboard)

⑤ Stitched Heart Card

Designer: Stephanie Barnard, courtesy of Inque Boutique

1. Make card from red cardstock.
2. Stitch large heart using white thread.
3. Stamp the letter "I" on card front and adhere heart punches.
4. Stamp the letters "y", "o" and "u" on white cardstock; trim and staple to card edge.

Finished size: 5½" x 7"

⑤ I Love You Card

Designer: Danielle Flanders

1. Make card from cardstock; trim bottom edge in wave. Ink edges.
2. Cut cardstock; trim long edges with decorative-edge scissors. Repeatedly stamp Love. Tie ribbon to longer ribbon length. Adhere. Stitch edges and stems. Adhere.
3. Tie thread through button; adhere.
4. Spell "You" on I love sticker.
5. Affix stickers with foam tape.

Finished size: 6" x 5¼"

SUPPLIES: *Cardstock:* (red, white) *Rubber stamps:* (Fresh Uppercase, Fresh Lowercase alphabet from See D's collection) Inque Boutique *Dye ink:* (Grand Cranberry, black) Inque Boutique *Tool:* (heart punch)

SUPPLIES: *Cardstock:* (Icy Blue, Maraschino) Bazzill Basics Paper *Clear stamp:* (Love) Heidi Swapp *Pigment ink:* (white) Tsukineko *Watermark ink:* Tsukineko *Accent:* (red button) Doodlebug Design *Stickers:* (circles, heart, I love, Roxie Basic alphabet) KI Memories *Fibers:* (aqua polka dot ribbon) American Crafts *Adhesive:* (foam tape) Plaid *Tool:* (decorative-edge scissors) Provo Craft

Tried & True Card

Designer: Angelia Wigginton

1. Make card from patterned paper.
2. Cut patterned paper pieces; distress edges. Adhere.
3. Punch holes in label. Tie twine through holes. Adhere.

Finished size: 5¾" x 4¼"

Cherish Card

Designer: Julia Stainton

1. Make card from cardstock.
2. Apply rub-ons.
3. Zigzag-stitch edge.
4. Adhere label.

Finished size: 5½" x 4¼"

SUPPLIES: *Patterned paper:* (Elsa, Princess' Pea from Perhaps collection) BasicGrey; (Gray Circles) Fontwerks *Accent:* (love chipboard label) Target *Fibers:* (twine)

SUPPLIES: *Cardstock:* (black) Bazzill Basics Paper *Accent:* (cherish label) Making Memories *Rub-on:* (floral scene, flourish) Daisy D's

⁵Love Vase Cover

Designer: Mou Saha

1. Make sure monogram negatives are same size. Adhere chipboard strips to increase size of smaller negatives.
2. Cover with patterned paper.
3. Adhere patterned paper behind letters.
4. Punch holes and tie panels together with raffia.
5. Place vase inside.

Finished size: 5¼" x 5¼" x 10½"

⁵L is for Love Gift Bag

Designer: Patty Lennon

1. Cover bag front with patterned paper.
2. Adhere patterned paper strips.
3. Tie ribbon on tag; adhere with foam tape. Attach brad to flower; adhere with foam tape.

Finished size: 4" x 5¼"

SUPPLIES: *Patterned paper:* (Capulet from Fair Verona collection; Chocolate Bunnies, May Flowers from Chocolate Bunnies collection) Rusty Pickle *Accents:* (chipboard monogram negatives) Rusty Pickle *Fibers:* (pink raffia) Michaels *Tool:* (⅛" circle punch) *Other:* (chipboard)

SUPPLIES: *Patterned paper:* (I Love You, Love Ornament from Love Letters collection; Cream Scroll Die Cut from Antique Cream collection) Creative Imaginations *Accents:* (love chipboard tag) Creative Imaginations; (cream flower) Prima; (gold brad) Making Memories *Fibers:* (cream ribbon) Making Memories *Adhesive:* (foam tape) *Other:* (kraft gift bag)

BONUS IDEA

Hang the hearts separately
for a mobile effect.

⁙5⁙ Heart Ornaments

Designer: Betsy Veldman

① Cut four equally-sized hearts from patterned paper, following
pattern on p. 282; score and fold along center.

② Adhere together.

③ Punch hole in top.

④ String buttons and beads on thread; knot and loop
through hole.

⑤ Decorate as desired.

Finished size: variable

SUPPLIES: *Patterned paper:* (Crush, Tender, Embrace, Affection, Adore from
Beloved collection) Tinkering Ink *Accents:* (alphabet die cuts) Tinkering Ink;
(assorted buttons) Autumn Leaves; (felt flowers) American Crafts; (assorted beads)
Rub-ons: (All Mixed Up alphabet) Doodlebug Design *Stickers:* (hearts) Doodlebug
Design *Fibers:* (red floss) DMC *Die:* (scalloped square) Provo Craft *Tools:* (die cut
machine) Provo Craft; (1⁄16" circle punch)

⑤ Heart Candy Jar

Designer: Lindsey Botkin

1. Adhere patterned paper around jar.
2. Adhere patterned paper strip.
3. Tie ribbon on rickrack. Adhere rickrack around jar. Attach pin.
4. Punch circle from patterned paper; adhere to lid. Cut hearts from patterned paper; adhere.
5. Fill jar with candy.

Finished size: 2" diameter x 6¼" height

You Rock Card

Designer: Danielle Flanders

1. Make card from cardstock; trim with decorative-edge scissors. Ink edges.
2. Cut patterned paper; trim right side with decorative-edge scissors. Mat with cardstock; trim right side with decorative-edge scissors. Adhere. Zigzag-stitch long edges.
3. Cut assorted pieces from patterned paper; adhere.
4. Affix sticker.
5. Stamp Love.
6. Adhere ribbon and flower. Tie thread through button; adhere.

Finished size: 8" x 5"

SUPPLIES: *Patterned paper:* (Long-Stemmed Love, Love Lines from Sweetheart collection) Cloud 9 Design *Accents:* (pin with flower charm) Making Memories *Fibers:* (white velvet rickrack, pink polka dot ribbon) May Arts *Tool:* (1¾" circle punch) Creative Memories *Other:* (jar) Prima; (candy)

SUPPLIES: *Cardstock:* (Maraschino, white) Bazzill Basics Paper *Patterned paper:* (Roxie Cliques, Roxie Funky Fun, Roxie Quilt) KI Memories *Clear stamp:* (Love) Heidi Swapp *Pigment ink:* (white) Tsukineko *Solvent ink:* (Jet Black) Tsukineko *Accents:* (red button) Doodlebug Design; (blue flower) Bazzill Basics Paper *Sticker:* (you rock) KI Memories *Fibers:* (pink, red stitched ribbon) Morex *Tools:* (large decorative-edge scissors) Provo Craft; (small decorative-edge scissors) Fiskars

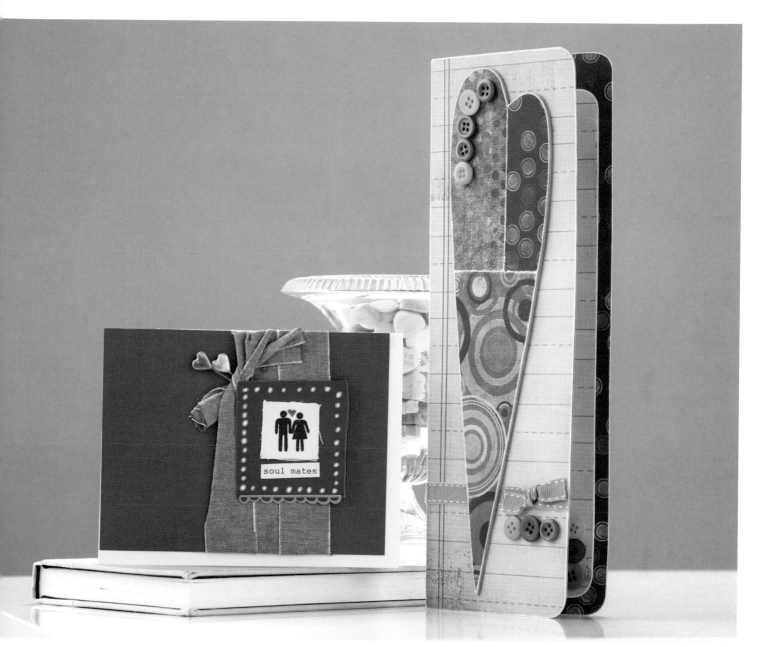

⑤ Soul Mates Card

Designer: Teri Anderson

① Make card from cardstock.

② Cut cardstock block; wrap with fabric. Knot and attach pins.

③ Cut motif from specialty paper; adhere to sticker. Cut "soul mates" from patterned paper; adhere.

④ Affix sticker to fabric; affix border strip.

⑤ Adhere block to card.

Finished size: 5¾" x 4½"

⑤ Tall Heart Card

Designer: Courtney Kelley

① Make card from cardstock; cover with patterned paper. Round outside corners and sand edges.

② Tie ribbon length to ribbon; adhere.

③ Cut patterned paper pieces to cover heart; sand edges and adhere.

④ Adhere buttons.

⑤ Adhere heart.

Finished size: 3¾" x 10½"

SUPPLIES: *Cardstock:* (tan) Bazzill Basics Paper; (cream) Provo Craft *Patterned paper:* (Betty Patchwork) KI Memories *Specialty paper:* (Betty You + Me fabric) KI Memories *Accents:* (heart pins) Jo-Ann Stores; (pink fabric strip) Rusty Pickle *Stickers:* (pink square, scalloped border strip) KI Memories

SUPPLIES: *Cardstock:* (Maraschino) Bazzill Basics Paper *Patterned paper:* (Groovy, Splendid, Sublime from Kewl collection) Fancy Pants Designs *Accents:* (chipboard heart) Fancy Pants Designs; (assorted buttons) Autumn Leaves *Fibers:* (aqua stitched ribbon) Fancy Pants Designs *Tool:* (corner rounder punch) Creative Memories

VALENTINES TRIMMED IN STYLE

Show off radiant ribbons, luscious laces, and fantastic fibers on heartfelt greetings and gifts for Valentine's Day. These loving creations will tug at the recipient's heart strings.

You Captured My Heart Card

Designer: Alisa Bangerter

❶ Make card from cardstock. Cover with reverse side of Doc Holiday paper; sand edges.

❷ Cut patterned paper slightly smaller than card front; sand edges and adhere. Attach eyelets.

❸ Cover "You" with patterned paper; trim and adhere.

❹ Cut out heart shape from reverse side of Doc Holiday; crumple, sand, and adhere with foam squares. Make a lasso from jute and adhere.

❺ Thread lace through buckle and adhere.

❻ Stamp "Captured my heart" on reverse side of Calamity Jane paper; trim, sand, and adhere with foam squares.

Finished size: 5" x 7"

SUPPLIES: *Cardstock:* (brown) *Patterned paper:* (Calamity Jane, Doc Holiday, Kissin' Kate from Wanted collection) Cosmo Cricket *Rubber stamps:* (Antique Alphabet) PSX *Dye ink:* (Chocolate Chip) Stampin' Up! *Accents:* (chipboard letters, buckle) Cosmo Cricket; (pewter eyelets) Making Memories *Fibers:* (crochet lace) Making Memories; (jute) Magic Scraps *Adhesive:* (foam squares) Making Memories

5 STEPS Me & You Card

Designer: Wendy Johnson

❶ Make card from cardstock.

❷ Adhere patterned paper rectangle.

❸ Adhere rickrack around chipboard heart; adhere.

❹ Adhere acrylic square and chipboard heart.

❺ Adhere ribbon and rickrack.

Finished size: 5½" x 6"

SUPPLIES: *Cardstock:* (white) Bazzill Basics Paper *Patterned paper:* (Vineyard Pinstripe) Heidi Grace Designs *Accents:* (chipboard hearts, me & you acrylic square) Heidi Grace Designs *Fibers:* (green velvet rickrack, blue velvet ribbon) BasicGrey

Floral Be Mine Card

Designer: Valerie Pingree

1. Make card from cardstock.
2. Cut patterned paper to fit front. Cut slots for ribbon. Thread ribbon and adhere ends on back.
3. Attach brad to flower; adhere.
4. Die-cut nameplate from cardstocks. Spell "Be mine" with rub-ons. Attach with brads.
5. Adhere piece to card.

Finished size: 4½" x 7½"

SUPPLIES: *Cardstock:* (black, white) *Patterned paper:* (Pink Climbing Vine from Sloane collection) Anna Griffin *Accents:* (white silk flower) Bazzill Basics Paper; (rhinestone brad) Karen Foster Design; (black brads) Lasting Impressions for Paper *Fibers:* (black stitched ribbon) Wal-Mart *Font:* (Pharmacy) www.dafont.com *Die:* (oval nameplate) QuicKutz *Tools:* (die cut machine) QuicKutz; (slot punch) Making Memories

Hugs & Kisses Card

Designer: Linda Dotterer

1. Make card from cardstock.
2. Cover with patterned papers; adhere rickrack over seam.
3. Stamp sentiment on white; trim and round corners. Mat with cardstock and adhere.

Finished size: 4¼" x 5½"

SUPPLIES: *Cardstock:* (Petunia) Bazzill Basics Paper; (white) *Patterned paper:* (Groovy, Ticking from Kiss Me collection) KI Memories *Rubber stamps:* (Hugs & Kisses from Alphabet Soup set) Stampin' Up! *Dye ink:* (Rose Red) Stampin' Up! *Fibers:* (black rickrack) Wrights *Tools:* (corner rounder punch) EK Success

5 Be Mine Tag

Designer: Melissa Phillips

Paint paper edges with pink and the light ivory.

1. Make tag from Pink Stripe paper. Punch hole.
2. Cut Polka Dot paper rectangle; stitch around edges. Adhere brown lace. Adhere piece.
3. Paint hearts light ivory. Let dry, sand edges, and adhere. Adhere flowers and buttons.
4. Paint be mine label with light ivory and wipe off excess. Adhere with foam squares.
5. Paint washer with light ivory and wipe off excess. Tie with lace and jute to tag.

Finished size: 2½" x 4¾"

SUPPLIES: *Patterned paper:* (Pink Stripe, Polka Dot from Pretty Little Girl collection) My Mind's Eye *Dye ink:* (Hot Cocoa) Ranger Industries *Paint:* (light ivory, pink) Delta *Accents:* (chipboard hearts) Heidi Swapp, (be mine metal label, treasure metal washer) Making Memories; (tan flowers) Prima; (pink buttons) *Fibers:* (brown, pink lace) Fancy Pants Designs; (jute) *Adhesive:* (foam squares)

5 XO Card

Designer: Terri Davenport

1. Make card from cardstock.
2. Cut patterned paper slightly smaller than card front; adhere.
3. Adhere rectangle of patterned paper.
4. Adhere cardstock circle and chipboard letters.
5. Adhere trim.

Finished size: 4¼" x 5½"

SUPPLIES: *Cardstock:* (Ebony) Bazzill Basics Paper *Patterned paper:* (Hold the Remote Control, Hart Strings from He Sings at Weddings collection) Imagination Project *Accents:* (white chipboard alphabet) Imagination Project *Fibers:* (black trim)

Ribbon L-O-V-E Card

Designer: Melissa Phillips

Ink all paper edges.

1. Cut cardstock to 8½" x 5½". Fold bottom up 2" and fold top down 2¾". Round corners.

2. Cover flaps with patterned paper. Apply "Adore you" rub-on to top flap.

3. Cut heart shape from Gracen Dot paper; cover half with Black Open Dot paper; and zigzag-stitch seam. Cut frame from Loves Me paper and adhere.

4. Apply "I" rub-on to tag. Attach to ribbon with brad. Adhere to card.

5. Make "L" and "E" from paper strips; adhere.

6. Make "V" with ribbon. Zigzag-stitch and staple.

Finished size: 5½" x 3¾"

SUPPLIES: *Cardstock:* (white) DMD, Inc. *Patterned paper:* (Loves Me, XOXO Expressions) Carolee's Creations; (Gracen Dot) Making Memories; (Black Open Dot from Gallery collection) Chatterbox *Dye ink:* (black) *Accents:* (pewter heart brad) Creative Impressions; (white tag) Making Memories; (staple) *Rub-ons:* (I adore you) Making Memories *Fibers:* (black plaid, black dotted ribbon) May Arts *Tools:* (corner rounder punch)

Big Heart Love Card

Designer: Linda Beeson

1. Make card from cardstock.

2. Zigzag-stitch trim on white cardstock square. Adhere ends around back.

3. Double mat with red cardstock and patterned paper. Adhere.

4. Mat stickers with red; adhere.

Finished size: 5½" square

SUPPLIES: *Cardstock:* (black, red, white) Bazzill Basics Paper *Patterned paper:* (Red Text from Everyday Primary collection) Creative Imaginations *Stickers:* (flower, heart) We R Memory Keepers *Fibers:* (fancy red trim) May Arts *Adhesive:* (foam tape) 3M

My Valentine Card

Designer: Dee Gallimore-Perry

1. Make card from cardstock.
2. Cut patterned paper slightly smaller than card front; ink edges.
3. Apply sticker to cardstock; staple.
4. Staple chipboard heart.
5. Adhere piece to card. Adhere trim.

Finished size: 6" x 4½"

SUPPLIES: *Cardstock:* (brown, white) Bazzill Basics Paper *Patterned paper:* (Pink Gingham from French Country Garden Collection) Printworks *Dye ink:* (Van Dyke Brown) Ranger Industries *Accent:* (pink chipboard heart) Heidi Swapp; (staples) *Sticker:* (my valentine) Die Cuts With a View *Fibers:* (pink rickrack) Maya Road

Valentine Wishes Card and Gift Box

Designer: Lisa Johnson

CARD

Ink card, paper edges, and fibers with Creamy Brown.

1. Make card from cardstock. Cut Feminine Delights slightly smaller than card front.
2. Adhere lace.
3. Adhere torn Celebration Charm paper.
4. Attach rickrack to ribbon with brads. Adhere to piece; adhere piece to card.
5. Stamp hearts on cardstock with Orchid Pastel and Warm Red; trim, ink edges with Dark Brown, and accent with glitter. Adhere hearts with foam squares.

BOX

Ink box, paper edges, and fibers with Creamy Brown.

1. Adhere patterned paper to all sides.
2. Adhere ribbon and trims.
3. Attach stick pin.

Finished sizes: card 4¼" x 5½", box 4" cube

SUPPLIES: *Cardstock:* (kraft) Stampin' Up! *Patterned paper:* (Celebration Charm, Feminine Delight from Simply Classic collection) EK Success *Rubber stamps:* (Hailey's Solid Heart, Valentine Wishes) A Muse Artstamps *Chalk ink:* (Creamy Brown, Dark Brown, Orchid Pastel, Warm Red) Clearsnap *Accents:* (stick pin) Jo-Ann Stores; (brown brads) Creative Impressions; (glitter) Stewart Superior Corp. *Fibers:* (oatmeal, brown, pink rickrack; pink, red twill ribbon) Creative Impressions; (lace) Jo-Ann Stores *Adhesive:* (foam squares) *Other:* (gift box) The Paper Zone

Mom Loves You Card

Designer: Melissa Phillips

❶ Make card from cardstock. Cover with patterned paper; ink edges.

❷ Stitch red trim and adhere rickrack on edge.

❸ Cut reverse side of Love Letter paper slightly smaller than card front; stitch edges and adhere.

❹ Cut heart from reverse side of Small Red-Pink Flower Whimsy paper; stitch red trim. Adhere piece.

❺ Spell "You" with chipboard letters.

❻ Sand photo corner edges and stitch; adhere.

❼ Sand chipboard heart edges. Tie ribbon. Adhere piece.

❽ Spell "Mom", "loves" with rub-ons on chipboard strips. Sand edges and adhere.

Finished size: 5½" square

SUPPLIES: *Cardstock:* (white) DMD, Inc. *Patterned paper:* (Red Dot from Love Me collection) Sweetwater; (Love Letter from Brighton collection, Small Red-Pink Flower Whimsy from Festivale collection) Scenic Route Paper Co. *Dye ink:* (Old Paper) Ranger Industries *Accents:* (white chipboard heart, pink chipboard strips) Heidi Swapp; (pink chipboard alphabet) Li'l Davis Designs; (chipboard photo corner) Scenic Route Paper Co. *Rub-ons:* (Providence alphabet) Making Memories *Fibers:* (double-pink grosgrain ribbon) Scrapworks; (red fancy trim) Making Memories; (white rickrack) Wrights

✦5✦ I Love You Card

Designer: Sherry Wright

❶ Adhere ribbons and trims to card.

❷ Attach "I love you" with brads.

❸ Adhere hearts.

Finished size: 4¼" x 5½"

SUPPLIES: *Accents:* (plastic hearts, I love you) Heidi Grace Designs; (pink striped brads) Queen & Co. *Fibers:* (pink rickrack) Maya Road; (hot pink sequin trim) Self-Addressed; (pink organza ribbon) Offray *Other:* (pink card) Paper Salon

True Love Card Set

Designer: Kim Hughes

CARDS

❶ Cover cards with cardstock; adhere trim on seam.

❷ Adhere flower, leaf, and sticker.

HOLDER

❶ Make holder, following diagram on page 284.

❷ Adhere cardstock rectangle to front.

❸ Adhere trims on seam.

❹ Adhere flower. Tie ribbon to button; adhere.

Pattern and instructions on p. 284

Finished sizes: card 4¼" x 5½", holder 7½" x 5¼"

CARDS

SUPPLIES: *Cardstock:* (Lima Bean) SEI; (peach) Bazzill Basics Paper *Accents:* (flowers, leaves) Prima; (green button) Making Memories *Stickers:* (epoxy love words) Jo-Ann Stores *Fibers:* (cream stitched ribbon, pearl strand, lace, fancy trim, flower trim) Jo-Ann Stores *Adhesive:* (hook and loop circles) *Other:* (white cards) Paper Salon

5. Red & White I Love You Card

Designer: Valerie Pingree

1. Make card from cardstock.
2. Cut patterned paper to cover card front.
3. Wrap and tie ribbons. Adhere piece to card.
4. Round corner.

Finished size: 4¼" x 5½"

SUPPLIES: *Cardstock:* (white) *Patterned paper:* (Red Batik from Sloane collection) Anna Griffin *Fibers:* (I love you, black gingham, white grosgrain ribbon) Making Memories; (black striped ribbon) All My Memories; (black dotted ribbon) SEI *Tools:* (corner rounder punch) EK Success

I Love U Card

Designer: Valerie Pingree

1. Make card from cardstock.
2. Paint chipboard negative edges; let dry.
3. Cover with patterned paper; trim excess. Tie ribbon.
4. Adhere ribbon to edge and behind letter
5. Spell "I love" with stickers.
6. Adhere piece to card.

Finished size: 5½" x 4"

DESIGNER TIP

Apply Fray Check or clear nail polish to ribbon ends to avoid fraying.

SUPPLIES: *Cardstock:* (white) *Patterned paper:* (Pink Paisley from Eliza collection) Anna Griffin *Dye ink:* (Van Dyke Brown) Ranger Industries *Paint:* (Valentine Pink) Plaid *Accent:* (chipboard letter "n" negative) Bazzill Basics Paper *Stickers:* (Sarah alphabet) American Crafts *Fibers:* (pink argyle, pink stripe, pink dotted ribbon) American Crafts *Tools:* (paper trimmer with scoring blade) EK Success

XOXO Gift Bag

Designer: Wendy Johnson

Ink all paper and chipboard edges.

❶ Mat patterned paper rectangle with cardstock and adhere to bag front.

❷ Adhere trim.

❸ Tie ribbon to paper clip; attach to bag.

❹ Sand chipboard heart. Punch hearts from patterned paper; adhere.

❺ Wrap silver cord around handles.

Finished size: 4" x 5¼"

SUPPLIES: *Cardstock:* (Raven) Bazzill Basics Paper *Patterned paper:* (Velvet Paisley from Ooh La La collection) Bo-Bunny Press *Dye ink:* (Basic Black) Stampin' Up! *Accents:* (XOXO paperclip) Carolee's Creations; (pink chipboard heart) Pressed Petals *Fibers:* (black/white striped ribbon) Making Memories; (white polka dot organdy ribbon) May Arts; (silver cord) Stampin' Up!; (black/silver trim) Wrights *Tools:* (heart punch) EK Success *Other:* (white bag with handles) DMD, Inc.

Pretty in Pink Card

Designer: Stefanie Hamilton

❶ Make card from cardstock. Cover with patterned paper.

❷ Adhere rectangle of reverse side of Love Petals paper.

❸ Adhere ribbon and lace on seam.

❹ Adhere flower, trims, and charm.

Finished size: 6" x 4¼"

SUPPLIES: *Cardstock:* (dark pink) *Patterned paper:* (Loopy Love Hearts) Doodlebug Design; (Love Petals from Twitterpated collection) SEI *Accents:* (heart charm) Making Memories; (pink paper flower) Prima *Fibers:* (love words printed ribbon) Doodlebug Design; (white lace, pink trim) Wrights

Love Notes Mailbox

Designer: Susan Stringfellow

SIDES

❶ Adhere patterned paper around mailbox.

❷ Cut patterned paper strip and fold into pleats; adhere.

❸ Adhere ribbon and trim.

❹ Cut images from patterned paper, ink and stitch edges; adhere.

❺ Tie flowers with ribbon; adhere.

❻ Die-cut tag and heart; adhere. Ink, attach jump ring, and adhere to flowers.

FRONT

❶ Die-cut "Love notes" from cardstock; ink and adhere.

❷ Die-cut tag and heart; adhere. Ink; attach jump ring.

❸ Attach jump ring to charm. Attach to tag's jump ring.

❹ Tie ribbon on jump ring; adhere.

Finished size: 5¼" x 3¾" x 3¼"

OTHER SIDE

SUPPLIES: *Cardstock:* (ivory) *Patterned paper:* (Pink Polka Dot, Heart and Lace Stripe) Karen Foster Design; (Old Fashioned Valentines from Twitterpated collection) Rusty Pickle *Dye ink:* (Antique Linen) Ranger Industries *Color medium:* (black pen) Faber-Castell *Accents:* (pastel paper flowers) Prima; (antique gold jump rings) Making Memories; (gold key charm) *Fibers:* (red gingham ribbon) American Crafts; (half-pearl trim) Wrights *Dies:* (Katie alphabet, small heart, small tag) QuicKutz *Tools:* (die cut machine) QuicKutz *Other:* (red mailbox) Michaels

Felt Love Gift Bag

Designer: Amy Farnsworth

❶ Adhere pieces of ribbons and trims in heart shape on felt.

❷ Paint chipboard white; adhere behind bookplate.

❸ Thread ribbon through bookplate and tie around felt. Adhere piece.

❹ Affix sticker.

Finished size: 8" x 10¼"

SUPPLIES: *Paint:* (white) Plaid *Accents:* (chipboard rectangle) BasicGrey; (silver bookplate) 7gypsies *Stickers:* (love) Doodlebug Design *Fibers:* (black floral ribbon) Maya Road; (white grosgrain, black gingham, polka dot ribbon; loopy trim) May Arts; (black rickrack) Doodlebug Design *Other:* (black gift bag) DMD, Inc.; (pink polka dot felt rectangle)

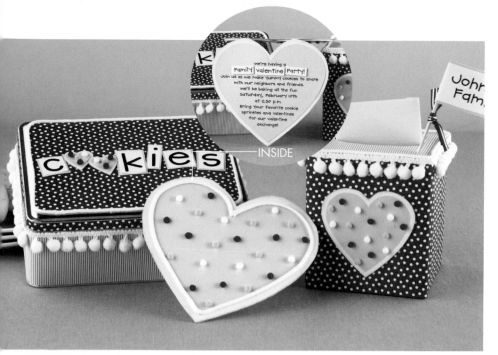

— INSIDE

SUPPLIES: *Cardstock:* (cream, pink, white) Prism *Patterned paper:* (Loopy Love Pinstripes, Ladybug Picnic) Doodlebug Design *Color medium:* (brown chalk) Craf-T Products *Accents:* (mini pink, red, white pompoms) Westrim Crafts *Fibers:* (red stripe ribbon, white cord, white pompom fringe) Wrights *Font:* (CK Handprint) Creating Keepsakes *Adhesive:* (foam squares) *Tools:* (heart punch) EK Success *Other:* (tin, tissue box, bamboo skewer)

COOKIE PARTIES

- Have all of your guests bring a batch of their favorite cookies and recipes to share.

- Invite guests over to make Valentine's Day cookies. Ask each guest to bring decorative sprinkles and valentines to hand out to each other.

SUPPLIES: *Cardstock:* (Juneberry, white) Bazzill Basics Paper *Patterned paper:* (Plum Dot from Olivia collection) Making Memories *Rubber stamps:* (Happy Valentines) Inkadinkado; (Hugs and Kisses from All-Year Cheer I set) Stampin' Up! *Solvent ink:* (Blazing Red) Tsukineko *Accents:* (decorative pewter brad) Making Memories; (pink silk flower) *Fibers:* (burgundy lace) Making Memories; (white string) *Adhesive:* (foam squares) Therm O Web *Die:* (mini tag) QuicKutz *Tools:* (die cut machine) QuicKutz

Valentine Cookie Party

Designer: Wendy Johnson

INVITATION

1. Make invitation from cardstock. Cut into heart shape; chalk edges.
2. Adhere cardstock heart.
3. Adhere cord and pompoms.
4. Print invitation wording on pink cardstock; cut into heart and adhere to inside.
5. Print "Family Valentine party" on white cardstock; trim and adhere over invitation words with foam squares.

TIN

1. Cover top and sides with patterned paper.
2. Punch hearts from white cardstock and mat with cream cardstock. Chalk edges. Adhere pompoms.
3. Print "ckies" on white cardstock; trim and mat with pink cardstock.
4. Adhere trims to top and sides, and letters to top with foam squares.

BOX

1. Cover box with patterned paper.
2. Cut heart shape from cardstock; mat with cream cardstock, chalk edges, and adhere pompoms. Adhere to box.
3. Print family name on white; trim, mat, and adhere to skewer. Tie ribbon, and pierce into box.
4. Adhere trims.

Finished sizes: invitation 5⅞" square, tin 8" x 6¼" x 3", box 4½" x 5" x 4½"

5 Purple Lace Flower Card
Designer: Susan Neal

1. Make card from cardstock.
2. Adhere patterned paper rectangle. Stitch top edge.
3. Stamp Happy Valentines on white cardstock; mat with Juneberry cardstock and adhere.
4. Adhere lace behind flower. Attach to card with brad.
5. Die-cut tag from cardstock; stamp Hugs and Kisses. Tie to brad with string.

Finished size: 3¾" x 8½"

INSIDE

Tingley All Over Card

Designer: Wendy Johnson

FRONT

❶ Make card from cardstock. Cut white cardstock slightly smaller than card front; adhere.

❷ Draw swirls; adhere beads.

❸ Print "I'm nauseous and tingley all over…"; trim, mat with cardstock, and adhere. *Note: Alternate strips adhered with foam squares for variety.*

❹ Cut small slit in top fold; wrap twice and adhere fiber.

INSIDE

❶ Cut and adhere cardstock squares.

❷ Print sentiment on cardstock; trim and adhere.

❸ Punch two hearts from cardstock; adhere.

Finished size: 4" square

SUPPLIES: *Cardstock:* (red, white) Provo Craft; (Raven) Bazzill Basics Paper *Color medium:* (black marker) Tombow *Accents:* (red seed beads) Darice *Fibers:* (black/red specialty yarn) Bernat *Fonts:* (Times New Roman) Microsoft; (CK Toggle) Creating Keepsakes; (Fairy Princess, Rickety, Tuxedo) www.twopeasinabucket.com; (Geeoh Hmk Bold) Hallmark *Adhesive:* (foam squares) *Tools:* (small heart punch) EK Success

Hearts That Love Card

Designer: Susan Neal

❶ Make card from cardstock.

❷ Cut patterned paper square; sand edges and adhere. Adhere cardstock rectangle.

❸ Adhere leather trim.

❹ Ink stamp with Cardinal and then Redwood; stamp on white cardstock, trim, and double mat with cardstock and ribbon. Adhere piece to card.

❺ Punch heart from cardstock; overlap and adhere.

❻ Die-cut flowers from cardstock; adhere.

❼ Adhere cord around brad into swirl; let dry and adhere.

Finished size: 5½" x 4¼"

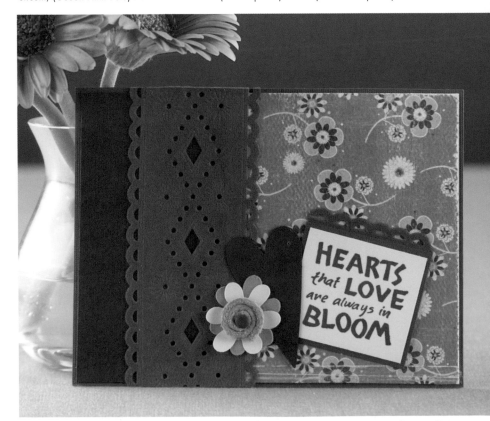

SUPPLIES: *Cardstock:* (Amaretto, Red Hot, Tweed, white) Bazzill Basics Paper *Patterned paper:* (Side Saddle from Cowgirl collection) Crate Paper *Rubber stamps:* (Hearts That Bloom) Rubber Soul *Dye ink:* (Cardinal, Redwood) Clearsnap *Accent:* (red brad) Lasting Impressions for Paper *Fibers:* (leather cord) Tandy Leather Company; (leather trim) Jo-Ann Stores *Die:* (flower) Provo Craft *Tools:* (die cut machine) Provo Craft; (primitive heart punch) McGill

You Make My Heart Flutter Card

Designer: Nicole Keller

① Make card from cardstock.

② Adhere torn strip of patterned paper.

③ Trace heart on patterned paper; cut out and mat with cardstock.

④ Apply wings rub-ons to cardstock; cut out and adhere behind heart. Adhere.

⑤ Decorate with pens, paint, rub-ons, and rhinestones.

Finished size: 6" square

Crazy Hearts Treat Container

Designer: Nicole Keller

① Apply rub-ons to top and bottom of container.

② Stamp hearts on cardstock; cut out and layer with foam tape. Adhere.

③ Print sentiment in circle shape on cardstock; die-cut. Attach brads and adhere stamped heart. Punch hole and tie to container with ribbon.

Finished size: 4¼" x 6¼"

SUPPLIES: *Cardstock:* (black, white) Bazzill Basics Paper *Patterned paper:* (Le Monde) 7gypsies; (Roxie Funky Fun) KI Memories *Paint:* (white) Sanford *Color media:* (dark, light pink pens) Sakura; (black marker, white pen) Sanford *Accents:* (pink rhinestones) K&Company *Rub-ons:* (wings) Hambly Screen Prints; (hearts) KI Memories *Template:* (heart) Westrim Crafts

SUPPLIES: *Cardstock:* (Bluff, Bubblegum, Cupcake, white) Bazzill Basics Paper *Clear stamps:* (hearts from Hearts and Stars set) Autumn Leaves *Dye ink:* (Jet Black) Ranger Industries *Accents:* (pink patterned brads) Queen & Co. *Rub-ons:* (flourishes) Making Memories *Fibers:* (striped ribbon) Doodlebug Design *Font:* (your choice) *Adhesive:* (foam tape) Plaid *Die:* (scalloped circle) Spellbinders *Tool:* (die cut machine) Spellbinders *Other:* (container) Prima

All Yours

Designer: Stefanie Hamilton

❶ Make card from Raven cardstock.

❷ Cut piece of Crimson cardstock slightly smaller than card; adhere.

❸ Adhere tape across center of card.

❹ Mat label with Lily White cardstock and velvet paper; adhere to card.

❺ Tie ribbon bow; adhere to card.

❻ Place stickpin through center of bow.

Finished size: 5½" x 5"

SUPPLIES: Cardstock: (Raven, Crimson, Lily White) *Bazzill Basics Paper* Specialty paper: (Black velvet) *SEI* Accents: (love printed tape) *7gypsies*; (fabric label) *Making Memories*; (jeweled stick pin) *EK Success* Fibers: (black and white grosgrain ribbon) *Scrapworks*

⑤ Together Forever

Designer: Ann Mabee

① Make card from Black cardstock.

② Cut rectangle of Life Noir paper; adhere to card.

③ Punch tag from Red cardstock; adhere to front of card. Adhere sticker to tag. Punch hole in tag; knot length of ribbon through hole.

④ Adhere love stickers to card.

⑤ Cut two strips of Red cardstock; adhere to card over Life Noir paper. Punch two sets of holes in strips; tie length of ribbon through holes. Adhere buttons to strips.

Finished size: 5½" x 4¼"

⑤ XO Always

Designer: Linda Beeson

① Make card from White cardstock.

② Cut strip of Unconditional Tiny Type paper; adhere to card.

③ Stamp Carved Heart 3 on White cardstock with Red ink; trim at slight angle. Mat piece with Red cardstock; adhere to card.

④ Stamp X and O on card with Black Soot. Stamp Always over X and O with Red ink.

Finished size: 5½" square

SUPPLIES: Cardstock: (Black, Red) *Bazzill Basics Paper* Patterned paper: (Life Noir) *7gypsies* Accents: (black buttons) *Jesse James & Co.* Stickers: (love sentiments) *7gypsies* Fibers: (red sheer ribbon) *Offray* Tools: (tag punch) *EK Success;* (⅛" circle punch)

SUPPLIES: Cardstock: (White, Red) *Bazzill Basics Paper* Patterned paper: (Unconditional Tiny Type) *KI Memories* Rubber stamp: (Carved Heart 3) *Hampton Arts;* (Always from Too Terrific Tags set) *Stampin' Up!;* (Antique alphabet) *Inkadinkado* Dye ink: (Black Soot) *Ranger Industries* Pigment ink: (Red) *Tsukineko*

Draw Close

Designer: Patti Milazzo

1. Make card from White cardstock.
2. Cut two rectangles of Midnight Paisley paper. Ink edges with Charcoal and adhere to card. *Note: Adhere one piece reverse side up.*
3. Adhere rickrack over seam.
4. Cut two hearts from red cardstock, using template; ink edges with Charcoal and adhere to card.
5. Ink wood tag and label holder with Warm Red; spray with sealer.
6. Tie length of floss to tag; adhere to card.
7. Stamp "You & me" on Midnight Paisley with Charcoal; trim. Adhere piece behind label holder. Attach brads to label holder; attach to card.

Finished size: 4½" x 6"

⁵ Love Tag

Designer: Karen Day

1. Cover tag with Wedding March paper; ink edges.
2. Cut heart from Love in Bloom Black paper; adhere to tag.
3. Die-cut "Love" from Red Roses paper; adhere to tag.
4. Punch hole in top of tag; knot length of ribbon through hole.

Finished size: 2¾" x 6"

SUPPLIES: Cardstock: (White) *Bazzill Basics Paper;* (red) Patterned paper: (Midnight Paisley from A Day to Remember collection) *Bo-Bunny Press* Rubber stamps: (Antique Uppercase, Lowercase alphabets) *PSX* Chalk ink: (Warm Red, Charcoal) *Clearsnap* Finish: (clear acrylic sealer) *Plaid* Accents: (wood label holder, wood tag) *Go West Studios;* (black mini brads) *Making Memories* Fibers: (red rickrack) *Wrights;* (tan floss) *Karen Foster Design* Template: (Heart) *Provo Craft*

SUPPLIES: Patterned paper: (Red Roses, Love in Bloom Black, Wedding March from True Love collection) *Flair Designs* Chalk ink: (Chestnut Roan) *Clearsnap* Accent: (tag) *DMD, Inc.* Fibers: (red velvet ribbon) *Flair Designs* Dies: (Studio alphabet) *QuicKutz* Tool: (die cut machine) *QuicKutz*

DESIGNER TIP
When applying thin amounts of color in a straight line, consider using a paint pen. This will give you more hands-on control than an ink pad or paint brush, while still achieving a vibrant result.

Cupid's Damask

Designer: Heather Thompson

❶ Make card from cardstock.

❷ Outline cardstock with gold pen; adhere. Trim sticker to fit cardstock and affix.

❸ Color middle frame with pen, adhere cardstock to center frame; affix frames to card.

❹ Apply rub-on.

❺ Adhere cupid.

Finished size: 4¼" x 5½"

Elegant I Love You

Designer: Tristann Graves

❶ Make card from cardstock. Cover with patterned paper.

❷ Cut journaling spot from patterned paper; adhere.

❸ Adhere epoxy sticker with foam tape. Affix border.

❹ Adhere rhinestones.

Finished size: 5" square

SUPPLIES: *Cardstock:* (Black Tie shimmer, kraft) Bazzill Basics Paper *Color medium:* (gold leafing pen) Krylon *Accent:* (white chipboard cupid) CherryArte *Rub-on:* (yours) BasicGrey *Stickers:* (black damask) Heidi Swapp; (red chipboard frame)

SUPPLIES: All supplies from Creative Imaginations unless otherwise noted. *Cardstock:* (white) no source *Patterned paper:* (Five Antique Notes, Script Noir from Antique Cream collection) *Accents:* (pink rhinestones) Heidi Swapp *Stickers:* (epoxy I love you, lace/script border) *Adhesive:* (foam tape) Plaid

BONUS IDEA

Modify the size of this card to hold cash, gift cards, or special love notes.

BONUS IDEA

Try some different candy and sentiments:
Sour Patch Kids: "Pucker up and be my Valentine"
Gum: "Valentine, I chews you"
Jolly Ranchers: "You make my heart jolly"
Whoppers: "You're a Whopper of a Valentine"

Valentine Love Note

Designer: Jennifer Gallacher

❶ Make pocket card, following pattern on p. 157.

❷ Cut strip of White cardstock with decorative-edge scissors; adhere on inside of card along diagonal edge.

❸ Attach eyelets; staple sentiment tag to top. Stitch pocket closed.

❹ Make heart from Red Floral paper, following pattern on page 157. Mat with White. Trim side of heart; adhere to card. Attach photo turns with brads.

❺ Apply rub-on sentiment. Knot length of ribbon around card.

Finished size: 3½" x 7"

I'm a Sucker for You

Designer: Nicole Keller

❶ Make card from reverse side of Birthday Dots paper.

❷ Cut heart shape from reverse side of Little Lady Stripe paper, following pattern on p. 158.

❸ Ink edges of heart, sticker, and paper heart circle.

❹ Adhere heart to card. Adhere sticker and heart circle.

❺ Spell sentiment with rub-ons, applying U in heart circle.

❻ Adhere lollipop to card.

Finished size: 6" square

SUPPLIES: Cardstock: (Black, White) *Making Memories* Patterned paper: (Red Floral) *Deja Views* Accents: (sentiment tag) *Deja Views;* (white eyelets) *Making Memories;* (cream photo turns) *Making Memories;* (red brads) *Karen Foster Design;* (staples) Rub-on: (love sentiment) *Deja Views* Fibers: (red gingham ribbon) *Offray;* (white thread) Tools: (decorative-edge scissors) *Fiskars*

SUPPLIES: Patterned paper: (Little Lady Stripe, Birthday Dots) *My Mind's Eye* Chalk ink: (Charcoal) *Clearsnap* Accents: (paper heart circle) *My Mind's Eye* Rub-ons: (Expressions alphabet) *Doodlebug Design* Sticker: (pink square) *Provo Craft* Other: (lollipop)

DESIGNER TIP
Use a die or hole punch to cut out the centers of the O pieces to save time.

XO

Designer: Summer Ford

GAME PIECES

❶ Adhere XO Red paper to craft foam. Trace several X shapes on back of foam, using chipboard X. Cut out.

❷ Adhere Black cardstock to craft foam. Trace several O shapes on back of foam, using chipboard O. Cut out.

CARD

❶ Cover flap side of envelope with XO Red; ink edges.

❷ Paint chipboard X and O letters black; let dry. Cut square of White cardstock; ink edges and adhere letters to square. Stamp "&" on square with Black paint. Make labels with label maker; adhere to square.

❸ Adhere square to card. Adhere envelope closure to card; knot length of ribbon around envelope closure.

❹ Stamp stripes in grid pattern on envelope front in Black paint; let dry.

❺ Place X and O cutouts in envelope.

Finished size: 6" square

Smooch

Designer: Dee Gallimore-Perry

❶ Cut XOXO paper slightly smaller than card; cut square from center. Adhere paper to card.

❷ Adhere love sentiment sticker to card front. Adhere kiss sticker inside card window.

❸ Knot lengths of ribbons around card window opening.

❹ Adhere love sticker sentiment to cardstock; trim. Attach cardstock to ribbons with safety pin.

Finished size: 5" square

SUPPLIES: Cardstock: (White, Black) *The Paper Company* Patterned paper: (XO Red) *Die Cuts With a View* Foam stamps: (Misunderstood alphabet, strip from Patterns set) *Making Memories* Dye ink: (Black Soot) *Ranger Industries* Paint: (Black) *Plaid* Accents: (chipboard letters) *Making Memories*; (envelope closure) *Clearsnap* Fibers: (black polka dot sheer ribbon) *May Arts* Tool: (label maker) Other: (square envelope) *Bazzill Basics Paper*; (craft foam)

SUPPLIES: Cardstock: (White) *Bazzill Basics Paper* Patterned paper: (XOXO from Love collection) *Reminisce* Accents: (pink mini safety pin) *Making Memories* Stickers: (kiss, love sentiment) *Reminisce* Fibers: (pink gingham, pink polka dot, pink satin, red striped ribbon) Other: (True White card) *Deja Views*

:5: True Love

Designer: Amy Comstock Combs

1. Make card from cardstock.
2. Cut rectangles of Brighton Ice Blocks and Brighton Love Letter paper; ink edges with Walnut Stain and adhere to card, reverse side up.
3. Cut rectangle of cardstock; adhere to card.
4. Sand chipboard pieces; ink with Walnut Stain. Adhere circle piece to square piece. Stamp "Be my" on circle piece with Black.
5. Cut lengths of ribbon; loop and adhere to back of square piece. Adhere square to card.

Finished size: 5½" x 4¼"

Kiss Me

Designer: Dee Gallimore-Perry

1. Make card from cardstock.
2. Cut rectangles of Kiss Me Journaling paper slightly smaller than card; sand edges and adhere to card.
3. Trim images from Kiss Me Love Letters paper; adhere to card. Knot length of black gingham ribbon around metal clip; attach to card.
4. Adhere printed twill ribbon to card. Apply rub-ons.
5. Cut out date circle from Kiss Me Journaling; sand edges, stamp date on piece, and adhere to card.
6. Sand edges of paper letter; knot lengths of ribbon around letter. Trim sentiment from Kiss Me Love Letters; attach to ribbons with safety pin. Adhere letter with foam dots.

Finished size: 6" x 4½"

SUPPLIES: Cardstock: (Black) *Bazzill Basics Paper* Patterned paper: (Brighton Love Letter, Brighton Ice Blocks) *Scenic Route Paper Co.* Rubber stamps: (Rummage alphabet) *Making Memories* Dye ink: (Walnut Stain, Black) *Ranger Industries* Accents: (chipboard square, circle sentiments) *Scenic Route Paper Co.* Fibers: (white rickrack; white stitched grosgrain, red and white gingham, pink striped grosgrain, pink stitched ribbon) Other: (sandpaper)

SUPPLIES: Cardstock: (White) *Bazzill Basics Paper* Patterned paper: (Kiss Me Journaling, Kiss Me Love Letters) *KI Memories* Rubber stamp: (Date) *OfficeMax* Dye ink: (Basic Black) *Stampin' Up!* Accents: (paper letter) *KI Memories*; (pink metal clip) *Provo Craft*; (pink mini safety pin) *Making Memories* Rub-on: (love sentiments) *7gypsies* Fibers: (black, pink gingham ribbon) *Offray*; (printed twill ribbon) *Provo Craft* Adhesive: (foam dots) *Plaid* Other: (sandpaper)

Just for You

Designer: Sylvie Corre

Note: Ink edges of all pieces.

❶ Make card from Element paper.

❷ Cut rectangle of Medium Blue cardstock slightly smaller than card; adhere. Cut rectangle of 9-Iron paper; adhere.

❸ Cut strip of Olive Green cardstock; adhere to corner of 9-Iron piece.

❹ Cut square of Dill; adhere to card.

❺ Attach rivet to tag; knot length of ribbon through rivet. Adhere tag to card with foam squares.

❻ Die-cut two hearts from Element; adhere to tag. Adhere metal sentiment.

Finished size: 5¼" square

SUPPLIES: Cardstock: (Medium Blue, Olive Green) *Bazzill Basics Paper* Patterned paper: (Element, 9-Iron, Dill from Skate Shoppe collection) *BasicGrey* Chalk ink: (Dark Brown) *Clearsnap* Accents: (green tag) *BasicGrey;* (green rivet) *Chatterbox;* (metal sentiment) *All My Memories* Fibers: (green ribbon) *Chatterbox* Adhesive: (foam squares) Die: (Heart) *QuicKutz* Tools: (die cut machine) *QuicKutz*

5 STEP Crazy for You

Designer: Michelle Tardie

❶ Make card from cardstock.

❷ Cut Small Stripes paper slightly smaller than card front; adhere.

❸ Cut strip of Magenta/Small Circles paper with decorative trimmer; adhere to card. Apply stitching rub-ons over seam.

❹ Cut circle from solid side of Tall Man paper. Apply love word rub-ons and monkey sticker. Adhere to card.

Finished size: 5" square

SUPPLIES: Cardstock: (Coal) *Bazzill Basics Paper* Patterned paper: (Tall Man from Comstock Circus collection) *We R Memory Keepers;* (Small Stripes from Autumn Sweet collection, Magenta/Small Circles from Mad About Plaid collection) *Sweetwater* Rub-ons: (love words) *Making Memories;* (stitching) *K&Company* Sticker: (monkey) *Westrim Crafts* Adhesive: (foam squares) Tools: (circle cutter) *Provo Craft;* (decorative trimmer) *Creative Memories*

BONUS IDEA

Make this a birthday greeting by changing the vellum piece to read "Happy birthday to".

⬡ Harlequin Love You

Designer: Michon Kessler

1. Make card from Pink cardstock.
2. Cut piece of patterned paper to cover lower half of card; adhere. Ink edges of card.
3. Adhere length of ribbon over paper seam. Adhere sticker.
4. Paint chipboard letter with two coats; let dry.
5. Tie Kisses ties around chipboard letter; adhere to card.

Finished size: 5½" x 4¼"

⬡ My Heart Belongs to You

Designer: Charrie Shockey

1. Make card from brown cardstock.
2. Cut strip of cream cardstock; mat with hot pink cardstock. Trim edges of strip to match edges; adhere to card.
3. Spell "You" with stickers.
4. Print "My heart belongs to" on vellum; tear along top and bottom edges. Attach with brads.

Finished size: 4" x 4½"

SUPPLIES: Cardstock: (Pink) *Prism* Patterned paper: (Flipside from Groovy collection) *Three Bugs in a Rug* Pigment ink: (Brown) *Clearsnap* Paint: (Brown spray) *Krylon* Accents: (chipboard letter) *Making Memories;* (heart sticker) *Three Bugs in a Rug* Fibers: (diamond pattern ribbon) *American Crafts* Other: (Valentine Kisses ties) *Hershey's*

SUPPLIES: Cardstock: (brown, hot pink, cream) Vellum: (Pink) *Hot Off the Press* Accent: (pink brads) *Making Memories* Stickers: (Towering Type alphabet) *K&Company* Font: (Arial) *Microsoft*

BONUS IDEA

Create a rail in a hill shape for an "Over the Hill" card. Or, try a pickup truck piled with boxes for a "We've Moved" card.

Dreamboat

Designer: Cari Kirla

❶ Make card from Light Blue cardstock.

❷ Emboss random pattern on card front, using heart stencil.

❸ Cut two slits in card front to create rail.

❹ Cut boat shapes from Red, Pink, and Black cardstock. Dry-emboss heart on Red piece. Assemble boat; attach eyelets. Die-cut Wave from Medium Blue cardstock; apply glitter glue and adhere to boat piece. Punch hearts from Pink and Red; apply glitter glue and adhere to piece.

❺ Cut thin strip of Red; slide strip through slits of rail. Adhere ends of strip together to create small loop. Test to be sure loop slides along rail.

❻ Adhere ribbon to back of loop. Adhere boat piece to front of loop. Punch small hearts from Red; adhere to ends of ribbon.

❼ Print sentiment on White cardstock; adhere to cover inside of card. (Note: Make sure not to adhere ribbons down, so that they may slide freely.) Note: Pull the ribbon to watch the boat sail.

Finished size: 6" square

To My Hubby

Designer: Alisa Bangerter

❶ Make card from cardstock.

❷ Cut Sweet Scarlet paper slightly smaller than card front; adhere.

❸ Spell "Hubby" with stickers on square of Sunbeam; apply rub-ons to spell "My". Adhere square to card.

❹ Cut various rectangles of Sunbeam; adhere to card. Adhere stickers.

❺ Sand card front to distress stickers.

❻ Adhere buttons. Knot length of thread; adhere to card.

Finished size: 5" x 7"

SUPPLIES: Cardstock: (Light Blue, Medium Blue, Red, Pink, Black, White) *Bazzill Basics Paper* Accents: (glitter glue) *Ranger Industries*; (white eyelets) Fibers: (white ribbon) Die: (Wave) *Provo Craft/Ellison* Tools: (die cut machine) *Provo Craft/ Ellison*; (heart stencil) *Plaid*; (small heart punch, medium heart punch)

SUPPLIES: Cardstock: (Sunbeam) *Bazzill Basics Paper* Patterned paper: (Sweet Scarlet) *Karen Foster Design* Accents: (blue, white buttons) *Making Memories* Rub-ons: (Expressions alphabet) *Doodlebug Design* Stickers: (love sentiments) *Karen Foster Design*; (Jumbo alphabet) *Chatterbox* Fibers: (white floss) Other: (sandpaper)

Postal Greeting

Designer: Lisa Strahl

1. Make card from cardstock; round corners.
2. Cut slightly smaller piece of reverse side of patterned paper; round corners, wrap with ribbon, and adhere.
3. Make envelope from patterned paper, using template; fold and seal flaps.
4. Stamp heart and wings on cardstock; cut out. Accent images with marker and gel pen; adhere to envelope flap. Adhere envelope.
5. Stamp sentiment and postal images.

Finished size: 5½" x 4¼"

In Love With You

Designer: Heather Nichols

1. Make card from cardstock.
2. Cut rectangle of cardstock; attach brads.
3. Stamp heart circle randomly on cardstock; ink edges and adhere to rectangle piece.
4. Wrap ribbon, tie knot, and adhere piece to card.
5. Stamp sentiment on cardstock; trim into square and adhere glitter along edges. Adhere to card with foam squares.
6. Thread button with linen thread; die-cut heart from cardstock and adhere button. Adhere heart with foam squares.

Finished size: 5½" x 4¼"

SUPPLIES: *Cardstock:* (Blush Red Dark) Prism; (white) *Patterned paper:* (Style, Trendy from Crate Avenue collection) Crate Paper *Acrylic stamps:* (Artsy Alphabet; heart, wings from Cherubs set; postmark, stamp border from French Mail set) Crafty Secrets *Specialty ink:* (Moulin Rouge, Noir hybrid) Stewart Superior Corp. *Color medium:* (Stardust gel pen) Sakura; (fine-tip black marker) *Fibers:* (green velvet ribbon) Stampin' Up! *Template:* (mini envelope) Stampin' Up! *Tool:* (corner rounder punch) EK Success

SUPPLIES: *Cardstock:* (Whisper White, Certainly Celery, Real Red, kraft) Stampin' Up! *Rubber stamp:* (sentiment) *Acrylic stamp:* (heart circle from My Heart Flowers set) Creative Imaginations *Solvent ink:* (Jet Black) Tsukineko *Pigment ink:* (Moonlight White) Tsukineko *Accents:* (red polka dot button) Doodlebug Design; (silver brads) Creative Imaginations; (green glitter) Making Memories *Fibers:* (red striped ribbon) May Arts; (linen thread) Stampin' Up! *Adhesive:* (foam squares) Stampin' Up! *Die:* (heart) Provo Craft *Tool:* (die cut machine) Provo Craft

BONUS IDEA

The collage style and mix-and-match color combinations on this card make it ideal for a huge variety of occasions and recipients. Send your congratulations, say thank you to a loved one, or invite your girlfriends to a fun night out. Just customize the colors and sentiment to your liking!

I Love You

Designer: Michelle Tardie

1. Make card from cardstock; ink edges.
2. Adhere strips, triangle of patterned paper.
3. Apply rub-on stitches along seams.
4. Spell "I love you" with rub-ons.

Finished size: 5" square

SWAK

Designer: Alissa Trowbridge

1. Make card from cardstock. Cover with patterned paper; ink edges.
2. Cut strip of patterned paper; ink edges and adhere.
3. Adhere chipboard letters and buttons.
4. Staple folded ribbon.
5. Cover chipboard lips with reverse side of patterned paper; ink edges and adhere.

Finished size: 6¾" x 3¼"

SUPPLIES: *Cardstock:* (Marrone) Prism *Patterned paper:* (Togetherness, Exchanged Glances, Quiet Contentment, Loving You, Shared Giggles from Just Us collection) Prima *Pigment ink:* (black) Clearsnap *Rub-ons:* (black stitches) Die Cuts With a View; (Hand Stamped Alphabet) Polar Bear Press; (love) Daisy D's; (Heidi alphabet) Making Memories

SUPPLIES: *Cardstock:* (white) Bazzill Basics Paper *Patterned paper:* (Dancing Diamonds, Party Time from Celebration collection) Polar Bear Press *Chalk ink:* (Warm Red) Clearsnap *Accents:* (chipboard letters, lips) Polar Bear Press; (staples, red buttons) *Fibers:* (black stitched ribbon) Michaels

5 STEP Sweet Treat

Designer: Anabelle O'Malley

❶ Make card from cardstock.

❷ Ink edges of patterned paper rectangle and strip; adhere.

❸ Adhere lace. Adhere ribbon.

❹ Attach flowers to chipboard frame with brads; adhere.

❺ Wrap ribbon around candy. Ink tag, attach tag, and adhere to ribbon. Adhere candy to card.

Finished size: 5" square

5 STEP 2/14/08

Designer: Layle Koncar

❶ Make card from cardstock.

❷ Trim circles and scalloped edge from patterned paper; adhere with foam tape.

❸ Stamp date label; write date with pen.

Finished size: 6" square

SUPPLIES: *Cardstock:* (Autumn Red Medium) WorldWin *Patterned paper:* (Scalloped Square from Love Story collection) Making Memoires; (Cute Dots from Tres Jolie collection) My Mind's Eye *Pigment ink:* (pink) Clearsnap *Accents:* (pink striped chipboard frame, valentine tag) Making Memories; (pink striped brads, red flowers) Queen & Co. *Fibers:* (red ribbon) Michaels; (pink heart ribbon) SEI; (red felt lace) Queen & Co. *Other:* (candy)

SUPPLIES: *Cardstock:* (white) Bazzill Basics Paper *Patterned paper:* (Love Dot, Petticoat, Shower from Betty collection) KI Memories *Dye ink:* (black) *Clear stamp:* (date label) Creating Keepsakes *Color medium:* (black pen) EK Success *Adhesive:* (foam tape)

Lined Heart

Designer: Polly McMillan

① Make card from patterned paper.

② Cut heart from notebook paper; adhere and trim.

③ Cut border from scalloped paper; adhere.

④ Die-cut hearts; adhere. Draw stitched border around one heart.

⑤ Apply rub-on. Adhere sticker with foam squares.

Finished size: 4" x 9"

Be My Star

Designer: Layle Koncar

① Cut heart card, following pattern on p. 161.

② Adhere slightly smaller piece of patterned paper.

③ Adhere strip of patterned paper.

④ Spell "Be my star" with stickers.

Finished size: 6" x 5¾"

SUPPLIES: *Patterned paper:* (Red Riding Hood from Perhaps collection) BasicGrey; (Black Scalloped from Antique Cream & Black collection) Creative Imaginations; (lined notebook paper) *Color medium:* (black marker) *Rub-on:* (tiny heart) Bo-Bunny Press *Sticker:* (be mine) Pebbles Inc. *Adhesive:* (foam squares) Making Memories *Dies:* (large, small heart) QuicKutz *Tool:* (die cut machine) QuicKutz

SUPPLIES: *Cardstock:* (black) Bazzill Basics Paper *Patterned paper:* (Laurel Sailmaker Lane) Scenic Route *Stickers:* (glitter alphabet) Making Memories

Posy Proposal
Designer: Lynette Carroll, courtesy of K&Company

1. Make card from cardstock.
2. Layer and adhere rectangles of patterned paper. *Note: Trim various edges with decorative-edge scissors.*
3. Cut flower stems from patterned paper; adhere.
4. Adhere flowers, acrylic dots, and rhinestone.
5. Cut strip of patterned paper; adhere rhinestone and spell "Mine" with stickers. Adhere with foam squares.
6. Spell "Be" with chipboard letters.

Finished size: 7" x 5"

Buckle Bling
Designer: Kelly Lunceford

1. Make card from cardstock.
2. Adhere rectangle of patterned paper.
3. Adhere strip of cardstock. Apply rub-on; adhere rhinestone.
4. Wrap ribbon around card front; attach ribbon slide. Knot ribbon.

Finished size: 5" square

SUPPLIES: All supplies from K&Company unless otherwise noted. *Cardstock:* (white) Bazzill Basics Paper *Patterned paper:* (Cream & Green Stripe, Lavender Stripe, Green Floral, Motif Border from Wedding Collection paper pad) *Accents:* (glitter flowers, glitter chipboard letters, acrylic dots, rhinestones) *Stickers:* (glitter alphabet) *Adhesive:* (foam squares) no source *Tool:* (decorative-edge scissors) no source

SUPPLIES: *Cardstock:* (Blush Blossom, Basic Black) Stampin' Up! *Patterned paper:* (Pink & Black Motif from Olivia collection) Making Memories *Accents:* (rhinestone ribbon slide) Li'l Davis Designs; (rhinestone) Making Memories *Rub-on:* (XOXO) Creative Imaginations *Fibers:* (fuchsia ribbon) May Arts

DESIGNER TIP

This card could easily be adapted for someone's birthday using the calendar die cut that matches the month of their birthday. Simply circle the date with a marker to personalize it!

⑤ Valentine Calendar Card

Designer: Kalyn Kepner

❶ Make card from cardstock; stitch and ink edges.

❷ Trim patterned paper; distress, ink, and zigzag-stitch edges. Tie ribbon around piece and adhere.

❸ Adhere calendar die cut; apply glitter glue. Circle number 14 with marker.

❹ Affix heart sticker. Adhere flower.

Finished size: 4¼" x 5½"

⑤ Love You Forever Card

Designer: Lisa Johnson

❶ Make card from cardstock; stamp flourish.

❷ Stamp flourish and sentiment on cardstock; ink edges. Adhere glitter.

❸ Mat stamped piece with cardstock, using foam tape. Adhere to card with foam tape.

❹ Stamp heart on cardstock, trim, and adhere with foam tape.

❺ Tie ribbon bow and adhere.

Finished size: 5½" x 4¼"

SUPPLIES: *Cardstock:* (Vanilla) Bazzill Basics Paper *Patterned paper:* (Unchained Melody from Baby 2 Bride collection) Graphic 45 *Chalk ink:* (Creamy Brown) Clearsnap *Color medium:* (red marker) *Accents:* (pink flower) Prima; (calendar die cut) Jenni Bowlin Studio; (red glitter glue) Ranger Industries *Sticker:* (felt heart) *Fibers:* (pink ribbon)

SUPPLIES: *Cardstock:* (kraft, Smokey Shadow, Vintage Cream, Hibiscus Burst) Papertrey Ink *Clear stamps:* (heart, sentiment from Heart Prints set; flourish from Fancy Flourishes set) Papertrey Ink *Dye ink:* (Creamy Caramel) Stampin' Up! *Specialty ink:* (Smokey Shadow, Hibiscus Burst hybrid) Papertrey Ink *Accent:* (iridescent glitter) Stewart Superior Corp. *Fibers:* (pink ribbon) Papertrey Ink *Tool:* (small heart punch) EK Success

Talk Nerdy to Me

Designer: Michele Boyer

❶ Make card from cardstock.

❷ Mat patterned paper with reverse side of patterned paper; adhere.

❸ Stamp image on cardstock; draw ground line with pen and shadow with marker. Trim.

❹ Stamp image on second piece of cardstock; color with markers and trim. Adhere image directly over first stamped image with foam tape.

❺ Double-mat stamped piece with cardstock and patterned paper; adhere.

Finished size: 4¼" square

Love Is in the Air

Designer: Ana Wohlfahrt

❶ Make card from cardstock.

❷ Randomly stamp Med. Heart Circle with Pink Petunia ink; repeat with Persimmon ink. Stamp sentiment.

❸ Pierce holes in top and bottom of card.

❹ Double-mat patterned paper with cardstock and adhere. Tie ribbon on card; tie cord to ribbon.

❺ Stamp Tree of Love and Lovebirds. Color image with markers and apply glitter glue.

❻ Trim stamped image, double-mat with cardstock, and adhere to card with foam tape.

❼ Punch circles from cardstock; attach to flower with brad and adhere.

Finished size: 4¼" x 5½"

SUPPLIES: *Cardstock:* (Bravo Burgundy) Stampin' Up!; (white) Papertrey Ink *Patterned paper:* (Polka Hearts from Smitten collection) Paper Salon *Pigment ink:* (Graphite Black) Tsukineko *Rubber stamp:* (Talk Nerdy to Me) Inkadinkado *Color media:* (Light Walnut, Sepia, Tender Pink, Warm Gray markers) Copic Marker; (black gel pen) Sakura *Adhesive:* (foam tape)

SUPPLIES: *Cardstock:* (Chocolate Chip, Groovy Guava, More Mustard, Purely Pomegranate, Pretty in Pink, Whisper White) Stampin' Up! *Patterned paper:* (Candy Girl from Hey Sugar collection) Cosmo Cricket *Rubber stamps:* (Lovebirds, Tree of Love, Love is in the Air, Med. Heart Circle) The Cat's Pajamas *Pigment ink:* (Onyx Black, Pink Petunia, Persimmon) Tsukineko *Color medium:* (brown, gray, green, pink, yellow markers) Copic Marker *Accents:* (sheer flower) Maya Road; (orange brad) Stampin' Up!; (gold glitter glue) Ranger Industries *Fibers:* (brown ribbon) Stampin' Up!; (copper cord) *Adhesive:* (foam tape) *Template:* (piercing) Stampin' Up! *Tools:* (½", ¾" circle punches) Stampin' Up!

Total Sweetheart

Designer: Kimberly Crawford

❶ Make card from cardstock.

❷ Adhere patterned paper. Mat bingo card with patterned paper and adhere.

❸ Cut patterned paper strip; mat with patterned paper.

❹ Stamp sentiment on matted strip; emboss. Attach brads and adhere.

Finished size: 5½" x 4¼"

Doodle Flower Love You

Designer: Layle Koncar

❶ Make card from patterned paper.

❷ Adhere cardstock square. Adhere doodle flower die cut.

❸ Spell sentiment with stickers.

Finished size: 4" square

SUPPLIES: *Cardstock:* (black) Bazzill Basics Paper *Patterned paper:* (Sparkle, Whirl from Mia collection; Fortitude from Prudence collection) Crate Paper *Clear stamps:* (sentiment from February set) Creative Café *Chalk ink:* (brown) Clearsnap *Embossing powder:* (clear) Stampendous! *Accents:* (bingo card) Jenni Bowlin Studio; (yellow rhinestone brads) BasicGrey

SUPPLIES: *Cardstock:* (black) Bazzill Basics Paper *Patterned paper:* (Surprise Rainbow Road) Scenic Route *Accent:* (doodle flower die cut) Scenic Route *Stickers:* (Puffy, Tiny alphabets) Making Memories

⁵⁵ₜₑₚₛ Destiny

Designer: Wendy Price

1. Make card from cardstock.
2. Die-cut five "X" and four "O" from cardstock; adhere with foam tape.
3. Stamp Just Leaves on cardstock; emboss. Cut out and adhere.
4. Adhere sticker with foam tape. Tie ribbon bow and adhere.

Finished size: 3½" square

⁵⁵ₜₑₚₛ Will You Be My Valentine?

Designer: Annette King

1. Make card from cardstock; round bottom corners.
2. Adhere patterned paper pieces. Adhere rickrack. Stitch card edges.
3. Paint chipboard heart; let dry. Apply glitter.
4. Tie ribbon on heart; adhere to card. Adhere pearls and metal label.

Finished size: 4½" x 5½"

SUPPLIES: *Cardstock:* (Wine Red 2) Die Cuts With a View; (red, black) DMD, Inc. *Rubber stamp:* (Just Leaves) Rubbernecker Stamp *Watermark ink:* Tsukineko *Embossing powder:* (white) Jo-Ann Stores *Stickers:* (destiny) Pebbles Inc. *Fibers:* (green ribbon) *Adhesive:* (foam tape) EK Success *Dies:* (Baby Face alphabet) Provo Craft *Tool:* (die cut machine) Provo Craft

SUPPLIES: *Cardstock:* (Tinted Dawn) The Paper Company *Patterned paper:* (Big Dot, Varnished Houndstooth from Rouge Paperie collection) Making Memories *Paint:* (white) Delta *Accents:* (chipboard heart) Heidi Swapp; (iridescent glitter) Martha Stewart Crafts; (black pearls) Kaisercraft; (metal sentiment label) Making Memories *Fibers:* (pink rickrack) Wrights; (black striped ribbon) *Tool:* (corner rounder punch)

XOXO Hearts

Designer: Betsy Veldman

❶ Make card from cardstock.

❷ Cut patterned paper strips. Trim one strip edge with decorative-edge scissors, ink edges, and adhere.

❸ Cut patterned paper strip; emboss with Swiss Dots and adhere.

❹ Cut three cardstock squares. Cut square cardstock frame and mask each square with frame before stamping hearts.

❺ Emboss stamped squares with dotted square; ink edges. Tie two with twine and adhere with foam tape.

❻ Die-cut tag from cardstock. Stamp sentiment and ink edges. Tie button and tag to stamped square with twine; adhere with foam tape.

Finished size: 7½" x 4¼"

SUPPLIES: *Cardstock:* (Dark Chocolate, Spring Moss, white) Papertrey Ink *Patterned paper:* (Hiya, Word from Everyday collection) American Crafts *Clear stamps:* (hearts, sentiment from Heart Prints set) Papertrey Ink *Chalk ink:* (Chestnut Roan) Clearsnap *Specialty ink:* (Spring Rain, Summer Sunrise, Berry Sorbet hybrid) Papertrey Ink *Accent:* (pink button) BasicGrey *Fibers:* (white twine) *Adhesive:* (foam tape) *Templates:* (dotted square, Swiss Dots embossing) Provo Craft *Die:* (tag) Provo Craft *Tools:* (die cut/embossing machine, decorative-edge scissors) Provo Craft

Elegant Hugs & Kisses

Designer: Sherry Wright

❶ Make card from cardstock.

❷ Distress edges of patterned paper piece; adhere.

❸ Adhere filigree felt. Affix sticker. *Note: Adhere one end of sticker with foam tape.*

❹ Adhere bird. Trim wing shape from swirl sticker; affix. Adhere rhinestones.

❺ Tie on ribbon and trim with decorative-edge scissors.

Finished size: 5" square

SUPPLIES: *Cardstock:* (red) Prism *Patterned paper:* (Pink Floral Die Cut from Sweet Pea collection) Creative Imaginations *Accents:* (cream filigree felt) Prima; (red felt bird) Fancy Pants Designs; (pink rhinestones) Kaisercraft *Stickers:* (XOXO, swirl) Creative Imaginations *Fibers:* (pink ribbon) Offray *Adhesive:* (foam tape) *Tool:* (decorative-edge scissors)

DESIGNER TIP

Emboss paper and accents with the positive and negative sides of embossing folders for a unique look.

Luv U

Designer: Melanie Douthit

❶ Make card from cardstock.

❷ Trim patterned paper slightly smaller than card front; adhere.

❸ Cut patterned paper; stitch edges. Mat with patterned paper. Trim mat with decorative-edge scissors, sand edges, and adhere.

❹ Tie on ribbon. Thread button with twine; adhere.

❺ Paint heart; let dry. Apply glitter.

❻ Cut cardstock to fit behind heart; emboss and adhere. Attach brads and adhere to card.

❼ Spell "Luv U" with stickers.

Finished size: 4¼" x 5½"

I Love You

Designer: Maren Benedict

❶ Make card from cardstock. Adhere patterned paper piece.

❷ Layer ribbon, wrap around card, and knot. Adhere rhinestone.

❸ Stitch card edges.

❹ Emboss love you tag on reverse side; adhere with foam tape.

❺ Cut heart from tag, emboss, and adhere with foam tape.

Finished size: 5½" x 4¼"

SUPPLIES: *Cardstock:* (white) Bazzill Basics Paper *Patterned paper:* (Patchwork Quilt, Wild Flowers, Bluebird from Urban Prairie collection) BasicGrey *Paint:* (golden yellow) Making Memories *Accents:* (chipboard heart) Cosmo Cricket; (yellow mini brads) Queen & Co.; (yellow glitter) Doodlebug Design *Stickers:* (Chalkboard alphabet) Jenni Bowlin Studio *Fibers:* (blue stitched ribbon) Doodlebug Design; (white twine) *Template:* (floral embossing) Provo Craft *Tool:* (embossing machine) Provo Craft; (decorative-edge scissors)

SUPPLIES: *Cardstock:* (Lemon Tart) Papertrey Ink *Patterned paper:* (Hop Scotch from Hello Sunshine collection) Cosmo Cricket *Accents:* (love you, heart tags) Cosmo Cricket; (red rhinestone) Heidi Swapp *Fibers:* (yellow ribbon) Papertrey Ink; (red ribbon) Target *Adhesive:* (foam tape) *Template:* (Swiss Dots embossing) Provo Craft *Tool:* (die cut/embossing machine) Provo Craft

Love Birds

Designer: Jessica Witty

❶ Make card from cardstock.

❷ Stamp birdhouses and swirl; watercolor with ink.

❸ Write "Do not disturb" on cardstock; trim and ink edges. Adhere twine to piece with foam tape; adhere to card. Attach brad.

❹ Stamp love birds on cardstock; trim. Tie with ribbon and adhere with foam tape.

Finished size: 5½" x 4"

SUPPLIES: *Cardstock:* (white) Papertrey Ink *Patterned paper:* (White Mini Dot from Kraft collection) Making Memories *Rubber stamps:* (birdhouse, love birds from Pretty Birds set; swirl from Cute Curls set) Cornish Heritage Farms *Dye ink:* (Basic Brown, Real Red, Bashful Blue) Stampin' Up! *Color medium:* (red pen) *Accent:* (brown brad) *Fibers:* (red gingham ribbon) Michaels; (hemp twine) Stampin' Up! *Adhesive:* (foam tape) *Tool:* (water brush)

DESIGNER TIP

Fabric paper works well with punches, and creates a quick, textured accent.

DESIGNER TIP

Draw a light pencil mark where you want the border to go, to help you apply the rub-on straight. The pencil mark won't show after the rub-on is applied.

my life

U+me =

A family's love is like a rainbow,
You can never find its end.

U + Me

Designer: Mary Jo Johnston

1. Make card from cardstock. Cover with patterned paper.
2. Punch fabric paper into circle; adhere.
3. Spell sentiment with stickers.
4. Affix label sticker; attach clip.

Finished size: 7" x 4½"

A Family's Love

Designer: Lea Lawson

1. Make card from cardstock.
2. Print sentiment on cardstock; trim and adhere.
3. Apply rub-on.
4. Adhere rhinestones and affix rainbow.

Finished size: 4" square

SUPPLIES: *Cardstock:* (white) Bazzill Basics Paper *Patterned paper:* (Notebook from Science Fair collection) Karen Foster Design *Specialty paper:* (Betty You+Me fabric) KI Memories *Accent:* (red clip) Design Originals *Stickers:* (Simply Sweet alphabet) Doodlebug Design; (my life label) KI Memories *Tool:* (1¾" circle punch) EK Success

SUPPLIES: *Cardstock:* (Mediterranean, white) Bazzill Basics Paper *Accents:* (blue rhinestones) Westrim Crafts *Rub-on:* (border) American Crafts *Sticker:* (rhinestone rainbow) Me & My Big Ideas *Font:* (Century Gothic) www.fonts.com

Black & White with Love

Designer: Daniela Dobson

1. Make card from cardstock.
2. Adhere patterned paper strip.
3. Apply rub-ons.
4. Adhere flower and rhinestone.

Finished size: 5½" x 3¼"

Fleur-de-lis Love

Designer: Melissa Phillips

1. Make card from cardstock. Adhere patterned paper.
2. Adhere cardstock piece and patterned paper strip.
3. Affix stickers and adhere accents.

Finished size: 3¾" x 5½"

SUPPLIES: *Cardstock:* (black) Frances Meyer *Patterned paper:* (Sentimental from Beloved collection) Tinkering Ink *Accents:* (black rhinestone) Doodlebug Design; (white crochet flower) *Rub-ons:* (leaf stem) Tinkering Ink; (sentiment circle) BasicGrey

SUPPLIES: *Cardstock:* (Red Devil, ivory) Bazzill Basics Paper *Patterned paper:* (Elizabeth Brocade Foiled, Elizabeth Floral from 5th Avenue collection) Making Memories *Accent:* (pearl) K&Company; (black fleur-de-lis, white label) American Crafts *Stickers:* (Chalkboard alphabet) Jenni Bowlin Studio

⑤ With Love

Designer: Sherry Wright

① Make card from cardstock; ink edges.

② Cut patterned paper slightly smaller; ink and stitch edges and adhere.

③ Adhere felt border and butterfly. Insert stick pin and adhere button.

④ Ink edges of chipboard bird; adhere.

⑤ Apply rub-on to brad. Attach brad and stick pin to crochet flower; adhere.

Finished size: 5¼" square

⑤ Love

Designer: Beatriz Jennings

① Make card from cardstock; paint edges.

② Cut patterned paper pieces, paint and stitch edges, and adhere.

③ Stamp Love.

④ Tie on ribbon. Adhere flowers and buttons.

Finished size: 4½" x 6"

SUPPLIES: *Cardstock:* (pink) Bazzill Basics Paper *Patterned paper:* (Turquoise Wallpaper from Tangerine Dream collection) Jenni Bowlin Studio *Chalk ink:* (turquoise, pink) Clearsnap *Accents:* (pink felt butterfly) Jenni Bowlin Studio; (blue chipboard bird) American Crafts; (pink, blue heart stick pins) Fancy Pants Designs; (cream felt border, blue brad) Queen & Co.; (ivory crochet flower) Imaginisce; (pink button) *Rub-on:* (sentiment circle) BasicGrey

SUPPLIES: *Cardstock:* (kraft) DMD, Inc. *Patterned paper:* (Yellow/Pink Gingham from Soft Tints collection) Hot Off The Press; (green damask from Super Slab) Provo Craft *Clear stamp:* (Love) Heidi Swapp *Pigment ink:* (black) Clearsnap *Paint:* (white) Delta *Accents:* (white flowers, buttons) *Fibers:* (brown polka dot ribbon) Offray

DESIGNER TIP

For extra interest on this card, adhere patterned paper behind the felt flowers.

Forever in My Heart

Designer: Jessica Witty

1. Make card from cardstock.
2. Cut patterned paper strip. Trim top edge to match felt branch curve; adhere strip and felt.
3. Stamp sentiment.

Finished size: 8½" x 4"

The World to Me

Designer: Jessica Witty

1. Make card from patterned paper; ink edges.
2. Adhere patterned paper piece. Tie on ribbon.
3. Stamp "The world" on patterned paper; trim, ink edges, and adhere.
4. Affix stickers to finish sentiment.

Finished size: 5½" x 4¼"

SUPPLIES: *Cardstock:* (kraft) Stampin' Up! *Patterned paper:* (Velvet Stocking from Blitzen collection) BasicGrey *Rubber stamp:* (sentiment from Forever in My Heart set) Stampin' Up! *Chalk ink:* (brown) Clearsnap *Accent:* (cream felt branch/bird) Prima

SUPPLIES: *Patterned paper:* (World Traveler Cream, Daydream, Market Paisley from Grayson Hall collection) Collage Press *Clear stamps:* (Grayson Poster Small alphabet) Collage Press *Chalk ink:* (Charcoal) Clearsnap *Stickers:* (Tiny alphabet) Making Memories *Fibers:* (white/green striped ribbon) May Arts

Vintage Valentines

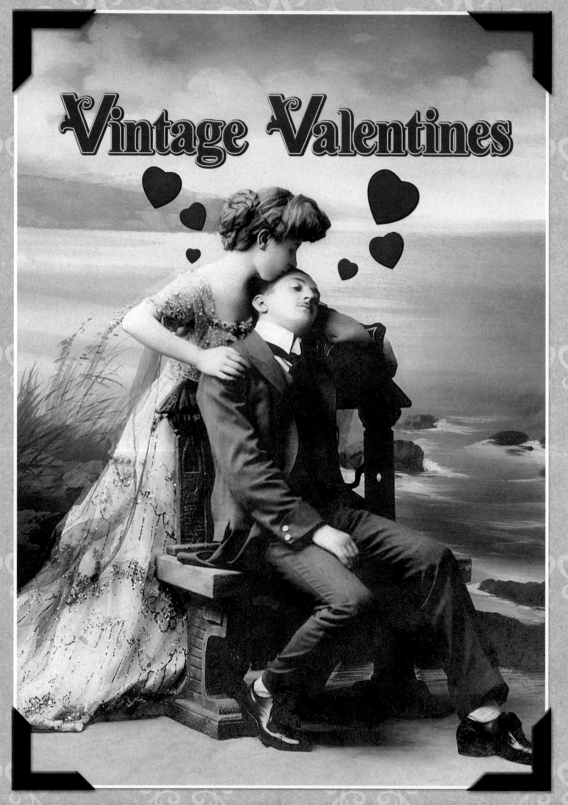

THERE IS NOTHING OUTDATED ABOUT IT: VINTAGE IS IN.

WE'LL SHOW YOU HOW TO PUT THOSE TREASURED TRINKETS
TO USE. CLEAR OUT THAT ATTIC CORNER AND CREATE
MEMORABLE VALENTINES FOR EVERYONE ON YOUR LIST.

:5: Be Mine Doily Card

Designer: Heidi Van Laar

1. Make card from cardstock. Cover with patterned paper.
2. Trim patterned paper; mat with cardstock and adhere.
3. Cut center from doily, place die cut through opening, and mat with felt. Trim with decorative-edge scissors and adhere to card.
4. Tie ribbon bow and adhere.
5. Stamp sentiment on cardstock, cut into tag shape, and attach to bow with pin.

Finished size: 5½" square

:5: Cupid Valentine's Day Card

Designer: Beatriz Jennings

1. Make card from cardstock; paint edges.
2. Trim patterned paper, ink edges. Adhere to card and stitch edges.
3. Trim patterned paper. Stamp sentiment and adhere lace. Mat with felt, trim with decorative-edge scissors, and stitch edges.
4. Tie ribbon around card; adhere matted piece.
5. Adhere cherubs and pearls.

Finished size: 4¾" x 5½"

SUPPLIES: *Cardstock:* (white) Georgia-Pacific; (Cream Puff, Ladybug) Bazzill Basics Paper *Patterned paper:* (Battenburg from Love Notes collection) Making Memories; (Powder Blue Dot from Double Dot collection) BoBunny Press *Clear stamp:* (Be Mine) Studio G *Chalk ink:* (Warm Red) Clearsnap *Accents:* (white heart stick pin) Making Memories; (vintage children die cut) *Fibers:* (red ribbon) Wrights *Tool:* (decorative-edge scissors) Fiskars *Other:* (cream felt) Kunin Felt; (red lace heart doily)

SUPPLIES: *Cardstock:* (kraft) Bazzill Basics Paper *Patterned paper:* (Sampler, Battenburg from Love Notes collection) Making Memories *Clear stamp:* (Valentine's day from Happy Days set) Inkadinkado *Dye ink:* (Antique Linen) Ranger Industries; (black) Clearsnap *Paint:* (cream) *Accents:* (white resin cherubs) Melissa Frances; (white pearls) *Fibers:* (red ribbon, cream lace) *Tool:* (decorative-edge scissors) *Other:* (cream felt)

Forever & Always Card

Designer: Kalyn Kepner

1. Make card from cardstock; ink edges.
2. Trim and tear patterned paper. Ink edges, adhere, and zigzag-stitch straight edges.
3. Affix ampersand sticker. Write sentiment with marker.
4. Adhere pearls to flowers. Layer two flowers and attach with brad.
5. Adhere flowers.

Finished size: 4¼" x 6"

Perfect Blend Card

Designer: Heidi Myers

1. Make card from cardstock.
2. Die-cut bracket frame and draw border with marker.
3. Stamp stand mixer and sentiment; emboss image.
4. Shade image using ink and water brush.
5. Adhere ribbon and button.

Finished size: 3¾" x 4¼"

SUPPLIES: *Cardstock:* (kraft) Bazzill Basics Paper *Patterned paper:* (Gingerbread from Good Cheer collection) October Afternoon *Chalk ink:* (Chestnut Roan) Clearsnap *Color medium:* (brown marker) *Accents:* (blue velvet flower) Imaginisce; (pink, cream, white flowers) Prima; (cream, green, pink pearls) BasicGrey; (decorative brad) K&Company *Stickers:* (pink chipboard ampersand) Heidi Swapp

SUPPLIES: *Cardstock:* (Cool Caribbean) Stampin' Up!; (white) The Paper Company *Rubber stamps:* (stand mixer, sentiment from Mix & Mingle set) Stampin' Up! *Dye ink:* (Barely Banana, Cool Caribbean, Going Grey, Soft Sky, Summer Sun) Stampin' Up! *Embossing powder:* (clear) Stampendous! *Color medium:* (Real Red marker) Stampin' Up! *Accent:* (brass button) Melissa Frances *Fibers:* (red polka dot ribbon) American Crafts *Die:* (bracket frame) Provo Craft *Tool:* (water brush) Stampin' Up!

⟨5 steps⟩ Birdie XOXO Box

Designer: Anne Jo Lexander

Ink all paper edges.

1 Cover box with patterned paper.

2 Punch patterned paper strips and adhere to box sides.

3 Die-cut and emboss labels from patterned paper. Apply rub-ons to small label. Adhere medium label, adhere ribbon, and adhere small label with foam tape. Adhere rhinestones and rhinestone medallion.

4 Spray flowers and vintage book pages with shimmer spray. Ink edges of yellow flower petals.

5 Roll book pages; adhere to box. Adhere flowers, feathers, tulle, and charms.

Finished size: 5¾" x 5¼" x 1¼"

⟨5 steps⟩ Patchwork Love Card

Designer: Kalyn Kepner

1 Make card from cardstock.

2 Die-cut squares from patterned paper and adhere to cardstock panel. Stitch each square edges.

3 Adhere panel to card; zigzag-stitch edges.

4 Affix stickers to spell "Love". Adhere flowers.

5 Cut slit in side of card. Thread ribbon through slit and tie around card front.

Finished size: 5" square

SUPPLIES: *Patterned paper:* (Queen of Hearts, Lovey Dovey, I'm Yours from Splendid collection) Fancy Pants Designs *Dye ink:* (Tea Dye, Walnut Stain) Ranger Industries *Specialty ink:* (Iridescent Gold, Vintage Pink, Coffee Shop shimmer spray) Tattered Angels *Accents:* (yellow flowers) Papirloftet; (cream flowers, pink/yellow/blue rhinestone medallion) Prima; (green rhinestones) Kaisercraft; (peach feather; silver oval, square charms) *Rub-ons:* (birds, xoxo) Fancy Pants Designs *Fibers:* (ivory ribbon) *Dies:* (small, medium labels) Spellbinders *Tool:* (border punch) Martha Stewart Crafts *Other:* (box, white tulle, vintage book pages)

SUPPLIES: *Cardstock:* (light green, Vanilla) Bazzill Basics Paper *Patterned paper:* (Unchained Melody, Sentimental Baby, Birdy Baby Blue from Baby 2 Bride collection) Graphic 45; (Gingerbread from Good Cheer collection) October Afternoon *Dye ink:* (Creamy Brown) Clearsnap *Accent:* (pink flowers) Prima *Stickers:* (Newsprint alphabet) Heidi Swapp *Fibers:* (cream scalloped ribbon) Chatterbox; (pale green ribbon) *Die:* (mosaic tile) QuicKutz

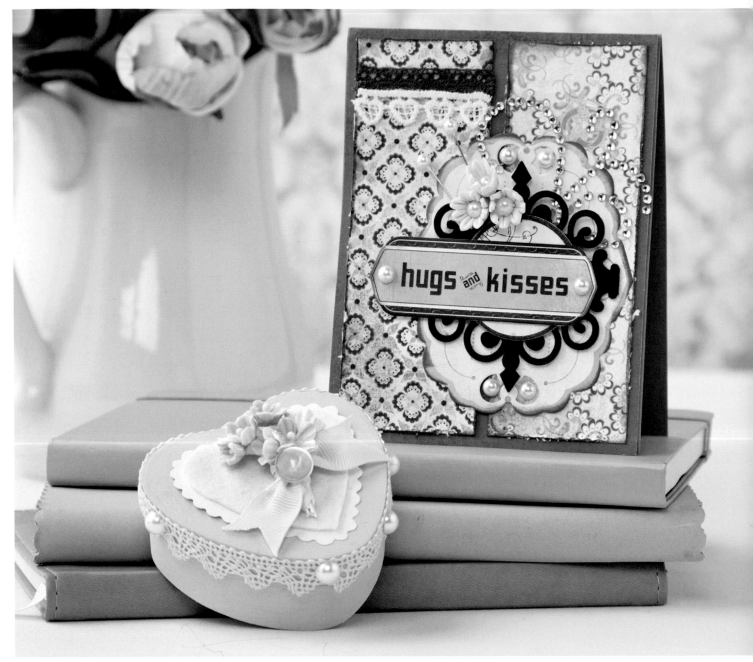

Valentine Heart Box

Designer: Annabelle O'Malley

1. Paint box; let dry.
2. Trim heart from felt; mat with cardstock and trim with decorative-edge scissors. Adhere to lid.
3. Tie flowers with ribbon; tie twine through button and adhere to ribbon. Adhere flowers to lid.
4. Adhere trim to lip of lid; adhere pearls.

Finished size: 3" x 3" x 1¼"

SUPPLIES: *Cardstock:* (cream) Bazzill Basics Paper *Paint:* (Hydrangea Pink) Delta *Accents:* (pink flowers) Caramelos; (cream button) Papertrey Ink; (white pearls) Zva Creative *Fibers:* (pink ribbon, white twine) Papertrey Ink; (cream lace trim) MJ Trimming *Tools:* (decorative-edge scissors) Fiskars *Other:* (cream felt, heart box)

Hugs & Kisses Card

Designer: Sherry Wright

1. Make card from cardstock. Cover with patterned paper.
2. Distress and ink edges of patterned paper; adhere to cardstock.
3. Adhere trim. Affix label sticker and adhere rhinestone swirl.
4. Adhere felt medallion and affix sentiment sticker.
5. Insert pins and flowers. Adhere pearls.

Finished size: 4¼" x 5½"

SUPPLIES: *Cardstock:* (tan) Prism *Patterned paper:* (Peanut Butter, Hand Dipped, Vanilla Fudge from Bittersweet collection) BasicGrey *Chalk ink:* (Chestnut Roan) Clearsnap *Accents:* (clear rhinestone swirl, brown felt medallion) Prima; (white pearls) Queen & Co.; (cream porcelain flowers, white pearl stick pins) *Stickers:* (sentiment, label) BasicGrey *Fibers:* (brown/white trim) Offray

DESIGNER TIP

You can remove printed text, sentiments, and handwriting from vintage card or advertising images by scanning them and using photo editing software.

5 STEPS | Heart You Postcard Card

Designer: Windy Robinson

1. Make card from cardstock.
2. Cut patterned paper slightly smaller than card. Trim with decorative-edge scissors, fold over card, and adhere.
3. Trace template on patterned paper; trim. Ink edges and adhere.
4. Stamp I Love You on postcard; emboss. Adhere heart. Layer with frame die cut and adhere to card.
5. Fold ribbon and adhere. Adhere trim, rickrack, flower, and pearls.

Finished size: 4½" x 5½"

5 STEPS Be Mine Card

Designer: Cindy Holshouser

1. Make card from cardstock; ink edges.
2. Zigzag-stitch patterned paper strips together; punch right edge. Mat with cardstock and ink edges; adhere.
3. Adhere crochet trim.
4. Ink edges of vintage image, adhere glitter, and adhere with foam tape.
5. Die-cut and emboss tag from cardstock. Stamp be mine. Thread with crochet trim, adhere button, and adhere to card with foam tape.

Finished size: 4¼" x 5½"

SUPPLIES: *Cardstock:* (Quartz) Bazzill Basics Paper *Patterned Paper:* (Individual Blooms from Uniquely You collection) My Mind's Eye; (Varnished Houndstooth from Paperie collection) Making Memories *Clear stamp:* (I Love You) Imaginisce *Dye ink:* (red) Technique Tuesday *Chalk ink:* (Charcoal) Clearsnap *Embossing powder:* (clear) Stampendous! *Accents:* (postcard) 7gypsies; (white frame die cut) My Mind's Eye; (red metal heart) Colorbok; (pink flower) Prima; (white pearls) Hero Arts *Fibers:* (pink polka dot ribbon) May Arts; (red trim) Creek Bank Creations; (pink rickrack) *Template:* (label die cut) My Mind's Eye *Tool:* (decorative-edge scissors) Provo Craft

SUPPLIES: *Cardstock:* (Sweet Blush, Vintage Cream) Papertrey Ink *Patterned paper:* (Time from Documented collection) Teresa Collins; (Tiny Dots from Me & My Cousins collection) My Mind's Eye *Clear stamps:* (be mine from Heart Prints set) Papertrey Ink *Dye ink:* (Antique Linen) Ranger Industries *Specialty ink:* (Burnt Umber hybrid) Stewart Superior Corp. *Accents:* (cream button) Jenni Bowlin Studio; (silver glitter) Hero Arts; (vintage image) *Fibers:* (cream crochet trim) *Die:* (tag) Spellbinders *Tool:* (border punch) Fiskars

Be Mine Polka Dot Card

Designer: Betsy Veldman

① Make card from cardstock.

② Ink edges of patterned paper and adhere to card.

③ Trim patterned paper, stitch and ink edges, and adhere. Tie on ribbon.

④ Stamp sentiment and finial on journaling label; affix chipboard frame and adhere pearl.

⑤ Adhere lace to label and adhere to card with foam tape.

⑥ Adhere vintage image with foam tape.

Finished size: 4¼" x 6"

⑤ Love Bingo Valentine Card

Designer: Anabelle O'Malley

① Make card from cardstock; stitch edges.

② Mat bingo card with felt; trim with decorative-edge scissors. Adhere to card.

③ Apply rub-on to cardstock, trim and stitch edges. Adhere with foam tape.

④ Wrap twine around card; tie in bow.

⑤ Insert pin.

Finished size: 4¼" x 4½"

SUPPLIES: *Cardstock:* (Pure Poppy) Papertrey Ink *Patterned paper:* (floral from Love Note collection notebook) Making Memories; (red polka dot) *Clear stamps:* (be mine from Heart Prints set, finial from Recipe Box Label set) Papertrey Ink *Chalk ink:* (Creamy Brown) Clearsnap *Specialty ink:* (Pure Poppy, Smokey Shadow hybrid) Papertrey Ink *Accents:* (journaling label) K&Company; (red pearl) Kaisercraft; (vintage image) Crafty Secrets *Stickers:* (chipboard frame) BasicGrey *Fibers:* (cream ribbon) Papertrey Ink; (yellow lace)

SUPPLIES: *Cardstock:* (cream) Bazzill Basics Paper *Accents:* (red heart stick pin) Caramelos; (bingo card) Jenni Bowlin Studio *Fibers:* (cream twine) Papertrey Ink *Rub-ons:* (sentiment) Hambly Screen Prints *Tool:* (decorative-edge scissors) Fiskars *Other:* (cream felt)

Antique Valentine Jar

Designer: Jessica Witty

1. Trim patterned paper strip to fit jar; ink edges and adhere.
2. Ink ribbon and tie around jar. Adhere vintage image.
3. Ink edges of tag; apply sentiment rub-on.
4. Tie tag to ribbon.

Finished size: 3" diameter x 5½" height

Cupid Love Wall Hanging

Designer: Ivanka Lentle

1. Coat plaque with gesso; let dry. Paint with beige paint, let dry, then paint with black.
2. Adhere cardstock. Cut patterned paper panel and ink edges.
3. Fray edges of fabric image. Mat with patterned paper, ink edges, and adhere to patterned paper panel with foam tape.
4. Tie on ribbon and adhere panel to plaque.

Finished size: 10¾" x 5¼"

SUPPLIES: *Patterned paper:* (Addie Pattern Stripe from Noteworthy collection) Making Memories *Dye ink:* (Antique Linen) Ranger Industries *Accent:* (vintage image) *Rub-on:* (sentiment) Crate Paper *Fibers:* (yellow polka dot ribbon) Papertrey Ink *Other:* (white tag) Avery; (antique glass jar)

SUPPLIES: *Cardstock:* (black) The Paper Company *Patterned paper:* (Vine Scroll from Brothers collection) My Mind's Eye *Chalk ink:* (black) Clearsnap *Paint:* (beige, black) Making Memories *Finish:* (gesso) Plaid *Accent:* (vintage fabric image) Crafty Secrets *Fibers:* (green ribbon) Waste Not Paper *Other:* (wood plaque)

Love You Doll Card

Designer: Susan Dupre

1 Make card from patterned paper; ink edges.
2 Ink inside and outside edges of frame die cut. Trim patterned paper to fit behind frame, layer, and adhere to card. Adhere lace.
3 Ink edges of tag. Tie on ribbon and adhere to card. Spell "Love you" with stickers.
4 Adhere flower.

Finished size: 5½" x 7¼"

You Warm My Heart Card

Designer: Julie Campbell

1 Create card from cardstock.
2 Trim cardstock slightly smaller than card front and adhere.
3 Stamp sentiment on cardstock; trim and adhere.
4 Cut patterned paper piece, adhere patterned paper strip, and stitch seam. Tie on twill.
5 Cut cardstock piece; sand edges. Adhere chipboard toast and draw trail. Adhere red pearls. Adhere twill tab.
6 Attach cardstock piece behind patterned paper piece with brad. Adhere patterned paper piece to card, leaving cardstock piece free to move on brad.
7 Trim patterned paper, punch corners, and mat with cardstock. Punch corners and adhere chipboard toaster. Adhere with foam tape.

Finished size: 4¼" x 5½"

SUPPLIES: *Patterned paper:* (Marigold) The Paper Loft; (Mary, Mary, Quite Contrary from Playtimes Past collection) Graphic 45 *Dye ink:* (Chestnut) Colorbok *Stickers:* (black chipboard alphabet) *Accents:* (red polka dot frame die cut) My Mind's Eye; (red flower) Prima; (little girl tag) Graphic 45 *Fibers:* (green polka dot ribbon, white lace)

SUPPLIES: *Cardstock:* (Robin's Egg) Memory Box; (Suede Brown Dark) Prism; (Vintage Cream) Papertrey Ink *Patterned paper:* (Farmer's Market, Ribbon Sandwich from Early Bird collection) Cosmo Cricket; (Darling Dear from Vintage Yummy collection) Sassafras Lass *Rubber stamp:* (You Warm My Heart) Rubber Soul *Dye ink:* (Rich Cocoa) Tsukineko *Color medium:* (black pen) *Accents:* (chipboard toaster, toast) Cosmo Cricket; (red pearls) Kaisercraft; (silver brad) *Fibers:* (brown twill) Papertrey Ink *Tool:* (ticket corner punch) Stampin' Up!

⟨5⟩ Flower Heart Card

Designer: Melyssa Connolly

❶ Trim cardstock piece. Adhere patterned paper strip and stitch edges.

❷ Adhere ribbon and lace around piece. Adhere to card.

❸ Punch card and tie on ribbon.

❹ Paint flower centers; let dry. Adhere pearls.

❺ Cut heart shape from cardstock; adhere flowers. Adhere to card with foam tape.

Finished size: 5½" x 4¼"

⟨5⟩ Sweetheart Bag

Designer: Lisa Dorsey

❶ Die-cut box from patterned paper; assemble.

❷ Affix circle sticker and adhere label to front of box.

❸ Adhere rhinestone in center of flower; cut pearls from garland and adhere behind flower. Adhere flower to box.

❹ Add magnet closures to box flap.

❺ Tie ribbon bow, attach pearl brad, and adhere.

Finished size: 2½" x 4" x 1¾"

SUPPLIES: *Cardstock:* (White Daisy) Close To My Heart *Patterned paper:* (pink floral from Scrapbook Walls collection) Chatterbox *Paint:* (Petal Pink dimensional) Ranger Industries *Accents:* (cream flowers) Prima; (white pearl seed beads) *Fibers:* (cream ribbon, white lace) *Tool:* (⅛" circle punch) Fiskars *Other:* (frosted acrylic card) SheetLoad ShortCuts

SUPPLIES: *Patterned paper:* (Primrose Garden from Sweet Charity collection) Webster's Pages; (Addie Brocade Dot from Noteworthy collection) Making Memories; (Jade from Treasure collection) My Mind's Eye *Dye ink:* (Antique Linen) Ranger Industries *Accents:* (sweetheart label) Crafty Secrets; (cream metal flower, pearl brad) Chatterbox; (pink rhinestone) Me & My Big Ideas; (white pearl garland) Hirschberg Schutz & Co. *Sticker:* (affection circle) Melissa Frances *Fibers:* (pink ribbon) *Die:* (scalloped bag) Ellison *Other:* (magnetic closure) BasicGrey

Give Them Chocolate

Death by Chocolate Fondue Pattie Donham

Just the thought of liquid chocolate makes my mouth water. I like to use both milk chocolate and semi-sweet chocolate bits so that everyone's chocolate preference is satiated. And, when you add the whipping cream and liqueur, the texture is so silky it will make you swoon!

INGREDIENTS

1 pkg. (11 oz.) Ghirardelli semi-sweet chocolate bits
1 pkg. (11 oz.) Ghirardelli milk chocolate bits
½ pint whipping cream
½ c. Kahlua liqueur

DIRECTIONS

Place chocolate bits in a large bowl, and pour cream and liqueur over chocolate, stirring it in. Melt slowly in a microwave, stirring frequently with a wood spoon until melted. Pour into a fondue pot, and light the flame underneath the pot to keep it warm.

Serve with marshmallows, crushed graham crackers, strawberries, crushed nuts, pineapple and apple chunks, and/or shredded coconut.

⁵ STEPS Sweet Treat Ensemble

Designer: Kim Hughes

ACCENT PIECES

❶ Trim two flowers and punch ten multi-sized circles from patterned papers. ❷ Stamp hearts, lips, and three strawberries on patterned paper; trim. ❸ Emboss strawberries and hearts. Color strawberry leaves with pen.

CARD

❶ Make card from cardstock. ❷ Cut patterned paper slightly smaller than card front; adhere. ❸ Print sentiment on cardstock. Trim and adhere. ❹ Adhere patterned paper. *Note: Trim one edge in wave.* Stitch edges. ❺ Adhere wavy strip of patterned paper over paper seams. ❻ Adhere accent pieces.

PLACE MAT

❶ Cut patterned paper slightly smaller than cardstock. Adhere. Stitch edges. ❷ Cut wavy strip of patterned paper. Adhere. ❸ Adhere accent pieces.

NAPKIN WRAP

❶ Cut strip of patterned paper. Stitch edges. Adhere ends together. ❷ Adhere accent pieces.

Finished sizes: card 4¼" x 5½", place mat 12" x 12", napkin wrap 5¾" x 1"

SUPPLIES: *Cardstock:* (white) Bazzill Basics Paper; (brown) Prism *Patterned paper:* (Front Porch, Courtyard, Window Box from Summer Cottage collection; Surfboard from Under the Boardwalk collection) Daisy Bucket Designs *Rubber stamps:* (lips, strawberry, scalloped heart, swirl heart, ladybug from Hugs and Kisses set) Cornish Heritage Farms *Watermark ink:* Tsukineko *Chalk ink:* (Dark Brown) Clearsnap *Embossing powder:* (Chocoholic Brownie) Cornish Heritage Farms *Color medium:* (light green pen) Sakura *Font:* (Mademoiselle) www.twopeasinabucket.com *Tools:* (½", ¾" circle punches) EK Success

Chocolate Sauce Cindy Schow

This is a recipe I like to make and keep in the fridge for when I want a quick dessert. It's easy to make and has a nice rich chocolate flavor. Mmm...it makes me hungry just thinking about it!

INGREDIENTS

6 tbsp. butter
2 c. sugar
¼ c. cocoa
1 c. evaporated milk

DIRECTIONS
Combine all ingredients in pot; boil 5 minutes. Remove from heat. Serve warm with vanilla ice cream, brownies, cake, or your favorite dessert.

So Sweet Together Tag
Designer: Tresa Black

❶ Make tag from cardstock; round corners and distress edges. ❷ Print "Chocolate ice cream sauce" on cardstock; trim and adhere. ❸ Distress edges of patterned paper piece; adhere. Stamp together on cardstock; emboss. Trim, distress edges, and adhere. ❹ Attach ribbon loop to tag with brad. ❺ Print "So sweet" on cardstock, punch into circle, and adhere to metal-rimmed tag. ❻ Punch hole, tie with ribbon, and adhere to tag.

Finished size: 3½" x 6¼"

BONUS IDEA

Change the tag color scheme to coordinate with the container you use for the sauce. Or, use a clear glass container to show off the rich chocolate color of the sauce.

SUPPLIES: *Cardstock:* (Pansy Purple, Baby Pink) Close To My Heart *Patterned paper:* (Friendship Hearts from Girls Will Be Girls collection) Adornit-Carolee's Creations *Clear stamp:* (together from Friendship Word Puzzle set) Close To My Heart *Watermark ink:* Tsukineko *Embossing powder:* (White Daisy) Close To My Heart *Accents:* (metal-rimmed tag) Avery; (silver mini brad) Making Memories *Fibers:* (pink grosgrain ribbon) Offray *Fonts:* (Angelica) www.dafont.com; (Tall Pen) Close To My Heart *Tools:* (⅛", 1" circle punches, corner rounder punch)

Turtle Cheesecake Heather D. White

This Turtle Cheesecake is so rich and decadent that your guests will think you bought it from a fancy bakery. Luckily you will have the recipe to prove that it was all you!

INGREDIENTS

Cheesecake:

1¾–2¼ c. chocolate graham cracker crumbs

⅓ c. butter, melted

3 (8 oz.) pkgs. cream cheese, softened

1 can (14 oz.) sweetened condensed milk

½ c. sugar

3 large eggs

3 tbsp. lime juice

1 tsp. vanilla extract

1½ c. semi-sweet chocolate chips

Topping:

2 tbsp. chocolate flavored syrup

2 tbsp. caramel syrup or ice cream topping

½ c. coarsely chopped pecans

¼ c. semi-sweet mini chocolate chips

YIELDS 12 SERVINGS

DIRECTIONS

Preheat oven to 300 degrees. Grease 9" spring form pan.

CRUST

Combine crumbs and butter in medium bowl. Press onto bottom and 1" up sides of prepared pan.

FILLING

Beat cream cheese and sweetened condensed milk in large mixer. Add sugar, eggs, lime juice, and vanilla extract; beat until combined. Microwave chocolate chips in medium, microwave-safe bowl on HIGH for 1–2 minutes; stir. If necessary, microwave at additional 10–15 second intervals, stirring just until chocolate chips are melted.

Stir 2 c. of cheesecake batter into melted chocolate chips; mix well. Alternately spoon batters into crust, beginning and ending with yellow batter. Bake for 1 hour and 10–20 minutes or until edge is set and center moves slightly. Cool in pan on wire rack for 10 minutes; run knife around edge of cheesecake. Cool completely. Drizzle chocolate syrup and caramel syrup over cheesecake. Sprinkle with pecans and mini chocolate chips. Refrigerate for several hours or overnight. Remove side of pan before serving.

Please join us for a special
Valentine Celebration Dinner
on February 14, 2007
at half past 6:00 at the Crosby's.
You won't want to miss
the grand finale which features
a delectable Turtle Cheesecake.
Please R.S.V.P

Collin Crosby

⑤ Valentine Celebration Dinner Designer: Amber Crosby

INVITATION

❶ Make invitation from In the Groove paper; round corners.
❷ Print dinner details on Natural cardstock. Trim, round corners, and punch hole through each side. Thread two lengths of peach ribbon through each hole. Adhere to invitation, wrapping ribbon ends in back. ❸ Adhere strip of Dez Dots paper; adhere gems. ❹ Punch heart from Andrew's Varsity Letter paper. Adhere to larger heart cut from Pink cardstock. Adhere to invitation.

PLACE CARD

❶ Make place card from Natural cardstock; round corners.
❷ Cut In the Groove paper slightly smaller than place card; round corners and adhere. ❸ Adhere strip of Dez Dots paper; adhere gems. ❹ Print guest's name on Natural; trim and attach to place card with brads. ❺ Punch heart from Pink cardstock; adhere.

CANDLE

❶ Cut In the Groove paper to fit around candle; adhere. Adhere peach ribbon around top edge. ❷ Adhere strip of Dez Dots paper to center. Adhere polka dot ribbon around bottom edge. Adhere gems to bottom row of dots. ❸ Punch heart from Andrew's Varsity Letter paper. Adhere to larger heart cut from Pink cardstock. Adhere to invitation.

BONUS IDEA

Decorate a small matching box containing a piece of cheesecake for each guest to take home. For an extra treat, attach a tag with the cheesecake recipe!

Finished sizes: invitation 6" x 7½", place card 4¼" x 3¼", candle 2¾" diameter x 5¼" height

SUPPLIES: *Cardstock:* (Natural) Bazzill Basics Paper; (Pink) American Crafts *Patterned paper:* (Dez Dots, In the Groove from Desperately Seeking Summer collection; Andrew's Varsity Letter from Leaves at Breakfast collection) Imagination Project *Accents:* (pink brads) Die Cuts With a View; (matching acrylic gems) Making Memories *Fibers:* (pink polka dot ribbon) American Crafts; (peach ribbon) Making Memories *Font:* (Garamond) www.myfonts.com *Tools:* (heart punch) The Punch Bunch; (corner rounder punch) Carl Manufacturing *Other:* (white candle)

Got Chocolate? Candy Bar Wraps

Designer: Melissa Phillips

Everyone loves chocolate, so indulge someone special today! Simply cover a chocolate bar with your own wrap and slip it into their briefcase, purse, backpack, or lunch for a sweet surprise! Or give one to a neighbor, colleague, or service person to say "Thanks for being you."

Falling in Love with Photos

5 STEPS Eyes for You Card

Designer: Kim Kesti

❶ Make card from cardstock; adhere patterned paper.

❷ Mat doily with cardstock; trim and adhere.

❸ Mat photo with cardstock; trim with decorative-edge scissors. Apply rub-ons.

❹ Adhere charm to sticker. Adhere sticker with foam tape.

❺ Punch holes and tie ribbon.

Finished size: 5" x 5¼"

SUPPLIES: *Cardstock:* (Powder, Tickled Pink, Sparkle Bling) Bazzill Basics Paper *Patterned paper:* (Antique Floral Wallpaper from Modern Romance collection) Daisy D's *Accent:* (gold arrow) Nunn Design *Rub-ons:* (flourishes) BasicGrey *Sticker:* (sentiment) 7gypsies *Fibers:* (blue organdy ribbon) Michaels *Adhesive:* (foam tape) *Tools:* (decorative-edge scissors) Fiskars; (⅛" circle punch) *Other:* (cupid photo, doily)

SUPPLIES: *Cardstock:* (red, brown) *Dye ink:* (black) Stewart Superior Corp. *Accent:* (black safety pin) Prym-Dritz *Fibers:* (red organdy ribbon) Offray *Font:* (CK Retro Block) Creating Keepsakes *Adhesive:* (foam squares) Making Memories *Tools:* (decorative-edge scissors, 1/16" circle punch) Fiskars *Other:* (candy photo)

Sweet Heart Card

Designer: Alisa Bangerter

1. Mat photo with cardstock; trim with decorative-edge scissors.
2. Tie ribbon in bow and adhere.
3. Print sentiment on cardstock. Trim into tag shape, ink edges, punch hole, and attach to ribbon with safety pin.

Finished size: 6¼" x 6¾"

BONUS IDEA

Create an interactive card that your younger valentines would love by covering your photo with patterned paper and cutting flaps to reveal the sugary treats beneath.

Great Together Card

Designer: Teri Anderson

1. Make card from patterned paper.
2. Adhere photo and patterned paper strip; cover seam with ribbon.
3. Adhere brackets and heart. Affix stickers to spell "Great together".
4. Print "Valentine, we're" on cardstock; trim, ink edges, and adhere.

Finished size: 5½" square

SUPPLIES: *Cardstock:* (white) *Patterned paper:* (Suffuse, Concentrate from Infuse collection) BasicGrey *Pigment ink:* (pink) Tsukineko *Accents:* (light, dark pink acrylic brackets) American Crafts; (pink chipboard heart) Heidi Swapp *Stickers:* (Infuse alphabet) BasicGrey *Fibers:* (pink grosgrain ribbon) Offray *Font:* (CK Holiday Spirit) Creating Keepsakes *Other:* (flower photo)

SUPPLIES: *Cardstock:* (white) Bazzill Basics Paper *Patterned paper:* (XOXO) The Paper Studio *Specialty paper:* (photo) *Font:* (CK Script) Creating Keepsakes *Software:* (photo editing) *Other:* (digital wedding rings photo)

Always Card

Designer: Jennifer Miller

❶ Make card from cardstock; adhere patterned paper strip.

❷ Open photo in photo editing software; type sentiment. Print on photo paper; adhere.

Finished size: 5" square

For You Gift Bag

Designer: Kim Hughes

❶ Remove handles from gift bag; adhere ribbon.

❷ Mat photo with patterned paper. Adhere scalloped cardstock strip; adhere to bag.

❸ Adhere scalloped cardstock strip to patterned paper piece; adhere to bag.

❹ Cut heart from cardstock and write sentiment using marker. Punch hole and attach to ribbon with safety pin.

Finished size: 5¼" x 8½"

SUPPLIES: *Cardstock:* (Natural, white scalloped) Bazzill Basics Paper *Patterned paper:* (Sweet Summer Plaid from Whimsy collection) Bo-Bunny Press *Color medium:* (purple marker) EK Success *Accent:* (yellow safety pin) Creative Impressions *Fibers:* (white twill ribbon) Creative Impressions *Tool:* (¹⁄₈" circle punch) McGill *Other:* (conversation heart photo, kraft gift bag)

Gotta Love Me Card

Designer: Kathleen Paneitz

1 Make card from patterned paper.

2 Mat photo with cardstock; adhere.

3 Thread ribbon through tag; tie bow and adhere.

4 Adhere hearts.

Finished size: 5¾" x 4"

Tic-Tac-Toe Card

Designer: Terri Davenport

1 Make card from cardstock.

2 Cut game board from cardstock; adhere cardstock strips.

3 Affix X stickers. Punch out photos and adhere.

4 Mat with patterned paper and adhere.

5 Adhere patterned paper strip.

6 Spell "We love you" with rub-ons.

Finished size: 4¼" x 5½"

SUPPLIES: *Cardstock:* (white) *Patterned paper:* (Love Affair) Li'l Davis Designs *Accents:* (chipboard tag) Me & My Big Ideas; (epoxy hearts) Making Memories *Fibers:* (black gingham ribbon) Offray *Other:* (photo)

SUPPLIES: *Cardstock:* (Cardinal, Ebony) Bazzill Basics Paper; (white) *Patterned paper:* (Flamingo, Pashmina Stripe from Pashmina collection) Luxe Designs *Rub-ons:* (All Mixed Up alphabet) Doodlebug Design *Stickers:* (Halloween Hoopla alphabet) SEI; (Cookie Cutter alphabet) KI Memories *Tool:* (¾" circle punch) EK Success *Other:* (photos)

Editor: Brandy Jesperson

Say "I Do" to Photos

Learn how easy it is to incorporate photos into your upcoming wedding. From favors to centerpieces and guest books to thank you cards, *Paper Crafts* designers show you how pictures can add an extra dose of personality and elegance to your special day.

5 Something Blue Favor

Designer: Wendy Sue Anderson

1. Paint tin; let dry.
2. Adhere ribbon to lid.
3. Print wedding date on cardstock. Trim, mat with cardstock, and adhere photo.
4. Adhere piece to sticker.
5. Adhere sticker to lid with foam tape.

Finished size: 3¾" x 2¼" x ¾"

SNAP SHOT

For many couples, the groom seeing the bride in her wedding dress before the ceremony is no longer considered a sign of bad luck. In fact, the new trend is to have formal wedding pictures taken of the couple in their gown and tuxedo before the day of the wedding. If this trend is for you, reserve some of your photos for simple favors that your guests are sure to treasure.

SUPPLIES: *Cardstock:* (light blue, cream) *Paint:* (black) Krylon *Sticker:* (houndstooth rectangle) Making Memories *Fibers:* (printed blue ribbon) Making Memories *Font:* (Beautiful ES) www.betterfonts.com *Adhesive:* (foam tape) *Other:* (mint tin, photo)

⚙5 Kissing Couple Thank You Card

Designer: Layle Koncar

❶ Make card from patterned paper.

❷ Double mat photo with cardstock and adhere to card.

❸ Apply rub-ons to cardstock, punch, ink edges, and adhere with foam tape.

Finished size: 5¼" x 6½"

SNAP SHOT

Make your thank you notes more personal by including a photo from your wedding day. Your recipients will appreciate your gratitude and enjoy the special touch your photo will add.

SUPPLIES: *Cardstock:* (teal, white) *Patterned paper:* (Laurel Rookery Road) Scenic Route *Pigment ink:* (Seafoam) Tsukineko *Rub-ons:* (thank you circle, flower) Scenic Route *Adhesive:* (foam tape) *Tool:* (1¾" circle punch) *Other:* (photo)

5 Bridal Shower Thank You Card

Designer: Layle Koncar

1. Make tri-fold card from patterned paper.
2. Apply rub-on to photo.
3. Adhere photo to reverse side of patterned paper with foam tape. Adhere piece to top flap of card.

Finished size: 6" square

SNAP SHOT

Use this simple photo card for your bridal shower and bachelorette party thank you notes. With its simple design, it's easy to mass produce and you can even use a stock photo from the internet if you don't have time to take a similar photo yourself.

SUPPLIES: *Patterned paper:* (Baby Blossoms from Botanical Bliss collection) Tinkering Ink *Rub-on:* (thank you) Scenic Route *Adhesive:* (foam tape) *Other:* (photo)

⁵ Unity Candle Guest Book

Designer: Anabelle O'Malley

❶ Mat patterned paper with cardstock; adhere.

❷ Adhere trim and flourishes to cover.

❸ Adhere flower and rhinestones.

❹ Mat photo with cardstock; adhere with foam tape.

❺ Adhere buttons and affix alphabet to spell "Guests".

Finished size: 9" x 8½"

SNAP SHOT

Create a focal point on your guest book with a photo of a unity candle, church doors, or a close up of your wedding bands. Use a picture with a lot of meaning to make your book even more of a keepsake once the wedding is over.

SUPPLIES: *Cardstock:* (black) *Patterned paper:* (flocked black and white) The Paper Company *Accents:* (blue, green, white buttons) Autumn Leaves; (clear rhinestones) EK Success; (white silk flower) Bazzill Basics Paper; (black felt flourishes) Queen & Co. *Stickers:* (Wedding Silver alphabet) K&Company *Fibers:* (teal lace trim) Offray *Adhesive:* (foam tape) *Other:* (green photo album) SEI; (photo)

To Love
Someone Centerpiece

Designer: Susan Neal

PHOTO PANEL

❶ Cut chipboard to finished size; cover with cardstock.

❷ Cut frame from patterned paper.

❸ Adhere photo behind frame and adhere piece to panel.

❹ Die-cut flourish from cardstock; adhere. Adhere rhinestone.

Finished size: each panel 3¾" x 5¾"

SENTIMENT PANEL

❶ Repeat Photo Panel steps 1-2.

❷ Print sentiment on cardstock, adhere behind frame, and adhere to panel.

❸ Die-cut flourish from cardstock; adhere. Adhere rhinestones.

ASSEMBLE

❶ Make each panel twice.

❷ Punch holes in each corner and tie together with ribbon.

SIMPLE SENTIMENT

To love someone deeply gives you strength. Being loved by someone deeply gives you courage.

– Lao Tzu

SNAP SHOT

Place this elegant photo centerpiece over a square candle or vase on the center of each table. For a more dramatic effect, make multiple centerpieces in different sizes for a staggered look.

SUPPLIES: *Cardstock:* (light blue, white) *Patterned paper:* (Baby 2 Brides Frames) Graphic45 *Accents:* (clear rhinestones) *Fibers:* (tan ribbon) Offray *Font:* (CBX Kreider) Chatterbox *Dies:* (flourishes) Provo Craft *Tool:* (die cut machine) Provo Craft *Other:* (chipboard, photo)

Here comes the *Bride*

Immerse yourself in the excitement of an upcoming wedding by making a greeting card, throwing a delightful shower, or creating heartfelt announcements. A handmade treasure is sure to delight any bride and groom.

5 STEPS Mr. & Mrs. Card
Designer: Jenn Diercks

1. Make card from cardstock.
2. Stamp floral motif repeatedly on cardstock. Trim, mat with cardstock, and punch edges. Adhere.
3. Stamp Mr. & Mrs. and frame on cardstock. Cut out, mat with cardstock, and punch edges. Dot scallops with pen. Adhere.
4. Adhere pearls.
5. Tie ribbon around front flap.

Finished size: 4¼" x 5½"

5 STEPS Bliss Card
Designer: Maren Benedict

1. Make card from cardstock.
2. Adhere patterned paper; zigzag-stitch edges.
3. Tie ribbon around front flap. Adhere brad.
4. Stamp cardstock; die-cut into circle. Die-cut larger circle and scalloped circle from cardstock; layer and adhere. Adhere rhinestones. Adhere with foam tape.

Finished size: 4¼" x 5½"

SUPPLIES: All supplies from Stampin' Up! unless otherwise noted. *Cardstock:* (Basic Black, Whisper White) *Rubber stamps:* (Mr. & Mrs. from All Holidays set; floral motif, frame from Frames with a Flourish set) *Dye ink:* (Basic Black) *Color medium:* (white pen) Sanford *Accents:* (pearls) *Fibers:* (lime green ribbon) *Adhesive:* (foam tape) *Tool:* (scalloped edge punch)

SUPPLIES: *Cardstock:* (Basic Black, Gable Green, Whisper White) Stampin' Up! *Patterned paper:* (black floral) Amanda Blu *Rubber stamp:* (bliss from June 2008 Bliss & A Birdie set) Unity Stamp Co. *Dye ink:* (Tuxedo Black) Tsukineko *Accents:* (green rhinestones) Me & My Big Ideas; (black felt brad) Queen & Co. *Fibers:* (white ribbon) May Arts *Adhesive:* (foam tape) *Dies:* (circles, scalloped circle) Spellbinders *Tool:* (die cut machine) Provo Craft

5 STEPS — Ever After Card

Designer: Ashley Harris

1. Make card from cardstock.
2. Adhere patterned paper to card; trim.
3. Affix bead strips.
4. Thread heart on ribbon, wrap ribbon around front card flap, and tie ends through other side of heart. Adhere.
5. Apply rub-on to cardstock; punch out and adhere.

Finished size: 6" x 4"

5 STEPS — Love Card

Designer: Melanie Douthit

1. Make card from cardstock.
2. Cut patterned paper square; mat with cardstock and adhere.
3. Cut patterned paper square; mat with cardstock. Tie with ribbon and adhere.
4. Adhere flowers. Thread button with floss; adhere.
5. Die-cut pieces from cardstock; adhere.

Finished size: 5½" square

SUPPLIES: *Cardstock:* (Cream Puff, French Vanilla) Bazzill Basics Paper *Patterned paper:* (black floral journaling die cut from 5th Avenue collection notebook) Making Memories *Accents:* (red chipboard heart) Heidi Swapp; (black bead strips) Glitz Design *Rub-on:* (happily ever after) BasicGrey *Fibers:* (black ribbon) Michaels *Tool:* (scalloped oval punch) Marvy Uchida

SUPPLIES: *Cardstock:* (black, white) *Patterned paper:* (Elegant Expressions, Grapevine Gossip from Simply Stated collection) Dream Street Papers *Accents:* (cream button) Making Memories; (cream, white flowers) *Fibers:* (cream ribbon) Offray; (cream floss) *Die:* (label, frame, love) Provo Craft *Tool:* (die cut machine) Provo Craft

Celebrate Shower Invitation

Designer: Maren Benedict

STAMPED PIECE

1. Stamp celebrate and sentiment on cardstock.
2. Mask off "e" and stamp umbrella. Stamp umbrella again on patterned paper; cut out, and adhere with foam tape.
3. Trim, punch corners, and adhere to slightly larger cardstock piece with foam tape.
4. Attach brads.

CARD

1. Make card from cardstock.
2. Cut slightly smaller piece of cardstock; stamp flowers. Cut into four pieces; adhere.
3. Adhere stamped piece with foam tape.
4. Tie ribbon around front flap.

Finished size: 5½" x 4¼"

Wedded Bliss Gift Bag

Designer: Susan Neal

1. Cut patterned paper slightly smaller than bag.
2. Adhere cardstock strip; zigzag-stitch edge.
3. Adhere patterned paper strip; stitch edge.
4. Stamp cardstock; cut out. Spell "Bliss" with stickers. Adhere with foam tape.
5. Print "Wedded" on cardstock. Trim into tag, punch hole, and tie with thread. Adhere.
6. Attach crochet flowers with brads.
7. Adhere to gift bag.

Finished size: 5¼" x 8½"

SUPPLIES: All supplies from Stampin' Up! unless otherwise noted. *Cardstock:* (Certainly Celery, Chocolate Chip, Whisper White) *Patterned paper:* (Tempting Turquoise Dots from Designer Series collection) *Rubber stamps:* (umbrella and sentiment from A Little Birdie Told Me set; flower from Fabulous Flowers set; celebrate from Celebrate Everything set) *Dye ink:* (Certainly Celery, Chocolate Chip, Tempting Turquoise) *Accents:* (silver brads) *Fibers:* (brown ribbon) May Arts *Adhesive:* (foam tape) *Tool:* (ticket corner punch)

SUPPLIES: *Cardstock:* (Green Tea) Bazzill Basics Paper; (white) *Patterned paper:* (Freshly Mown Lawn, Patio Umbrella from Daydream collection) October Afternoon *Clear stamp:* (journaling label from Journaling set) Making Memories *Pigment ink:* (Celadon) Clearsnap *Accents:* (aqua, green crochet flowers) Fancy Pants Designs; (clear rhinestone brads) Making Memories *Stickers:* (Good Cheer alphabet) October Afternoon *Fibers:* (white crochet thread) *Font:* (Maiandra GD) www.fonts.com *Adhesive:* (foam tape) *Tool:* (⅛" circle punch) *Other:* (white gift bag)

Diamond Ring Card

Designer: Sherry Wright

1. Make card from cardstock.
2. Cut patterned paper slightly smaller than card.
3. Cut patterned paper; distress and ink edges. Adhere.
4. Distress and ink edges of sticker; affix.
5. Cut flowers from patterned paper; adhere.
6. Thread ring on ribbon; tie around piece. Adhere.

Finished size: 5¼" x 6¼"

Special Happiness Card

Designer: Michelle Woerner

CARD

1. Make card from cardstock.
2. Stamp Pretty Pattern Backgrounder on cardstock. Trim, ink edges, and adhere.
3. Die-cut corner flourish from cardstock; adhere.

STAMPED PIECE

1. Stamp flower and newlyweds on cardstock. Trim, ink edges, and mat with cardstock.
2. Wrap with ribbon; thread ends through buckle and knot.
3. Stamp sentiment on cardstock. Trim and attach behind bookplate with brads. Adhere.
4. Accent with glitter glue.
5. Adhere with foam tape.

Finished size: 4¼" x 5½"

SUPPLIES: *Cardstock:* (brown, light blue) *Patterned paper:* (Twigs from Feather Your Nest collection, Tranquility from Classic Garden collection) Webster's Pages *Chalk ink:* (Chestnut Roan) Clearsnap *Accent:* (ring) Darice *Sticker:* (with this ring) Melissa Frances *Fibers:* (brown ribbon) Offray

SUPPLIES: All supplies from Stampin' Up! unless otherwise noted. *Cardstock:* (Chocolate Chip, Sage Shadow, Very Vanilla) *Rubber stamps:* (flower from Fabulous Flowers set); (Pretty Pattern Backgrounder) Cornish Heritage Farms *Clear stamps:* (newlyweds, sentiment from Wedding set) Inkadinkado *Accents:* (silver bookplate, brads, buckle); (iridescent glitter glue) Ranger Industries *Fibers:* (brown ribbon) *Adhesive:* (foam tape) *Die:* (corner flourish) Provo Craft *Tool:* (die cut machine) Provo Craft

Always & Forever Card

Designer: Anabelle O'Malley

❶ Make card from cardstock.

❷ Cover with patterned paper; ink edges.

❸ Cut patterned paper; ink and zigzag-stitch edges. Adhere.

❹ Cut cardstock; punch edges and adhere.

❺ Cut patterned paper; ink and stitch edges. Adhere.

❻ Cut flowers from patterned paper; adhere. Adhere rhinestones.

❼ Affix stickers.

Finished size: 5¼" square

Beautiful Bride Card

Designer: Melissa Phillips

CARD

❶ Make card from patterned paper; ink edges.

❷ Cut patterned paper slightly smaller than card; repeatedly stamp How Do I Love Thee. Ink edges and adhere.

❸ Cut patterned paper strip; trim with decorative-edge scissors. Ink edges and adhere. Stitch top edge.

❹ Ink edges of photo corner sticker; affix. Adhere rhinestones.

❺ Tie ribbon around front flap. Apply rub-on to oval tag sticker; ink edges. Punch hole and tie to bow with cord and button.

❻ Adhere trim.

STAMPED PIECE

❶ Stamp gown on two patterned paper pieces. Cut top and skirt from one image. Ink edges and adhere over second image. Trim; ink and stitch edges.

❷ Mat with patterned paper. Trim with decorative-edge scissors. Adhere with foam tape.

❸ Cut tulle; gather at top and adhere to waistline of gown. Attach flower and brad.

Finished size: 4¾" x 6"

SUPPLIES: *Cardstock:* (Apple Green) Bazzill Basics Paper *Patterned paper:* (Nestled, Front Porch, Verandah from Vintage Home collection; Flutterby from Feather Your Nest collection) Webster's Pages *Chalk ink:* (Creamy Brown) Clearsnap *Accents:* (orange rhinestones) Kaisercraft *Stickers:* (always & forever) K&Company; (label) Webster's Pages *Tool:* (lace border punch) Fiskars

SUPPLIES: *Patterned paper:* (Addie Brocade Dot from Noteworthy collection) Making Memories; (Ambiente Chelsey, Julie) Melissa Frances; (Love is Blue from Baby 2 Bride collection) Graphic45; (Endeared from Sugared collection, Admire from Blush collection) BasicGrey *Rubber stamps:* (Brush Gown with Full Ruffled Hem, How Do I Love Thee) Rubbernecker Stamps *Dye ink:* (Old Paper, Walnut Stain) Ranger Industries *Accents:* (green rhinestones) Kaisercraft; (pink brad) BasicGrey; (white velvet flower) Maya Road; (blue button, cream tulle) *Rub-on:* (bride) BasicGrey *Stickers:* (photo corner) BasicGrey; (oval tag) Melissa Frances *Fibers:* (cream lace trim) Melissa Frances; (cream ribbon) Wrights; (hemp cord) *Adhesive:* (foam tape) *Tools:* (⅛" circle punch, decorative-edge scissors)

BONUS IDEA

Decorate the inside of the card with a photo, ribbon, photo corners, and a charm.

Forever & Ever Card

Designer: Kandis Smith

1. Make card from cardstock; sand edges.

2. Cut patterned paper. Sand and stitch edges; adhere.

3. Cut patterned paper; adhere. Sand and zigzag-stitch sides.

4. Cut cardstock strip; sand edges. Adhere rickrack and lace trim. Stitch. Adhere.

5. Adhere hatpin, flowers, and pearls. Spell "And ever" with stickers.

6. Stamp frame on cardstock; cut out and attach brads. Adhere patterned paper piece. Spell "Forever" with stickers. Adhere frame with foam tape.

Finished size: 5½" x 8"

Monogram Announcement

Designer: Tracy Houser, courtesy of Anna Griffin

1. Make card from patterned paper.

2. Print monogram on cardstock. Punch out and adhere to patterned paper square with foam tape. Adhere chipboard square to back. Adhere with foam tape.

3. Cut slit in card fold and tie ribbon around front flap.

Finished size: 5¼" x 7"

SUPPLIES: *Cardstock:* (blue, cream) *Patterned paper:* (blue diamonds, blue floral) Chatterbox *Clear stamps:* (frame from Frames & Messages set) Hero Arts *Dye ink:* (Indigo) Clearsnap *Accents:* (beaded hatpin, light blue brads) Scrappin' Creations; (blue, cream flowers; pearls) Hero Arts *Stickers:* (Tiny Alpha alphabet) Making Memories *Fibers:* (blue rickrack) Crate Paper; (cream lace trim) *Adhesive:* (foam tape)

SUPPLIES: *Cardstock:* (cream) *Patterned paper:* (Grey Voile from Georgette collection) Anna Griffin *Fibers:* (pink ribbon) *Font:* (Brock Script) www.dafont.com *Adhesive:* (foam tape) *Tool:* (scalloped square punch) Family Treasures *Other:* (chipboard)

Love Conquers All Card

Designer: Beatriz Jennings

1. Make card from cardstock.
2. Cut patterned paper; round bottom corners. Ink edges and adhere.
3. Cut patterned paper; ink edges and adhere.
4. Zigzag-stitch edges.
5. Stamp corners.
6. Cut slit in fold; insert ribbon. Tie ribbon around front flap.
7. Stamp love conquers all on cardstock; apply ink. Cut out and adhere.
8. Thread button with floss; adhere button and flowers.

Finished size: 5¼" x 3¾"

Our Wedding Card

Designer: Anabelle O'Malley

1. Make card from patterned paper.
2. Adhere patterned paper piece.
3. Stitch edges.
4. Adhere border strips.
5. Affix stickers.
6. Adhere pearls.

Finished size: 4½" square

SUPPLIES: *Cardstock:* (cream, white) *Patterned paper:* (Flutterby from Feather Your Nest collection, Cream from Raspberry Truffle collection) Webster's Pages *Clear stamps:* (love conquers all from Gypsy Style set) Autumn Leaves; (corner from Wild Daisy Road set) Heidi Grace Designs *Dye ink:* (Old Paper) Ranger Industries *Pigment ink:* (black) Clearsnap *Accents:* (blue/white button) Making Memories; (white flowers) *Fibers:* (light blue ribbon) Martha Stewart Crafts; (white floss) *Tool:* (corner rounder punch) EK Success

SUPPLIES: *Patterned paper:* (Purple Majesty from Reflections of Nature collection) Webster's Pages *Accents:* (white border strips) Doodlebug Design; (pearls) Kaisercraft *Stickers:* (our wedding) K&Company; (flourishes) American Crafts

Happily Ever After Card

Designer: Sonja Skarbo

1. Make card from cardstock.
2. Stamp flowers and border.
3. Adhere border strip.
4. Stamp sentiment.
5. Attach brad.

Finished size: 6½" x 5"

With This Ring Card

Designer: Janette Olen

1. Make card from cardstock; punch top corners.
2. Cut cardstock slightly smaller than card; punch top corners. Adhere.
3. Cut cardstock strip; punch border and adhere.
4. Tie ribbon around front flap.
5. Stamp bride and groom on cardstock. Trim and apply ink around image. Mat with cardstock. Adhere rhinestones. Adhere with foam tape.
6. Stamp sentiment.

Finished size: 5½" x 4¼"

SUPPLIES: All supplies from Close To My Heart unless otherwise noted. *Cardstock:* (kraft) no source *Clear stamps:* (flowers from Friendship Blessings set; border, sentiment from Soul Mates set) *Dye ink:* (black) *Pigment ink:* (Pink Carnation, White Daisy) *Accents:* (black border strip) Doodlebug Design, (black velvet flower brad) Creative Imaginations

SUPPLIES: *Cardstock:* (Basic Black) Stampin' Up!; (white) *Rubber stamps:* (bride and groom from Wedding Silhouettes set) Artful Inkables; (sentiment from Wedding Background) Delta *Pigment ink:* (Graphite Black) Tsukineko *Specialty ink:* (Spring Moss hybrid) Papertrey Ink *Accents:* (clear rhinestones) The Paper Studio *Fibers:* (green ribbon) Papertrey Ink *Adhesive:* (foam tape) *Tools:* (Sunburst border punch) Fiskars; (corner scallop punch) Marvy Uchida

INSIDE

Umbrella Bridal Shower

Designer: Alisa Bangerter

INVITATION

1. Make invitation from cardstock; cover with patterned paper.

2. Cut umbrella, following pattern. Cover with patterned paper. Adhere trim. Adhere to invitation with foam tape.

3. Cut handle from gift bag; tie with ribbon and adhere to form umbrella handle.

4. Print text on cardstock. Trim, chalk edges, and adhere with foam tape.

FRAME

1. Paint frame.

2. Cover with patterned paper.

3. Adhere trim.

4. Tie ribbon around side.

5. Print sentiment on cardstock. Trim, chalk edges, and adhere.

FAVOR

1. Adhere patterned paper to umbrella container.

2. Tie ribbon on handle.

3. Print sentiment or guest's name on cardstock. Trim, chalk edges, and adhere.

Finished sizes: invitation 3½" x 6", favor 2¾" x 4¼" x 2¾", frame 8" square

SUPPLIES: *Cardstock:* (cream) *Patterned paper:* (Patio Umbrella from Daydream collection; Fruit Stand, Picnic Basket, Walk in the Park from Detours Collection) October Afternoon *Color medium:* (aqua chalk) Craf-T Products *Paint:* (cream) Delta *Fibers:* (aqua pompom trim) Fancy Pants Designs; (green ribbon) Making Memories *Adhesive:* (foam tape) *Font:* (CK Jessica) Creating Keepsakes *Other:* (frame) Delta; (umbrella container) Wilton; (chipboard, gift bag)

All Dressed in White

Nothing is as sweet or as perfect as two people in love. Send your best wishes to the bride and groom as they start their happily ever after with a handmade tribute to wedded bliss.

BONUS IDEA

Create this card for other occasions by using a variety of colors for spring, or pink or blue for baby.

⁵ Ribbon & Lace Wedding Card

Designer: Alisa Bangerter

❶ Make card from cardstock.

❷ Adhere trims and lace.

❸ Make tag from cardstock; write "true love" on tag.

❹ Adhere tag to card with foam tape; tie bow with ribbon and adhere.

❺ Attach wedding rings with heart pin to bow.

Finished size: 7" x 5"

Happy Ever After Gift Bag & Tag

Designer: Alice Golden

BAG

❶ Cut patterned paper to fit bag; sand edges.

❷ Apply sticker to wide ribbon; wrap around piece and adhere.

❸ Attach flowers with brads; adhere piece to bag.

TAG

❶ Cut rectangle from patterned paper; sand edges.

❷ Wrap wide sheer ribbon around piece; adhere.

❸ Affix sticker on cardstock; cut out and adhere to piece.

❹ Attach flower with brad.

❺ Mat piece with cardstock; punch hole at top.

❻ Tie tag to bag with ribbon; attach flower with brad.

Finished sizes: bag 8" x 10¼", tag 2½" x 5½"

SUPPLIES: *Cardstock:* (white) *Color medium:* (silver gel pen) Sanford *Accents:* (white pearl heart pin) Jo-Ann Stores; (silver wedding rings) Darice *Fibers:* (assorted white lace, trim) Trimtex, Carolace Industries, Wrights, Making Memories; (white sheer ribbon) Offray *Adhesive:* (foam tape) Making Memories

SUPPLIES: *Cardstock:* (White Prismatic) Prism *Patterned paper:* (Wedding Lace) Karen Foster Design *Accents:* (white flowers, cream fabric-covered brads) Imaginisce *Stickers:* (promise, happy ever after) Deja Views *Fibers:* (white sheer ribbon) Karen Foster Design; (wide white sheer ribbon) May Arts *Other:* (gift bag)

BONUS IDEA

Create this bag to hold a gift for your favorite ballerina—use pink or purple tulle with a matching satin ribbon in place of the rhinestones and lace.

Bridal Veil Gift Bag

Designer: Alisa Bangerter

❶ Trim top corners of bag.

❷ Cut 5" x 10" rectangle of tulle; sew gather stitch down 2" from top and gather.

❸ Cut 8" x 10" rectangle of tulle; sew gather stitch along 10" edge and gather.

❹ Adhere gathered tulle pieces to bag, with gathers overlapping. *Note: Small gathered piece extends above top of bag.*

❺ Adhere lace and rhinestone strand over gathers; adhere pearls to lace.

❻ Tie heart charm to bag with ribbon.

Finished size: 5½" x 8½"

SUPPLIES: *Accents:* (love heart charm) Hirschberg Schutz & Co.; (pearl beads) Darice *Fibers:* (white lace, rhinestone string) Wrights; (white sheer ribbon) Offray; (white tulle) *Other:* (white gift bag) DMD, Inc.

Mr. & Mrs. Card

Designer: Alicia Thelin

ACCENT

❶ Stamp Mr. & Mrs. on cardstock; emboss.

❷ Punch stamped text; punch ⅛" circle at top and bottom.

❸ Thread beads and stamped circle on hat pin; knot ribbon.

❹ Punch scallop circle from cardstock; adhere hat pin to circle with foam tape.

CARD

❶ Make card from cardstock.

❷ Stamp flourishes on card front; emboss.

❸ Adhere ribbons around card front.

❹ Adhere accent.

Finished size: 3" x 6"

BONUS IDEA

■ Save time! Make several of these cards at once to keep on hand for upcoming weddings.

■ Replace the "Mr. & Mrs." stamp with another stamped image to create this card for any occasion.

■ Stamp a flourish from your stamp set on the flap of the envelope and emboss it to create a coordinating envelope that adds a touch of class and flair.

SUPPLIES: All supplies from Stampin' Up! unless otherwise noted. *Cardstock:* (Shimmery White, Soft Sky, Whisper White) *Rubber stamps:* (Mr. & Mrs. from Fundamental Phrases set, flourish from Flowers & Flourish set) *Watermark ink:* Tsukineko *Embossing powder:* (white) *Accents:* (hat pin; clear faceted, pearl beads) *Fibers:* (blue stitched grosgrain, white taffeta ribbon) *Adhesive:* (foam tape) *Tools:* (scallop circle, 1¾" circle, ⅛" circle punches)

BONUS IDEA

Choose a patterned paper that coordinates with the wedding colors. Then the bride and groom can use the frame to display one of their wedding photos.

BONUS IDEA

Personalize your card for the bride and groom by stamping their monogram on the card in place of the sentiment.

Forever Frame

Designer: Julia Stainton

❶ Paint edges of frame; let dry.

❷ Adhere patterned paper to frame; sand edges.

❸ Apply rub-ons.

❹ Adhere flowers and rhinestones.

Finished size: 12" square

Wishing You Happiness Card

Designer: Sharon Laakkonen

❶ Make card from cardstock.

❷ Adhere trim; cut scallop edge following lace as guide.

❸ Stamp sentiment.

❹ Adhere rhinestone flourish, flowers, metal hearts, and rhinestone flowers to card.

Finished size: 6" x 5¾"

SUPPLIES: *Patterned paper:* (Mint Julep from Savannah collection) Autumn Leaves *Paint:* (white) Making Memories *Accents:* (white flowers) Prima; (clear rhinestones) Doodlebug Design *Rub-ons:* (forever) Royal & Langnickel; (flourish) Me & My Big Ideas *Other:* (wood frame) Michaels

SUPPLIES: *Cardstock:* (white) *Clear stamps:* (wishing you, happiness from Just Between Friends set) Fiskars *Dye ink:* (Black Soot) Ranger Industries *Accents:* (metal hearts) Nunn Design; (green flowers, black rhinestone flourish) Prima; (white rhinestone flowers) *Fibers:* (black crotchet lace trim) Prima

Elegant Bridal Shower

Designer: Carolyn Peeler, courtesy of Melissa Frances

INVITATION

Ink all paper edges.

❶ Make card from cardstock.

❷ Tie ribbon around card.

❸ Open a new project in software. Add label, flourishes, and invitation text; print on cardstock and trim.

❹ Cut patterned paper; mat with patterned paper and stitch edges.

❺ Adhere printed piece to block; stitch long sides. Adhere block with foam tape.

❻ Adhere cardstock rectangles. Tie buttons with string; adhere.

Finished sizes: invitation 5½" square, favor box 2" x 2" x 2"

SUPPLIES: *Cardstock:* (Dark Coffee Brown, Light Totally Tan, Light Heritage) WorldWin *Patterned paper:* (Abigail, Lillian from From This Moment On Wedding collection) Melissa Frances *Accents:* (white vintage buttons) *Digital elements:* (label from Swank Labels kit) www.twopeasinabucket.com; (flourishes) *Font:* (Copperplate Gothic Bold) www.myfonts.com *Software:* (photo editing) Adobe *Fibers:* (textured cream ribbon) May Arts; (cream crotchet lace trim) *Adhesive:* (foam tape) Fiskars

FAVOR BOXES

Ink all paper edges.

❶ Adhere patterned paper strip around box; cut notch. Adhere trim.

❷ Create label using software (see Invitation step 3); print on cardstock and trim. Adhere to top of box.

SUPPLIES: *Patterned paper:* (Dawning Damask, Roman Columns from Now & Forever collection) Imaginisce *Accents:* (pearl brad) K&Company; (antique gold flower charm, bookplate; ivory flower) Imaginisce; (magnetic snaps) BasicGrey *Rub-on:* (guests) K&Company *Other:* (journal) Target

Damask Guest Book

Designer: Alice Golden

JOURNAL CLASP

❶ Cut 1¼" x 12" rectangle from patterned paper; fold in half.

❷ Adhere one end to inside back cover.

❸ Adhere one side of snap to front cover.
Note: Place snap to line up with end of clasp.

❹ Adhere remaining snap side to front end of clasp.

❺ Attach charm and flower to clasp with brad.

JOURNAL COVER

❶ Cover journal front with patterned paper.

❷ Apply rub-on to patterned paper; trim and adhere behind bookplate.

❸ Adhere bookplate to cover.

Finished size: 8¼" square

Together Forever Card

Designer: Andrea Bowden,
courtesy of Stampin' Up!

❶ Make card from cardstock.

❷ Stamp sentiment on cardstock; trim.

❸ Emboss circles horizontally near sentiment using eyelet setter.

❹ Adhere ribbon around piece.

❺ Adhere pearl to flower; adhere to piece.

❻ Adhere piece with foam tape.

Finished size: 4¼" x 5½"

SUPPLIES: All supplies from Stampin' Up! unless otherwise noted. *Cardstock:* (Whisper White, Kraft) *Rubber stamps:* (sentiment from Together Forever set) *Dye ink:* (Chocolate Chip) *Accents:* (pearl, white flower) *Fibers:* (white taffeta ribbon) *Adhesive:* (foam tape)

Blossoms Wedding Favor

Designer: Lauren Meader

❶ Cut 3½" x 11" rectangle of cardstock; score at 3¾", 6", 10" and fold.

❷ Die-cut large and small flowers from cardstock.

❸ Stamp vine on folded cardstock; stamp flowers on die cut flowers.

❹ Adhere rhinestones to flowers; adhere flowers to favor with foam tape.

❺ Knot ribbon around flap.

❻ Cut plastic bag to fit inside favor; fill and close.

Finished size: 3½" x 4" x 2¼"

Always & Forever Card

Designer: Betsy Veldman

❶ Make card from cardstock.

❷ Emboss white glitter cardstock; cut rectangle and adhere.

❸ Die-cut flowers from cardstock; adhere.

❹ Adhere rhinestones.

❺ Wrap ribbon around card front.

❻ Adhere rhinestone trim to ribbon; tie bow and affix sticker.

Finished size: 6¼" x 5"

SUPPLIES: *Cardstock:* (Shimmery White) Stampin' Up! *Clear stamps:* (flowers, leaves from Beautiful Blooms set) Papertrey Ink *Dye ink:* (Romance) Bazzill Basics Paper *Accents:* (pink rhinestones) A Muse Artstamps *Fibers:* (pink taffeta ribbon) *Adhesive:* (foam tape) *Dies:* (large, small flowers) Provo Craft *Tool:* (die cut machine) Provo Craft *Other:* (frosted bags) Papertrey Ink

SUPPLIES: *Cardstock:* (white glitter) Die Cuts With a View; (white) *Accents:* (clear rhinestones) The Beadery; (always & forever chipboard) Die Cuts With a View *Fibers:* (white grosgrain ribbon) Offray; (clear rhinestone trim) Wrights *Die:* (flowers) Provo Craft *Template:* (swirls embossing) *Tool:* (die cut/embossing machine) Provo Craft

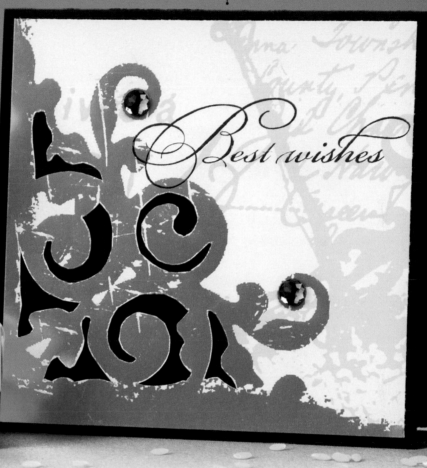

Scalloped Wedding Favor Bag

Designer: Kim Hughes

❶ Cut cardstock strip. Punch circles from reverse side of patterned paper; adhere to edge of strip.

❷ Adhere piece to bag.

❸ Adhere flower trim.

❹ Thread twine through button and knot; adhere button to flower. Adhere.

❺ Knot lace around bag handle.

Finished size: 2¼″ square

Silvery Best Wishes Card

Designer: Daniela Dobson

❶ Make card from cardstock.

❷ Cut patterned paper slightly smaller than card front; cut out pieces around flourish edge. Adhere to card.

❸ Adhere rhinestones.

❹ Stamp sentiment.

Finished size: 5″ square

SUPPLIES: *Cardstock:* (Paisley Impressions embossed) Doodlebug Design *Patterned paper:* (Wonder Floral from Bonjour collection) My Mind's Eye *Accents:* (blue flower) Prima; (white button) Autumn Leaves *Fibers:* (white waxed twine) Scrapworks; (white flower trim, white lace) *Other:* (white bag) Martha Stewart Crafts

SUPPLIES: *Cardstock:* (black) *Patterned paper:* (Love Bird Silver Foil from Elegance collection) Creative Imaginations *Clear stamps:* (best wishes from Sentiments set) Fiskars *Solvent ink:* (black) Tsukineko *Accents:* (black rhinestones) Doodlebug Design

BONUS IDEA

Use this same design for invites to a black tie New Year's Eve party or another black tie event. You can change the patterned papers to add more color or even display the theme for your party.

BONUS IDEA

Change this card for any occasion. Stamp an appropriate sentiment and brighten up the card by replacing the white flowers with colored ones.

Save the Date Invitation

Designer: Wendy Gallamore

1. Print wedding information on patterned paper.
2. Cut printed piece into oval; adhere to patterned paper.
3. Mat with cardstock.
4. Tie bow; adhere.

Finished size: 6¾" x 5¼"

Doodled Best Wishes Card

Designer: Daniela Dobson

1. Make card from cardstock.
2. Trim oval from sticker; affix sticker to card.
3. Stamp Best Wishes; let dry. Adhere to card with foam tape.
4. Adhere flowers and rhinestones.

Finished size: 6" x 4"

SUPPLIES: *Cardstock:* (Beetle Black) Bazzill Basics Paper *Patterned paper:* (manila stripe, vine flourish from Cityscape collection) Making Memories *Fibers:* (black grosgrain ribbon) Offray *Fonts:* (Avant Garde BK BT, Kuenstler Script) www.fonts.com *Tool:* (oval cutter) Creative Memories

SUPPLIES: *Cardstock:* (black) *Rubber stamp:* (Best Wishes) Inkadinkado *Solvent ink:* (black) Tsukineko *Accents:* (white flowers) Prima; (clear rhinestones) Darice *Stickers:* (oval doodle border) Doodlebug Design *Adhesive:* (foam tape)

Fancy Embossed
Best Wishes Card
Designer: Lisa Nichols

ACCENT
1. Stamp sentiment on sticker.
2. Cut rectangle from patterned paper; mat with cardstock.
3. Adhere ribbon around piece.
4. Affix sticker.

CARD
1. Make card from cardstock.
2. Adhere slightly smaller piece of cardstock.
3. Emboss cardstock using template. Cut square, mat with cardstock, and adhere with foam tape.
4. Adhere accent with foam tape.

Finished size: 5" square

Wedded Bliss Card
Designer: Mimi Schramm

1. Make card from cardstock.
2. Make flowers, following patterns on p. 283.
3. Adhere flowers to card in numerical order. *Note: Only place adhesive at flower centers.*
4. Bend petals up to create depth.
5. Adhere metal charm.

Finished size: 6" x 4¾"

SUPPLIES: All supplies from Stampin' Up! unless otherwise noted. *Cardstock:* (Basic Gray, Whisper White, Very Vanilla) *Patterned paper:* (floral from Charbon collection) *Rubber stamps:* (best wishes from Short & Sweet set) *Dye ink:* (Basic Gray) *Sticker:* (decorative oval frame) EK Success *Fibers:* (gray taffeta ribbon) *Adhesive:* (foam tape) *Template:* (floral embossing) Provo Craft *Tool:* (die cut/embossing machine) Provo Craft

SUPPLIES: *Cardstock:* (Cryogen White, Champagne, Silver Ore, black) Prism *Accent:* (white metal bliss charm) Making Memories

BONUS IDEA

Add a touch of color to your design. Select a few flowers and apply a soft pastel shade of chalk to the center before adding the button center. For greater contrast, swap out a few of the white flowers for a pastel or bright colored flower of your choice..

Wedding Bell Card

Designer: Trudee Sauer

❶ Make card, following pattern on p. 283.

❷ Stamp Paisley Backgrounder on card; emboss.

❸ Punch bottom edge of card with corner rounder punch to create scalloped edge.

❹ Stamp The Forest Chapel Vignette on cardstock; cut out.

❺ Die-cut and emboss scalloped oval from cardstock.

❻ Adhere stamped piece to die cut; adhere to card with foam tape.

❼ Punch holes at top of card; thread ribbon through holes and trim.

Finished size: 4¼" x 5½"

Flowered Heart Wedding Card

Designer: Nicole Lund

❶ Make card from cardstock; stitch edges.

❷ Adhere flowers in heart shape.

❸ Stamp love; emboss.

❹ Stitch buttons; adhere.

❺ Adhere seed pearls.

Finished size: 4¼" x 5½"

SUPPLIES: *Cardstock:* (Cryogen White) Prism; (beige shimmer) Bazzill Basics Paper *Rubber stamps:* (Paisley Backgrounder, The Forest Chapel Vignette) Cornish Heritage Farms *Dye ink:* (Sandalwood) Clearsnap *Pigment ink:* (white) Clearsnap *Embossing powder:* (white) Stampin' Up! *Fibers:* (white satin ribbon) May Arts *Adhesive:* (foam tape) *Die:* (oval scallop embossing) Spellbinders *Tools:* (small corner rounder punch) EK Success; (die cut/embossing machine) Spellbinders

SUPPLIES: *Cardstock:* (white) *Rubber stamps:* (love) *Pigment ink:* (white) Stampin' Up! *Embossing powder:* (white) Stampin' Up! *Accents:* (white flowers) Close To My Heart; (white seed pearls) Darice; (white buttons)

Bride & Groom

Designer: Julie Hillier

1. Make card from white cardstock.
2. Cut Pistachio cardstock slightly smaller than card front.
3. Stamp tree sprig background repeatedly on Pistachio piece. Ink edges and mat with Pinecone cardstock.
4. Adhere stamped piece to card front.
5. Apply bride & groom sticker to white; cut out and mount on Pinecone. Cut out with decorative-edge scissors.
6. Tie bow; adhere to top of sticker piece. Adhere sticker piece to card with foam squares.

Finished size: 5½" x 4¼"

SUPPLIES: *Cardstock:* (Pinecone, Pistachio) *Bazzill Basics Paper;* (white) *Rubber stamp:* (tree sprig background from Petite Patterns set) *Stampin' Up! Dye ink:* (Chocolate Chip) *Stampin' Up! Fibers:* (brown satin ribbon) *Offray Sticker:* (bride & groom) *K&Company Adhesive:* (foam squares) *Tools:* (decorative-edge scissors) *Fiskars*

BONUS IDEA

For a little bit of color and whole lot of flair, choose a colored ribbon to wrap around the card fold.

BONUS IDEA

This is a perfect card to tie on a gift for the happy couple. If you're looking to send this card of well wishes through the mail, try converting the design to a rectangle-shaped card for easy mailing.

To have and to hold

To Have & to Hold

Designer: Jennifer Miller

1. Print "To have and to hold" on white cardstock.
2. Make card from white cardstock. *Note: Make card so printed sentiment is centered on front.*
3. Apply wedding cake sticker to black cardstock; cut out and adhere to card front.
4. Wrap ribbon around card fold; tie bow.

Finished size: 4" x 5½"

Simplistic Bliss

Designer: Charrie Shockey

1. Make card from pink cardstock; ink edges.
2. Stamp Bride & Groom on white cardstock; cut image slightly smaller than card front and adhere.
3. Cut strip of patterned paper; adhere to card front along fold.
4. Adhere pearl beads to card front.
5. Punch hole at top of card front; thread ribbon through hole and knot.

Finished size: 5¼" x 4¼"

SUPPLIES: **Cardstock**: (white, black) **Fibers**: (black polka dot ribbon) *May Arts* **Font**: (AL Heavenly) *Autumn Leaves* **Sticker**: (wedding cake) *Pebbles Inc.*

SUPPLIES: **Cardstock**: (pink, white) **Patterned paper**: (Black & White Mini Bangles Reverse) *KI Memories* **Rubber stamp**: (Bride & Groom) *Ichiyo* **Dye ink**: (black) **Accents**: (pearl beads) *The Beadery* **Fibers**: (pink velvet ribbon) *Flair Designs*

Congratulations

Designer: Julie Hillier

1. Make card from white cardstock.

2. Cut Pinkini cardstock slightly smaller than card front; adhere.

3. Apply wedding cake sticker to square of white cardstock; stamp Congratulations with Rose Romance below sticker. Ink edges; mat with yellow cardstock.

4. Wrap pink ribbon around embellished piece; knot.

5. Adhere piece to square of Rosey Plaid paper; mat with yellow. Adhere to card front.

Finished size: 5¼" square

Newlyweds Become Oldyweds

Designer: Kim Kesti

1. Make card from cardstock.

2. Cut strip of The Stars At Night paper; adhere to card front.

3. Mat newlywed chipboard sentiment with cardstock.

4. Apply large dot and blue gingham fabric tape to top and bottom edge of patterned paper on card front. Apply pink polka dot fabric tape to card front.

5. Adhere buttons where fabric tape intersects.

6. Adhere newlywed chipboard sentiment to card front with foam squares.

Finished size: 6½" x 3½"

SUPPLIES: **Cardstock**: (Pinkini) *Bazzill Basics Paper*; (white, yellow) **Patterned paper**: (Rosey Cottage Plaid) *Chatterbox* **Rubber stamp**: (Congratulations) *Making Memories* **Dye ink**: (Rose Romance) *Stampin' Up!* **Stickers**: (wedding cake) **Fibers**: (pink satin ribbon) *Offray*

SUPPLIES: **Cardstock**: (Rosebud) *Bazzill Basics Paper* **Patterned paper**: (The Stars At Night from A Colorful Adventure collection) *Imagination Project* **Accents**: (pink, green, purple, white buttons) *Junkitz*; (large dot, pink polka dot, blue gingham fabric tape; newlywed chipboard sentiment) *Imagination Project* **Adhesive**: (foam squares)

L for Love

Designer: Lynette Carroll, courtesy of K&Company

1. Make card from cardstock.
2. Adhere patterned paper rectangles and strips.
3. Punch two circles and cut out scroll from patterned paper; adhere. Add sticker, lace, chipboard letter, and flower.

Finished size: 5" x 7"

Together

Designer: Heather Thompson

1. Make card from cardstock; adhere patterned paper.
2. Apply rub-ons to card and ribbon.
3. Paint heart; accent with glitter.
4. Adhere heart and ribbon to card.

Finished size: 4½" x 5½"

SUPPLIES: All supplies from K&Company unless otherwise noted. *Cardstock:* (white) Bazzill Basics Paper *Patterned paper:* (Wedding Dreamy Green Flat, blue floral, decorative blue, cream and brown floral, green and ivory striped, scrolls foil from Wedding collection) *Accents:* (glitter chipboard letter, flower) *Sticker:* (love epoxy) *Fibers:* (lace trim) no source *Tools:* (decorative-edge scissors, small circle punch) no source

SUPPLIES: *Cardstock:* (white) Bazzill Basics Paper *Patterned paper:* (Sherelle) Heart & Home *Paint:* (blue) Making Memories *Accents:* (glitter chipboard heart) Heart & Home; (glitter) Art Glittering System *Rub-ons:* (together) Heart & Home; (corner scrolls) Bo-Bunny Press *Fibers:* (velvet ribbon) BasicGrey

Now & Forever

Designer: Nicole Keller

1. Make card from cardstock.

2. Cover front with patterned paper; apply stitch rub-on. Distress card edges.

3. Create scallop border on cardstock strip with notch and die tool; adhere.

4. Print sentiment on cardstock, distress, and adhere.

5. Apply swirl rub-on to card and stitch rub-on to ribbon.

6. Adhere ribbon, lace, flower, and rhinestones.

Finished size: 6" square

Priceless

Designer: Dee Gallimore-Perry

1. Make card from cardstock.

2. Cover front with patterned paper and paper borders.

3. Cut images from patterned paper; mat with cardstock and adhere.

4. Print prices; trim and adhere.

5. Attach flowers with brads.

Finished size: 4¾" x 8"

SIMPLE SENTIMENT

The inside of the card reads, "Finding the love of your life. . . priceless."

SUPPLIES: Cardstock: (French Vanilla) Bazzill Basics Paper Patterned paper: (Chocolate Souffle from Coco collection) Webster's Pages Accents: (blue flower) Prima; (brown rhinestones) My Mind's Eye Rub-ons: (stitches) Autumn Leaves; (swirls) BasicGrey Fibers: (lace trim) Home Sew; (blue ribbon) Offray Font: (Adine Kirnberg Script) www.simplythebestfonts.com Tool: (notch and die tool) BasicGrey

SUPPLIES: Cardstock: (white) Bazzill Basics Paper Patterned paper: (Wedding Lace, Happy Couple Collage, Bride & Groom from Wedding collection) Karen Foster Design Accents: (flowers) Prima; (white brads) Queen & Co.; (paper borders) Doodlebug Design Font: (ShelleyAllegro BT) Microsoft

Designer Tip

Change the sentiment to create an elegant card for any occasion.

On Your Wedding Day

Designer: Sherry Wright

1. Make card from cardstock.

2. Cut patterned paper pieces, distress and ink edges, and adhere.

3. Attach rhinestone brad to felt scroll; adhere.

4. Stamp sentiment on patterned paper; trim, distress and ink edges, and adhere with foam tape.

5. Tie on ribbon. Affix bird sticker to button; adhere.

6. Trim two pieces of felt scroll; adhere.

Finished size: 5" x 6¼"

🌀 Romantic

Designer: Melissa Phillips

1. Make card from cardstock; paint edges.

2. Stamp and emboss hearts on cardstock. Punch hearts, and adhere flowers.

3. Adhere hearts to cardstock, ink edges, and stitch. *Note: Stitch trim to bottom of piece.*

4. Adhere piece to sheet music. Mat with cardstock; ink edges.

5. Adhere to card base.

Finished size: 5" x 5¾"

SUPPLIES: *Cardstock:* (Wheat) Bazzill Basics Paper *Patterned paper:* (Flutterby from Feather Your Nest collection, Full Bloom from Classical Garden collection) Webster's Pages *Rubber stamp:* (sentiment from Springtime Swirls set) Inque Boutique *Chalk ink:* (Chestnut Roan) Clearsnap *Accents:* (cream felt scroll) Prima; (clear rhinestone brad) Creative Imaginations; (cream button) *Sticker:* (bird) Cavallini Papers & Co. *Fibers:* (brown ribbon) Offray *Adhesive:* (foam tape)

SUPPLIES: *Cardstock:* (kraft, Sweet Blush, Vintage Cream) Papertrey Ink *Clear stamps:* (patterned hearts from Heart Prints set) Papertrey Ink *Pigment ink:* (Vintage Cream) Papertrey Ink *Embossing powder:* (Winter Wonderland) Stampendous! *Paint:* (ivory) Delta *Accents:* (cream flowers) *Fibers:* (cream ribbon, flower trim) *Tool:* (heart punch) Marvy Uchida *Other:* (sheet music)

Wedding Wishes

Designer: Daniela Dobson

1. Make card from cardstock.
2. Adhere chipboard pieces.
3. Apply rub-on.
4. Adhere rhinestones.

Finished size: 5½" x 5"

Mr. & Mrs.

Designer: Traci Gentry

1. Make card from cardstock.
2. Emboss cardstock. Trim and mat with cardstock. Wrap with knotted ribbon. Adhere.
3. Stamp cardstock. Punch into oval and mat with larger cardstock oval. Adhere with foam tape.

Finished size: 4¼" x 5½"

SUPPLIES: *Cardstock:* (black) *Accents:* (white chipboard corner, hearts) Creative Imaginations; (pink rhinestones) Darice *Rub-on:* (wedding wishes) American Crafts

SUPPLIES: All supplies from Stampin' Up! unless otherwise noted. *Cardstock:* (Basic Black, Whisper White) *Rubber stamp:* (Mr. & Mrs. from All Holidays set) *Dye ink:* (Basic Black) *Fibers:* (white polka dot ribbon) Really Reasonable Ribbon *Template:* (embossing heart pattern) Provo Craft; (large, small oval punches) *Adhesive:* (foam tape)

⁵ₛₜₑₚₛ Fancy Flowers

Designer: Breanna Laakkonen

❶ Make card from cardstock.

❷ Adhere die cut piece.

❸ Adhere flowers and buttons.

Finished size: 5½" x 4"

⁵ₛₜₑₚₛ Wedding Day

Designer: Sherry Wright

❶ Make card from cardstock.

❷ Adhere patterned paper.

❸ Adhere trim.

❹ Stamp cardstock; trim and adhere behind frame. Adhere.

Finished size: 5½" x 4¼"

SUPPLIES: *Cardstock:* (white) *Accents:* (black die cut felt border, yellow flowers) Prima; (green buttons) Autumn Leaves

SUPPLIES: *Cardstock:* (light blue) *Patterned paper:* (Elizabeth Brocade Foiled from 5th Avenue collection) Making Memories *Clear stamp:* (on your wedding day from Springtime Swirls set) Inque Boutique *Chalk ink:* (Charcoal) Clearsnap *Accent:* (chipboard frame) Cosmo Cricket *Fibers:* (black lace trim)

Bliss

Designer: Debbie Ikert

❶ Make card from cardstock; ink edges.

❷ Cut patterned paper; ink edges and adhere.

❸ Tie ribbon around front flap. Adhere pearls.

❹ Stamp cardstock. Cut into tag and ink edges.
Punch hole and tie to bow with thread.

Finished size: 5½" x 4¼"

Once Upon a Time

Designer: Julia Stainton

❶ Make card from patterned paper.

❷ Stamp images.

❸ Affix tape.

❹ Fold ribbon over edge and staple in place.

❺ Adhere crown and rhinestones.

Finished size: 5½" x 4¼"

SUPPLIES: *Cardstock:* (brown, cream) *Patterned paper:* (Gypsy Paisley–Hazelnut) Daisy D's *Clear stamp:* (bliss from Adorable set) Close To My Heart *Chalk ink:* (Chestnut Roan) Clearsnap *Accents:* (pearls) Kaisercraft *Fibers:* (cream ribbon) May Arts; (crochet thread) *Tool:* (⅛" circle punch)

SUPPLIES: *Patterned paper:* (Blue Lace from Delightful collection) My Little Yellow Bicycle *Rubber stamps:* (clock from Time to Stamp set, once upon a time from Storybook set, Vintage Ledger Scrapblock) Cornish Heritage Farms *Dye ink:* (Antique Linen) Ranger Industries *Specialty ink:* (Burnt Umber hybrid) Stewart Superior Corp. *Accents:* (acetate crown) Heidi Swapp; (clear rhinestones) Me & My Big Ideas; (staple) *Sticker:* (decorative tape) Prima *Fibers:* (red ribbon) Prima

Daughter-in-Law

Designer: Nicole Keller

SLEEVE

❶ Cut 7½" x 5½" rectangle from Paisley Blooms paper. Score 1½" in from each side; fold. ❷ Cut semi-circle every inch along edge; repeat on other side. *Note: Complete edge by using straight edge of tool. Punch hole at center of each semi-circle.* ❸ Ink edges; adhere lace to each side inside edge. ❹ Lace cream ribbon through holes on each side; knot at top left edge. ❺ Ink flowers; attach brads to flower centers. Adhere flowers to sleeve. ❻ Print "To our new daughter-in-law" on cream cardstock; cut into tag shape and ink edges. ❼ Punch hole at tag top; thread ribbon through hole and tie bow.

INSERT

❶ Cut rectangle of reverse side of Paisley Blooms. ❷ Apply floral tab sticker to top of rectangle. Place inside sleeve.

Finished sizes: sleeve 4½" x 5½", insert 4¼" x 5¼"

Mr. & Mrs.

Designer: Linda Beeson

❶ Make card from cardstock.
❷ Cut square of Dictonary paper; adhere to transparency and let dry.
❸ Trace ampersand on back of Dictonary piece; cut out.
❹ Adhere ampersand to rectangle of cardstock; spell "Mr." and "Mrs." with stickers. Adhere chipboard heart to ampersand.
❺ Mat embellished piece with Cayenne Dashed Lines paper; adhere to card front.

Finished size: 7½" x 4"

SUPPLIES: **Cardstock**: (cream) **Patterned paper**: (Paisley Blooms from Heirloom Blue collection) *Daisy D's* **Chalk ink**: (Brown) *Clearsnap* **Accents**: (pewter brads) *Making Memories;* (white flowers) *Prima* **Stickers**: (floral tabs) *Daisy D's* **Fibers**: (cream ribbon) *Offray;* (cream lace) **Font**: (Adorable) *www.dafont.com* **Tools**: (corner rounder punch) *EK Success;* (notch & dye punch) *BasicGrey;* (⅛" circle punch) *McGill*

SUPPLIES: **Cardstock**: (Raven) *Bazzill Basics Paper* **Patterned paper**: (Cayenne Dashed Lines from Flip Flops collection) *Paper Loft;* (Dictonary from Life's Journey collection) *K&Company* **Transparency sheet**; **Accents**: (chipboard heart) *Heidi Swapp* **Stickers**: (Jumbo alphabet) *Chatterbox* **Template**: (ampersand) *Deja Views*

Building a Marriage

Designer: Julie Medeiros

1 Make card from white cardstock.

2 Round bottom corners.

3 Print sentiment on white; cut out and mat with Fussy cardstock.

4 Cut window in card front with craft knife; adhere sentiment inside card to show through window.

5 Adhere flowers to card front; adhere pearls to center of flowers and let dry.

Finished size: 8½" x 4"

A Toast

Designer: Terri Davenport

1 Make card from cardstock.

2 Cut Rosey Paisley paper to fit card front; adhere.

3 Cut rectangle of Sky Dot paper; adhere to card front.

4 Cut strip of Sky Dot; adhere reverse side up on card front.

5 Apply rub-ons to spell "…Here's to our" and "Happily ever after" on card front.

6 Stamp Bubbly on Rosey Paisley; cut out and sand edges.

7 Adhere love file tab to stamped image; adhere image to card front. Sand edges of card front.

Finished size: 5½" x 4¼"

SUPPLIES: **Cardstock**: (Fussy) *Bazzill Basics Paper;* (white) **Accents**: (light, medium, dark pink flowers) *Prima;* (mini pearls) **Font**: (Castellar) *www.myfonts.com* **Adhesive**: (foam squares) **Tools**: (corner rounder punch) *Creative Memories*

SUPPLIES: **Cardstock**: (white) **Patterned paper**: (Sky Dot from Gallery collection; Rosey Paisley from Powder Room collection) *Chatterbox* **Rubber stamp**: (Bubbly) *A Muse Artstamps* **Dye ink**: (brown) **Accent**: (love file tab) *Daisy D's* **Rubons**: (Oda Mae, Kellerman alphabets) *Imagination Project* **Other**: (sandpaper)

DESIGNER TIPS

- Rub cardstock with waxed paper before embossing for a smoother gliding surface.

- When embossing on textured cardstock, make sure to emboss with the textured side face down.

- For a tighter, more uniform design, emboss the same single flower from the template from the same cardstock color. Only change flowers when you change cardstock colors

If I Searched

Designer: Heather Gagnier

PREPARE

❶ Make card from Remember Floral paper; Tear right edge of card front. ❷ Print "You…" on Baby Boy Stripe paper; print "If I searched the whole world over…" and "I could never find another you!" on white cardstock. ❸ Cut out sentiments; ink edges. ❹ Apply rub-on to reverse side of Baby Boy Stripe; cut out. ❺ Cut rectangle from Pinecone cardstock slightly larger than rub-on piece.

EMBELLISH

❶ Place "you" sentiment in metal index tab; adhere to card front. ❷ Adhere "If I searched the whole world over…" with foam squares to rub-on piece. Adhere "I could never find another you!" to Pinecone piece; adhere to card front. ❸ Attach rub-on piece over Pinecone piece with hinge. ❹ Cut strip of Remember Floral paper; tear edge and adhere reverse side up to card front along fold. Punch two rectangles along fold; thread ribbon through and knot on card front.

Finished size: 6" square

Wedding Wreath

Designer: Cath Edvalson

PREPARE

❶ Make card from Desert Sun cardstock. ❷ Punch several circles from each cardstock color. *Note: These circles will be used as centers for each flower.*

EMBOSS

❶ Dry-emboss bouquet on Leapfrog. *Note: Do not emboss ribbon or stems.* Cut out. Repeat four times. ❷ Emboss single flower on Amber, Desert Sun, and Lemonade five times each; cut out. *Note: Emboss more flowers on shade of your choice to fill holes when forming wreath.*

EMBELLISH

❶ Adhere Leapfrog flower bunches to card front with foam tape to create wreath. ❷ Adhere flowers of various shades to wreath shape. *Note: Adhere darker flowers first and lighter flowers last. Adhere various flowers around wreath with foam tape.* ❸ Adhere 2–4 circles in center of each flower.

Finished size: 5" square

SUPPLIES: **Cardstock**: (Pinecone) *Bazzill Basics Paper*; (white) **Patterned paper**: (Baby Boy Stripe; Remember Floral) *My Mind's Eye* **Dye ink**: (brown) **Accents**: (antique gold hinge) *Making Memories*; (metal index tab) *7gypsies* **Rub-on**: (Map Rubbings) *7gypsies* **Fibers**: (cream organza ribbon) *May Arts* **Font**: (Amazone BT) *www.flyerstater. com* **Adhesive**: (foam squares) **Tools**: (rectangle punch) *Beary Patch*

SUPPLIES: **Cardstock**: (Amber, Desert Sun, Lemonade, Leapfrog) *Bazzill Basics Paper* **Adhesive**: (foam squares) **Template**: (Bouquet #L9313) *Lasting Impressions for Paper* **Tools**: (1/16" circle punch)

Cutting the Cake

Designer: Kelli Crowe

❶ Make card from Kraft cardstock. Dry-brush card edges with Hibiscus; let dry and ink edges.

❷ Cut rectangle of each patterned paper. Angle and ink edges, making each piece slightly smaller in size.

❸ Cut rectangle from light kraft cardstock; round and ink edges.

❹ Adhere cardstock and patterned paper pieces to card front to create cake.

❺ Cut three lengths of rickrack; adhere at top of each patterned paper piece.

❻ Cut small rectangle from black cardstock; cut small triangle from white cardstock. Ink white edges. Adhere to card front; draw bride, groom, and heart around triangle and rectangle pieces. Color bride and groom faces with colored pencil.

Finished size: 4" x 7¼"

SUPPLIES: **Cardstock**: (Kraft) *Bazzill Basics Paper*; (light kraft, white, black) **Patterned paper**: (Birthday Geo Floral, Summer Chic Plaid) *KI Memories*; (Pink Damask) *Anna Griffin* **Dye ink**: (brown) **Paint**: (Hibiscus) *Making Memories* **Color medium**: (black pen) *EK Success*; (white colored pencil) **Fibers**: (pink dotted rickrack) *Li'l Davis Designs*

The Happy Couple

Designer: Cindy Bentley

❶ Make card from white cardstock.

❷ Cut Juneberry cardstock to fit front; adhere.

❸ Cut dark kraft cardstock slightly smaller than card front; stitch along edge.

❹ Apply stitched heart rub-ons; adhere acrylic letters and happy couple label to dark kraft piece.

❺ Attach photo turns with brads.

❻ Adhere embellished piece to card front.

Finished size: 4¼" x 5"

SUPPLIES: **Cardstock**: (Juneberry) *Bazzill Basics Paper*; (dark kraft, white) **Accents**: (black photo turns) *7gypsies*; (pewter brads) *Making Memories*; (acrylic letters) *Go West Studios*; (happy couple fabric label) *Me & My Big Ideas* **Rub-ons**: (stitched hearts) *Autumn Leaves* **Fibers**: (white thread)

⑤ Two Hearts Card

Designer: Rachel Schumacher

❶ Make card from cardstock.

❷ Round corners of patterned paper panel.

❸ Spell sentiment on cardstock with stickers.
Trim and adhere to panel.

❹ Stamp hearts on cardstock. Cut out and adhere
to panel with foam tape.

❺ Tie on ribbon. Adhere panel to card.

Finished size: 4" x 6"

⑤ Elegant Thank You Card

Designer: Maile Belles

❶ Make card from cardstock; round top right corner.

❷ Punch cardstock strip and adhere.

❸ Stamp flowers and leaves on cardstock. Cut out and
adhere with foam tape.

❹ Stamp thank you on card. Adhere rhinestones.

Finished size: 3½" x 7"

SUPPLIES: *Cardstock:* (cream) *Patterned paper:* (Vintage Black Branch from Vintage Cream & Black collection) Jenni Bowlin Studio *Rubber stamp:* (heart from Happy Hearts set) Stampin' Up! *Dye ink:* (Real Red) Stampin' Up! *Stickers:* (Tiny Alpha alphabet) Making Memories *Fibers:* (red ribbon) *Tool:* (corner rounder punch) Stampin' Up!

SUPPLIES: *Cardstock:* (Vintage Cream, kraft) Papertrey Ink; (black) Bazzill Basics Paper *Clear stamps:* (flowers, leaves from In Bloom set; thank you from Damask Designs set) Papertrey Ink *Dye ink:* (Real Red) Stampin' Up! *Specialty ink:* (Raspberry Fizz, Ripe Avocado, True Black hybrid) Papertrey Ink *Accents:* (black rhinestones) Kaisercraft *Tools:* (border punch) Fiskars; (corner rounder punch) EK Success

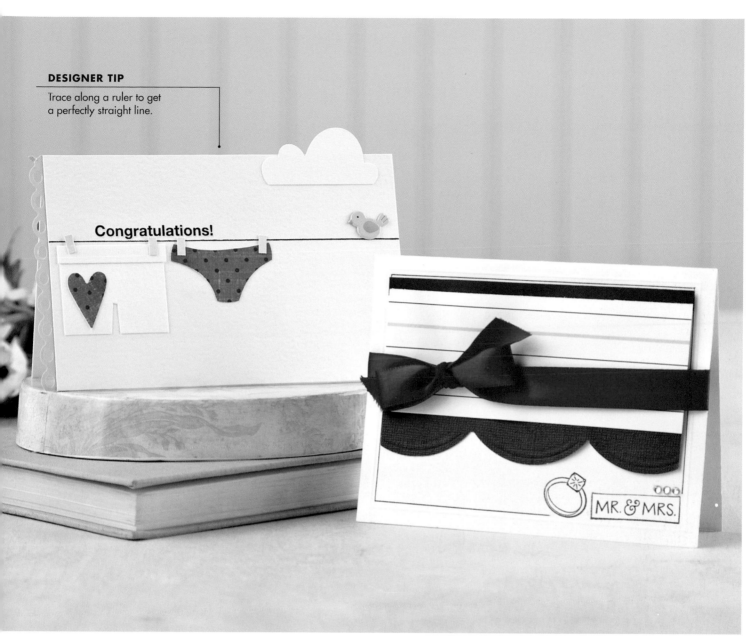

Congratulations!

5 STEPS Clothesline Congratulations Card

Designer: Kim Hughes

1. Make card from cardstock. Punch cardstock strip and adhere.
2. Draw line and apply rub-on.
3. Cut clothespins, boxers, and cloud from cardstock. Adhere.
4. Cut bikini bottoms and heart from patterned paper and adhere.
5. Attach brad.

Finished size: 6" x 3¾"

5 STEPS Mr. & Mrs. Card

Designer: Winter Sims

1. Make card from cardstock; score border.
2. Stamp ring and Mr. & Mrs. on card. Draw border.
3. Punch cardstock panel; adhere patterned paper. Adhere panel with foam tape.
4. Tie on ribbon and adhere rhinestones.

Finished size: 5½" x 4¼"

SUPPLIES: *Cardstock:* (Vanilla Cream, Restful Blue, white, teal) Prism *Patterned paper:* (Make Merry from Celebrate collection) Fancy Pants Designs *Color medium:* (black pen) Sakura *Accent:* (bluebird brad) Doodlebug Design *Rub-on:* (congratulations!) Making Memories *Tool:* (border punch) Fiskars

SUPPLIES: *Cardstock:* (white) The Paper Company; (black) Colorbok *Patterned paper:* (black stripes from Paper #2 stack) Scrapbook Wizard *Clear stamps:* (ring, Mr. & Mrs. from Series 14 set) Studio G *Solvent ink:* (Jet Black) Tsukineko *Color medium:* (black pen) *Accents:* (clear rhinestones) *Fibers:* (red ribbon) Offray *Tool:* (embossing border punch) EK Success

Happily Ever After

Designer: Kimberly Crawford

1. Make card from cardstock.
2. Stamp damasks on cardstock.
3. Tie piece with ribbon, stamp happily ever after, and adhere with foam tape.

Finished size: 4¼" x 5½"

Wedded Bliss

Designer: Susan R. Opel

1. Make card from cardstock.
2. Adhere ribbon to patterned paper; stitch beads and adhere.
3. Print sentiment on cardstock; trim to fit behind tag.
4. Cut out middle of tag. Adhere sentiment to back. Stitch beads.
5. Adhere tag with foam tape.

Finished size: 7" x 5"

SUPPLIES: *Cardstock:* (Summer Sunrise, Vintage Cream) Papertrey Ink *Clear stamps:* (happily ever after from Favor It Weddings set) Papertrey Ink; (large, small damasks from Bold Damasks set) Inkadinkado *Dye ink:* (black) Stewart Superior Corp. *Specialty ink:* (Summer Sunrise hybrid) Papertrey Ink *Fibers:* (white ribbon) *Adhesive:* (foam tape)

SUPPLIES: *Cardstock:* (white) *Patterned paper:* (gold frame from Georgette Christmas Mat Pack) Anna Griffin *Accents:* (white pearl beads) Crafts, Etc.; (tag) Anna Griffin *Fibers:* (white/gold ribbon) Hallmark *Fonts:* (Zachary) www.dafont.com; (Bickham Script Fancy 2) peacemanor.bravepages.com/fonts.html *Adhesive:* (foam tape)

⁵ Simple Love

Designer: Ashley Newell

❶ Make card from cardstock.

❷ Stamp ornate squares on cardstock; emboss and punch.

❸ Mat squares with cardstock; adhere with foam tape.

❹ Stamp love on cardstock, punch into circle, and adhere with foam tape.

❺ Adhere flowers and pearls.

Finished size: 5½" x 4¼"

⁵ Shabby Love

Designer: Kristen Swain

❶ Make card from patterned paper. Adhere strips of patterned paper.

❷ Punch edge of patterned paper strip; adhere. Adhere trim.

❸ Cut heart from patterned paper, sand, and adhere.

❹ Die-cut flourish from patterned paper; adhere. Adhere pearls and flower.

❺ Thread button with twine; adhere. Adhere sentiment.

Finished size: 4" x 7"

SUPPLIES: *Cardstock:* (Spring Moss, Aqua Mist, silver, white) Papertrey Ink *Rubber stamp:* (ornate square from Simple Delights set) Stampin' Up! *Clear stamp:* (love from Wonderful Wishes set) Verve Stamps *Dye ink:* (Kiwi Kiss) Stampin' Up! *Watermark ink:* Stampin' Up! *Embossing powder:* (silver) Papertrey Ink *Accents:* (white flowers, pearls) *Adhesive:* (foam tape) Stampin' Up! *Tools:* (square, circle punches)

SUPPLIES: *Patterned paper:* (Simple, Trendy, Glam, Style from Crate Avenue collection) Crate Paper *Accents:* (green button) BoBunny Press; (tan flower, sentiment) We R Memory Keepers; (white pearls) *Fibers:* (white lace trim, hemp twine) *Die:* (flourish) Provo Craft *Tools:* (die cut machine) Provo Craft; (scalloped border punch) Martha Stewart Crafts

Love Birds

Designer: Nicole Keller

1. Make card from cardstock; round top right corner.
2. Die-cut and emboss circle from cardstock. Apply rub-on, color, and adhere.
3. Punch hearts from cardstock; adhere. Affix sticker.
4. Die-cut "Love birds" from cardstock; adhere.
5. Stitch with floss.

Finished size: 4" x 8½"

SUPPLIES: *Cardstock:* (Vanilla) Bazzill Basics Paper; (kraft) DMD, Inc.; (brown, green) *Color medium:* (brown marker) EK Success *Rub-on:* (birds on twig) Hambly Screen Prints *Sticker:* (pink epoxy heart) Creative Imaginations *Fibers:* (brown floss) *Dies:* (circle) Spellbinders; (Daisy SkinniMini alphabet) QuicKutz *Tools:* (die cut/embossing machine) Spellbinders; (heart punch) EK Success; (corner rounder punch) McGill

Birdie Wishes

Designer: Layle Koncar

1. Make card from patterned paper. Stamp Old Letter Writing.
2. Adhere patterned paper and scalloped trim.
3. Apply rub-ons to cardstock, trim into oval, ink edges, and adhere with foam tape.

Finished size: 4½" x 6¾"

SUPPLIES: *Cardstock:* (teal) *Patterned paper:* (Sophia Leaves Flocked from 5th Avenue collection) Making Memoires; (Worn Blue Grid Background) Scenic Route *Rubber stamp:* (Old Letter Writing) Hero Arts *Dye ink:* (Jet Black) Ranger Industries *Rub-ons:* (love birds) Maya Road; (best wishes) Scenic Route *Fibers:* (black scalloped trim) Creative Imaginations *Adhesive:* (foam tape)

DESIGNER TIP

Use the technique in step five to add texture, dimension, and make your own unique flower centers on any card.

DESIGNER TIP

The 1+1=2 chipboard piece is from a school-themed line. Don't be afraid to think outside of the box with your supplies and use them for projects beyond their intended theme!

Happy Wishes

Designer: Sherry Wright

1. Make card from cardstock. Cover with patterned paper.

2. Trim patterned paper pieces, distress and ink edges, and adhere.

3. Stamp sentiment on patterned paper; punch into circle and adhere. Ink chipboard frame and adhere over sentiment.

4. Cut swirl from felt and adhere. Adhere flower brad. Punch flower from patterned paper; adhere with rhinestone flower.

5. Layer blue and orange flowers. Punch circles in brad; thread ribbon and trim. Adhere flowers, brad, and leaves.

Finished size: 4½" x 6"

1+1=2

Designer: Layle Koncar

1. Make card from patterned paper; ink edges.

2. Trim card center from patterned paper. Punch holes in scallops; adhere.

3. Apply rub-ons.

4. Adhere chipboard piece with foam tape.

Finished size: 5¾" x 4½"

SUPPLIES: *Cardstock:* (white) *Patterned paper:* (All My Heart from My Dearest collection, Gum Drop Garden from Sunshine Lollipop collection, The Countdown from Robotics collection) Sassafras Lass *Rubber stamp:* (best wishes from Silhouette Blooms I set) Cornish Heritage Farms *Chalk ink:* (orange) Clearsnap *Accents:* (blue felt swirl; white flower, orange circle brads; clear rhinestone flower) Queen & Co.; (blue flower) Heidi Swapp; (orange felt flower) Making Memories; (scalloped circle chipboard frame) American Crafts; (turquoise sequin leaves) Jenni Bowlin Studio *Fibers:* (blue ribbon) Offray; (orange trim) *Tools:* (circle punch) We R Memory Makers; (flower punch)

SUPPLIES: *Patterned paper:* (Fun Filled Forest from Hog Heaven collection) Sassafras Lass; (Sondra Drive from Sonoma collection) Scenic Route *Dye ink:* (Walnut Stain) Ranger Industries *Accent:* (equation chipboard tile) Scenic Route *Rub-ons:* (people, congratulations) Scenic Route *Adhesive:* (foam tape) *Tool:* (⅛" circle punch)

Wedding Essentials

The 6 most important layouts for any wedding scrapbook

by Karen Glenn

If you've planned a wedding, then surely you had one or two essential elements that you knew you wanted for the big day. Maybe they included having your father give you away or displaying white roses on every table. Or maybe you reveled in keeping the tradition of wearing something old, something new, something borrowed, and something blue. Whatever your essentials were, they were fundamental to making the experience everything you wanted it to be.

After the big day has come and gone, every bride wants to preserve all of these wonderful moments—from getting her hair done to driving away from the reception with cans behind the car. But if the thought of scrapbooking every memory seems more daunting than writing all those thank you cards, never fear! We have a solution: the six essential pages for any wedding album. Focus your efforts on these key layouts; then tuck the hundred photos you have left into photo sleeves. Before you know it, you'll have a beautiful album that captures the heart of the day, plus plenty of time left over to plan your second honeymoon.

Memories *from the* Groom

While so much of the focus of a wedding is centered on the bride, it's definitely a big day for the groom as well. So find a way to include his perspective in your album—even if all you can get him to do is tell you how pretty you looked.

The Groom Recollects...

Who helped you with planning or preparing your wedding? Amelia Bahr

What kind of flowers did you have at your wedding? White roses—Karen's favorite. I arranged to have some vases of them magically appear in our hotel room as well.

What kind of cake did you serve at your wedding? Cheesecake.

What detail of the day stands out most in your mind? The carriage ride from the temple to the wedding breakfast and dancing with Karen at the reception

What was your dominant emotion of the day? Excitement, followed by nervousness.

What do you remember about the ceremony or vows? The mirrors showing us for eternity and the promises we made before God.

What was the best advice or lingering words of wisdom you were given that day? Don't go to bed angry and pray together each night. Now I need to do better about following both.

What was the best wedding gift you received? Money from Karen's grandfather for a bed.

Of all the attendee(s) at your wedding, which meant the most to you? Bryan Romney, my best friend and best man.

What was the best thing anyone said to you that day? 'Yes' (Karen at the alter when she agreed to marry me).

One fun and easy way to get your groom to open up is to use a quiz. Quizzes are great for prompting memories and can be less intimidating for an uncertain spouse than handing him a blank piece of paper and asking him to write (trust me on this!). See my helpful, 14-question quiz on the following page!

2 Memories *from the* Bride

It doesn't matter whether you're tackling this project on your 1st anniversary or your 20th, there's no better time than now to record your memories and impressions. Feel free to share lots of favorite moments from your wedding or just one or two highlights—it's up to you!

The Bride Remembers...

Who helped you with planning or preparing your wedding? My mother, Jerry's mother (made my dress), Amelia Bahr (did the flowers) and Symbria Whitaker (catered the food).

What kind of flowers did you have at your wedding? White roses with eucalyptus for accent. No baby's breath to be found, mostly because Amelia hated baby's breath.

What kind of cake did you serve at your wedding? We didn't have a wedding cake, but we did serve Symbria's special cheesecake—delicious! It's been a family favorite ever since.

What detail of the day stands out most in your mind? Spending the night before, and early morning of, sleeping on Kristi's bed and being woken periodically for fittings for my dress.

What was your dominant emotion of the day? Nervousness.

What do you remember about the ceremony or vows? I remember kneeling at the alter and seeing our faces reflected in the mirrors for eternity. Lovely.

What was the best advice or lingering words of wisdom you were given that day? I don't know about 'best' advice, but I do recall the officiator at our wedding advising me not to ask Jerry to do chores—like emptying the garbage—the minute he walked in the door from work. I was somewhat irked that he assumed I would ever do such a thing!

What was the best wedding gift you received? Probably money for a mattress—from Papa.

Of all the attendee(s) at your wedding, which meant the most to you? My family.

What was the best thing anyone said to you that day? That I looked beautiful.

I used the exact same quiz, the same products, and the same design approach to create both of my "Memories from the..." layouts. The only thing that changes from the Groom to the Bride? The photo and the answers to the questions. I love seeing our responses side-by-side in my wedding album! Note that you can use the quiz directly on your layouts (as I did) or translate your answers into paragraph form.

materials patterned papers, pearl brads (Making Memories) • rub-ons (American Crafts) • Book Antigua and Vladimir Script fonts • 8½ x 11 page by Karen Glenn, Orem, UT

*journaling*TIP

If you're including a quiz on your layout, differentiate between the questions and answers by using a different typeface or by putting one or the other in bold or italics. This makes things quick and clear for your readers. For other great tips on using quizzes, check out the special issue *Scrapbook Shortcuts with Quizzes and Questions*, available on **simplescrapbooksmag.com**.

Wedding Day Quiz

If you could use a little help reflecting, try using this quiz to trigger memories from your special day. Don't feel like you have to answer every question. Use the ones that share what's important to you, and supplement with your own questions when applicable.

1. Do you recall the first time you saw your husband-to-be or wife-to-be on your wedding day?

2. What was your dominant emotion (nervousness, stress, blissful happiness, excitement, etc.)?

3. What kind of flowers did you have at your wedding?

4. What kind of cake did you serve at your wedding?

5. Of all the attendees at your wedding, who among them meant the most to you?

Within the image: "it's a beautiful day"

6. What detail of the day stands out most in your mind?

7. Who helped you with planning or preparing your wedding?

8. Do you remember anything going wrong?

9. What surprised you about the day (e.g., I was surprised at how tired my cheeks got from smiling so much)?

10. What do you remember about the ceremony or vows?

11. What was the best advice or best lingering words of wisdom you received that day?

12. What was the best wedding gift you received?

13. What was the best thing anyone said to you that day?

14. Is there anything you would change if you could do it over again?

Rather than answer every question from the quiz, Paula was inspired by just one question: "What detail of the day stands out most in your mind?" For Paula, it was a particular song—"It's a Beautiful Day"—that she and her husband danced to. Sit for a moment and reflect on your own big day. Ask yourself if there's one overriding experience, expression, feeling, or song that reflects the essence of your wedding day, and build your page around that.

m a t e r i a l s patterned papers (7gypsies, American Crafts, Autumn Leaves, BasicGrey, Chatterbox, Cosmo Cricket, Fancy Pants, Hambly, Imagination Project, KI Memories, My Mind's Eye, Reminisce, Scenic Route) • foam letters, felt and plastic hearts (American Crafts) • silk flower (Making Memories) • ribbon • 12 x 12 spread by Paula Gilarde, Bedford, MA

3 The Ceremony

No wedding album would be complete without a page about the ceremony. Make sure you record your memories of this pivotal life event—the moment you said "I do" and officially crossed the threshold from single girl to married woman.

Linda's stunning layout, with its clean lines, open space, careful alignment, and tiny embellishments, captures the beauty and majesty of her formal church wedding.

materials patterned papers (American Crafts, Bo-Bunny) • sticker, ribbon (American Crafts) • butterfly punch (Martha Stewart Crafts) • Futura font • 12 x 12 page by Linda Barber, Wayne, PA

Although Lindsay's photo is not from the ceremony itself, her journaling talks about the promises she and her husband made as they began their life together, and it records the specific date and time that those promises were made.

materials patterned papers (Close To My Heart) • brads (Bo-Bunny) • journaling card (Rusty Pickle) • letter stickers (American Crafts) • stamp (Technique Tuesday) • stamping ink • chipboard leaf • ric rac • staples • 12 x 12 page by Lindsay Bateman, Lac La Biche, AB, Canada

The Wedding Party

Whether your entourage was large or small, these are the people who were standing by you and supporting you on that special day, so celebrate them on a layout! You can choose to cover your entire wedding party or just one special individual, like a maid of honor or the mother of the bride.

Athena was excited that her photographer caught this adorable shot of "the smallest but most important" members of the wedding party—her daughter (the flower girl) and her nephew (the ring bearer)—shortly before her ceremony on the beach.

materials patterned papers (KI Memories) • trim, plastic letter (American Crafts) • rub-ons (American Crafts, Doodlebug, Making Memories) • paper flowers, photo corners (Prima) • stamps (Li'l Davis) • 8½ x 11 page by Athena Patacsil, Aurora, CO

Melissa used a sepia-toned photo and focused this wedding-party page on her best friends, aka her bridesmaids. Notice how she encircled the photo with pearls, which subtly highlights their closeness, and accented it with a beautiful spray of flowers.

materials 12 x 12 album (K&Company) • patterned papers (Imaginisce) • paper flowers (Prima) • chipboard letters (Doodlebug) • pearls (KaiserCraft) • brads (Making Memories) • album by Melissa Wright, St. John, NB, Canada

5 The Details

From the centerpieces designed by your aunt to the pearls handed down by your great-grandmother, your wedding included important little touches that enhanced the day and made your celebration unique. This is the page in your album that gives you a chance to show off these essential details!

The details Katrina chose to feature on this layout reflect things that were important to her and her husband-to-be, which included sunny daisies and adorable miniature bottles of Vermont maple syrup. To further enhance her theme, she used her wedding colors in the design of her page.

materials patterned paper, letter stamps (Melissa Frances) • letter dies (QuicKutz) • cardstock sticker (October Afternoon) • felt flower (American Crafts) • brad (Bazzill Basics) • border punch (Fiskars) • ribbon • stamping ink • LD Becca font • 12 x 12 page by Katrina Simeck, Colchester, VT

From the flowers to the cake to the setting—all of Lisa's wedding details had to be managed long-distance. Thank heavens for a wonderful mother and bridesmaids, who helped her to pull all of the pieces together to make her day (and this layout) unforgettable!

materials patterned papers (Creative Imaginations, Scenic Route) • chipboard letters (Heidi Swapp) • chipboard flower (Melissa Frances) • letter stickers (EK Success) • paper border (Doodlebug) • acrylic paint • lace • staples • Disproporz font • 12 x 12 page by Lisa Dickinson, Erie, CO

design TIP

Notice how both Katrina's and Lisa's layouts mirror the wedding-details theme by incorporating things like scallops, tiny flowers, bits of paper, lace, and ribbon.

6 The Reception

It's time to party! Finish off your wedding album with a layout highlighting your reception. Consider including your first dance together as husband and wife, the cutting of the cake, favorite gifts, and who caught the bouquet.

For the journaling on this reception layout, Mary wrote a simple, bulleted list of her favorite memories from the celebration, including when her groom fed himself the wedding cake first!

materials patterned paper, paper border (Doodlebug) • epoxy accent, metal embellishment, rub-ons, brads (Making Memories) • rhinestone (Darice) • ribbon (Offray) • tulle (Modern Elegance) • stamp (Paper Salon) • stamping ink • Carpenter and Sansumi fonts • 12 x 12 spread by Mary MacAskill, Calgary, AB, Canada

Love stories

THROUGH THE YEARS

Capture love stories from all generations ▪ My grandparents got married because of a piano. It's true. During World War II, a woman (who was nearly blind) asked my grandmother to scribe a letter to my grandfather (who was serving in the Navy) regarding the piano. That letter began a regular correspondence between the two. When my grandpa came home on a furlough, he proposed to my grandma, and the rest is history.

What stories do your parents, grandparents, aunts or uncles have? Now is the perfect time to celebrate love stories from all generations. Take a look at these stories, and start documenting the love stories in the generations connected to you.

Love Letters

It was the 60's. The era of peace, love and rock n' roll. The Beatles were big and the Sound of Music was the must-see movie. Lyndon Johnson was President of the United States and the price of a stamp was five cents. That five cent postage was the carrier of the love letters that would lead to 42 years of marriage (and counting), four children and twelve grandchildren. Those letters would bring two people together who had never met and were separated by the Vietnam War. I have never read any of the letters. I am not sure even where they are kept or how many there are. I don't know what they wrote about or what it was about those simple letters that made them want to spend the rest of eternity together. All I know is that when the letters ended their beautiful life began.

Write

ABOUT LOVE LETTERS.

Jackie Stringham documented her in-laws' courtship, which happened through letters while her father-in-law served in the Vietnam War. Do you or others have any letters from a courtship? Document what happened, and if you have the letters, include them as part of your layout!

Love Letters *by Jackie Stringham.*
Supplies *Cardstock:* Die Cuts With a View and Target; *Patterned paper:* My Mind's Eye and SEI; *Buttons:* Autumn Leaves; *Fonts:* Adobe Jenson and Bix Antique Script.

Document

WHAT YOU'VE LEARNED.

Look at a relationship close to you and talk about what you've learned from observing that relationship. Mou Saha shared what she learned from watching her parents' subtle acts of love and kindness for each other.

about love

a thing or two

Rajasthan, December 2007   Delhi, January 2000   Calcutta, August 1978

A thing or two that I know about love, I learned from my parents. They met back in 1972 and have been together since. He was taken by her beautiful doe-eyes and she was charmed by his honesty. She gave him the freedom to spend every evening rehearsing and performing his parts in stage shows as she appreciated that he worked hard all day to support the family. He read aloud every book so she could enjoy while she went about her chores at home. They had two children together, lost one and faced many challenges raising the other. Whenever she felt sick, he assumed the role of nurse-housekeeper-homeworkhelper-groceryshopper for months at a time. She was the quiet kind and a good handyman, he could not drive a nail in straight but could solve most disputes with his quick wit. Her strengths were her patience and forgiveness, his was his outgoing demeanor. She was often indecisive and he was almost always quick-tempered. He handed her every penny he earned and she stretched the money to make all the ends meet. They entertained guests often, kept their needs simple and were rarely out of sync. There were no grandiose romantic gestures, no boisterous happy anniversaries, but very quietly she decorated the house with his favorite tuberoses and he brought back dinner from her favorite restaurant every June 30th. The romance was subtle in waiting together nervously for a phone call that their first grandchild has landed safely on earth, going on pilgrimages together and helping each other up mountainous paths to make it to the shrine, just him making her a simple cup of evening tea every day since he retired... just a powerful understanding of each other's needs, a deep mutual respect and acceptance of each other in the light of what was, is now and what's to come. To me, these sure are the ingredients for a made-for-each-other-together-forever kind of romance.

A Thing or Two about Love *by Mou Saha.* **Supplies** *Cardstock and patterned paper:* Frances Meyer; *Letter stickers:* Luxe Designs (large) and Making Memories (mini); *Labels:* Luxe Designs; *Square punch:* Marvy Uchida; *Embroidery floss:* DMC; *Sanding block:* Making Memories; *Pen:* American Crafts; *Font:* Times New Roman.

Construct

A TIMELINE.

Amanda Probst documented her parents' courtship through the eyes of her mother. Amanda had her mother write their story, including some challenges they experienced, and then constructed a timeline on her layout.

TIP: Do you have too much text to include on your layout? Amanda had to cut some of what her mother wrote from the front of the layout, but she included everything on the back to preserve the entire story.

WHEN I FELL IN LOVE. I can still picture the evening that my Robert stole my heart. We had been playing Monopoly with two other friends for almost two hours. We decided to call it a game and the others left. Robert and I started talking. He was lying on the sofa and I was sitting on the floor. We talked about a variety of things and for some reason, during our conversation, we happened to look into each other's eyes. To this day, I'm not altogether sure what Rob saw, but for me, I saw my future. For a moment in time, I had a vision of us playing with a little baby...a one year old baby boy to be exact, our future son, Joseph. (It was many years after we were married that I realized just who that baby was, when that very same vision came to me, while playing with Joseph at home.) That was the day I fell deeply in love with my friend, Robert E. Smith.

THE DAY WE MET He had on black Converse tennis shoes, blue jeans, a black turtle neck, a multicolored plaid-style long sleeved shirt, and an olive green corduroy, double-breasted jacket.

BREAKING UP. The only time Rob and I broke up during our 4 years as a dating couple was when he had promised to take me to the Winter Ball at YVC in February of 1969. As I wasn't allowed to date while in high school, I didn't go to my prom, so going to this dance was very important to me. Unfortunately, it wasn't as important to Rob. He had the opportunity to attend an Iron Butterfly concert in Ellensburg which was the same Saturday as the dance. I broke up with him the day he told me he was going with his friends to the concert. In all honesty, I'm not certain how we got back together . . . I probably forgave him! It was hard to resist his smile, plus he asked me to wear his class ring and told me he loved me. I couldn't refuse. From then on, he became my whole reason for being.

AN OCEAN COULDN'T KEEP US APART The true test of our relationship came when my parents decided that I should go to Hawaii (poor me) for a few months. My sister was due to have her first baby in February and they thought it would be good for me to go and help. Of course, the alternative reason, as I found out later from my sister, was to get me away from Robert. Although my parents liked him, they thought we were getting too serious. The old adage "absence makes the heart grow fonder" came into play as Rob and I continually wrote to each other. All in all, it was a good experience plus it brought Rob and me even closer. I had left for Hawaii before Christmas 1969 and returned to the mainland in February of 1970. (I finally just had to come home and booked my own return flight without really consulting anyone. I didn't even go see my parents until about a week after I'd been back in Washington, and my dad simply accepted that this was the way things were.)

THE WAY TO A MAN'S HEART IS THROUGH HIS STOMACH. Thanksgiving of '70 was one to remember as that was the first turkey dinner I cooked for Rob. Rob loved to eat . . . almost anything you put in front of him, he ate. I loved cooking for him and that's one of the things I miss the most. That Thanksgiving, Rob didn't just eat my dinner, he ate two other dinners that same day! He had dinner with his family in Prosser, had dinner with me, and then we both went to my parents for dinner. Talk about a stuffed turkey!!

ASKING FOR MY HAND. As 1972 rolled around, it was time for Rob to ask my parents' permission for my hand in marriage. This happened soon after New Years Day. Rob felt he should talk to mom and dad by himself. I agreed, as I was a bit worried that they would start grilling me in front of Rob and put him in an embarrassing situation. When I asked him later how things went, he just smiled and said "fine"! Oh to be a fly on the wall at that time!

SEALING THE DEAL Rob and I enjoyed attending Mass at St. Paul's and once our pre-marital classes were completed, our engagement was announced in the Marriage Banns in the parish bulletin. Rob couldn't get out of it now, even if he had wanted to . . . it was in the church bulletin and that was final!

1968 ...THE STORY OF MY PARENTS' COURTSHIP, AS TOLD BY MY MOM 1972

Timeline by Amanda Probst. **Supplies** *Cardstock:* Prism Papers; *Felt letters:* KI Memories; *Pen:* Precision Pens, American Crafts; *Font:* Rockwell.

Back of layout

Record

THE STORIES OTHERS TELL.

Often, the only memory of a relationship is from the stories others tell. Because her grandfather died when she was two, Cindy Tobey learned of her grandparents' relationship through the stories her grandmother told. Here she records the story of "their song."

Their Song *by Cindy Tobey.* **Supplies** *Cardstock:* Bazzill Basics Paper; *Patterned paper:* Fancy Pants Designs and Making Memories; *Acrylic shape, felt, rub-ons and transparency overlay:* Fancy Pants Designs; *Ink:* Clearsnap; *Stickers:* 7gypsies and Making Memories; *Paint and ribbon:* Making Memories; *Chipboard:* BasicGrey and Deluxe Designs; *Pin embellishment:* American Crafts.

View

A RELATIONSHIP
OVER TIME.

Kelly Noel and Kelly Purkey both created layouts that focus on relationships over a period of years. This approach is a great way to reflect on how the relationship has changed or grown over the decades.

Time Flies *by Kelly Purkey.* **Supplies** *Cardstock:* American Crafts; *Patterned paper:* BasicGrey (green) and Heidi Grace Designs (brown dot and yellow); *Rub-ons:* Heidi Grace Designs; *Ink:* Stampin' Up!; *Ribbon and stickers:* American Crafts; *Epoxy stickers:* Cloud 9 Design, Fiskars; *Butterfly and circle punches and decorative-edge scissors:* Fiskars; *Font:* AL Uncle Charles; *Other:* Thread.

The Test of Time *by Kelly Noel.* **Supplies** *Cardstock:* Bazzill Basics Paper; *Patterned paper:* Creative Imaginations and KI Memories; *Brads:* American Crafts; *Buttons:* Autumn Leaves; *Flowers:* Imaginisce (orange) and Making Memories (pink and cream); *Stickers:* Heidi Grace Designs; *Chipboard:* American Crafts (letters) and Heidi Swapp for Advantus (clock); *Font:* My Old Remington.

Look

AT A RELATIONSHIP
BETWEEN GENERATIONS.

An aunt, uncle or grandparent can have a very different relationship with a child than a parent. Document what those relationships are like. Tiffany Tillman focused her layout on the relationship between her father and her daughter.

Got to Make This Moment Last *by Tiffany Tillman.* **Supplies** *Software:* Adobe Photoshop CS3; *Cardstock:* Worn and Weary by Tiffany Tillman; *Brushes and elements:* Feeling Groovy Element and Brush Pack by Michelle Coleman; *Font:* Serifa.

Vintage Valentine Sweets

When writing about stories from older generations, it's only fitting that you add a little vintage flair! Try some of these vintage-inspired products on your layouts.

Timeless Love buttons
Buttons Galore
MoreButtons.com

Vintage Valentine tags
Shabby Chic Crafts
ShabbyChicCrafts.com

Heart rub-ons
Hambly Screen Prints
HamblyScreenPrints.com

The Luxury Stack pearlized and metallic paper
Die Cuts With a View
DCWV.com

Vintage Valentine stamps and That's Amore stickers
Close To My Heart
CloseToMyHeart.com

Love Notes patterned paper and dimensional stickers
Making Memories
MakingMemories.com

Mellow Sweet paper embellishments
My Mind's Eye
MyMindsEye.com

Love Story Phrases rub-ons
American Crafts
AmericanCrafts.com ck

Stamp Kissing

Dress up your stamps with this fun technique that makes simple projects stunning. It gives your stamps added versatility and you have unlimited options for adding detail and interest.

Designer: Nichole Heady

BASIC STAMP KISSING

By pressing a dry patterned stamp onto a solid inked stamp, you can create a textured look. Solid stamps with large blank areas work best for this technique. Pigment ink coats stamps more thickly and will give you the clearest images. Because it also has a longer drying time, pigment ink is ideal when you need to stamp-kiss an inked stamp multiple times, as in the following project.

❶ Ink solid stamp.

❷ Press uninked patterned stamp onto inked solid stamp.

Wedding Congratulations Card

❶ Make card from cardstock.

❷ Cut cardstock slightly smaller than card; adhere.

❸ Stamp-kiss bottom portion of dress with Antique Pattern. Lift off patterned stamp; clean thoroughly. Stamp-kiss top portion of dress with Antique Pattern.

❹ Clean pigment ink off hanger portion of dress stamp with baby wipe; coat with watermark ink. Stamp inked dress image on cardstock. Emboss hanger portion.

❺ Mat stamped image with cardstock; adhere to card.

❻ Stamp Congratulations on cardstock; emboss. Create tag, attach flower with brad, and adhere to card with foam squares.

Finished size: 4½" x 6"

DESIGNER TIPS

• Place the inked stamp securely on a solid surface.

• When stamp kissing, press hard on the uninked stamp with all your weight. Carefully peel it off the inked stamp so the image remains crisp.

• Keep embossing powder from drifting into the pigment ink on this stamp by holding the stamped image upside down and applying powder to the hanger portion in small amounts at a time.

SUPPLIES: *Cardstock:* (Plum, Wizard Light, white) Prism *Rubber stamps:* (Solid Dress) Renaissance Art Stamps; (Congratulations) Plaid; (Antique Pattern) Penny Black *Pigment ink:* (Whisper White) Stampin' Up! *Watermark ink:* Tsukineko *Embossing powder:* (silver) Stampin' Up! *Accents:* (pink flower) Prima; (burgundy brad, oval metal tag frame) Making Memories *Adhesive:* (foam squares) Stampin' Up! *Tools:* (tag maker) Making Memories

Kiss and Twist

By giving your uninked patterned stamp a little "twist" after pressing it onto your solid inked stamp, you gain a completely different design. Small, detailed patterns or designs work better than solid images. Experiment with lots of patterns and see what develops!

❶ Ink solid stamp.

❷ Press and twist uninked stamp on inked solid stamp.

Close to My Heart Card

❶ Make card from cardstock.

❷ Cut cardstock slightly smaller than card front; stamp Large Petal multiple times with dye ink to form flower. *Note: Stamp off edge of cardstock.*

❸ Kiss and twist dots stamp on petal stamp. Clean dots stamp and kiss and twist repeatedly until inked stamp is filled with pattern. Overstamp existing petal on cardstock.

❹ Repeat step 3 until all petals are complete.

❺ Cut circle of cardstock; adhere behind epoxy circle. Adhere piece to stamped image with foam squares.

❻ Apply rub-on. Stitch edges of stamped piece and adhere to card.

Finished size: 5½" x 4¼"

SUPPLIES: *Cardstock:* (white, fuchsia) Prism *Rubber stamps:* (Large Petal) Memory Box; (dots from Petal Pushers set) Stampin' Up! *Pigment ink:* (Regal Rose) Stampin' Up! *Dye ink:* (Pretty in Pink) Stampin' Up! *Accent:* (epoxy circle) Making Memories *Rub-on:* (close to my heart) K&Company *Adhesive:* (foam squares) Stampin' Up!

Kiss With Non-Stamps

Once you start stamp kissing, you'll realize how easy it is to use virtually any patterned item to create the cool textured looks on your solid stamps. Even household items can get in on the fun; try crumpled plastic wrap, aluminum foil, cheesecloth, shoe soles, or a comb. The next project makes a work of art using an ordinary kitchen sponge!

❶ Ink solid stamp.

❷ Press patterned item against inked stamp.

Hugs & Kisses Tag

❶ Cut tag shape from cardstock.

❷ Punch circle from cardstock; adhere to tag top.

❸ Ink stamp; kiss with sponge. Stamp image on cardstock.

❹ Trim stamped image, ink edges, and mat with cardstock. Adhere to tag.

❺ Adhere epoxy charm.

❻ Fill tube with candy.

❼ Attach tag with ribbon; adhere ribbon to secure at top.

Finished sizes: tube 5" height x 1" diameter, tag 3½" x 1¾"

SUPPLIES: *Cardstock:* (Rose Red, Very Vanilla, Chocolate Chip) Stampin' Up! *Rubber stamp:* (Solid Cont. Heart) Northwoods Rubber Stamps *Pigment ink:* (Rose Red, Chocolate Chip) Stampin' Up! *Accent:* (kisses epoxy charm) Li'l Davis Designs *Fibers:* (brown polka dot ribbon) American Crafts *Tools:* (½" circle punch) *Other:* (plastic tube with lid, candy, sponge)

Anniversary Wishes

DESIGNER TIPS

■ Having trouble tying the perfect knot? Go online and type keywords such as "ribbon tying" into your web browser. You'll find links to a variety of detailed how-tos as well as step-by-step videos showing you how to get that professional look every time.

■ Prevent ribbon ends from fraying by quickly running them through a flame. Make sure to test a scrap of the ribbon first before heat-setting the real thing.

Together

Designer: Melissa Phillips

1. Make card from cardstock; round right corners.
2. Cut rectangles of patterned paper; adhere.
3. Adhere bingo card, tag, die cuts, and felt star.
4. Apply rub-on.
5. Thread button with string; adhere.

Finished size: 3½" x 5¼"

You Mean Everything

Designer: Cassie Larson

1. Make card from cardstock.
2. Cut rectangles of cardstock; adhere to card.
3. Stamp sentiments and bird.
4. Knot ribbon around card front.

Finished size: 4¼" x 5½"

SUPPLIES: *Cardstock:* (Cream Puff) Bazzill Basics Paper *Patterned paper:* (Strawberry Lemonade Dots from Carefree collection) Heidi Swapp; (Norms News from Hometown collection) October Afternoon; (Darcy from Windsor collection) SEI *Accents:* (glitter circle, mod flowers die cuts) Crate Paper; (brown felt star, bingo card) Jenni Bowlin Studio; (chipboard tag) SEI; (black button) *Rub-on:* (sentiment) SEI *Fibers* (white string) *Tool:* (corner rounder punch) Marvy Uchida

SUPPLIES: All supplies from Stampin' Up! unless otherwise noted. *Cardstock:* (Chocolate Chip, More Mustard, Pumpkin Pie) *Rubber stamps:* (bird, sentiments from Always set) *Dye ink:* (Chocolate Chip) *Fibers:* (floral ribbon) Michaels

BONUS IDEA

The vintage look of this card is a fitting complement to photographs from decades past. Create invitations for a golden anniversary party by changing the sentiment to "You're invited."

:5: Keepsake Photo

Designer: Ashley Newell

❶ Make card from cardstock; adhere photo.

❷ Thread ribbon through ribbon slide; wrap around card front and adhere.

❸ Stitch border and ink edges of card.

❹ Stamp sentiment on cardstock; trim, ink, and mat with cardstock. Adhere to card. *Note: Slip one corner underneath ribbon slide.*

Finished size: 5" x 7"

:5: Darling

Designer: Susan R. Opel

❶ Make card from cardstock.

❷ Cut strip of patterned paper; adhere.

❸ Tie on ribbon. Adhere rhinestones.

❹ Apply rub-ons; adhere rhinestones.

Finished size: 4" x 5½"

SUPPLIES: *Cardstock:* (Gold Shimmer, white) Papertrey Ink; (Bravo Burgundy) Stampin' Up! *Clear stamp:* (sentiment from Out on a Limb Sentiments set) Papertrey Ink *Chalk ink:* (Chestnut Roan) Clearsnap *Specialty ink:* (Pure Poppy hybrid) Papertrey Ink *Accent:* (brass ribbon slide) Stampin' Up! *Fibers:* (burgundy ribbon) Paper Mart *Other:* (photo)

SUPPLIES: *Cardstock:* (black) *Patterned paper:* (Black Diamonds from Black Tie Optional collection) Imaginisce *Accents:* (clear, green rhinestones) *Rub-ons:* (sentiment, flourish) Cosmo Cricket *Fibers:* (green ribbon) Michaels

To My Hubby

Designer: Nichol Magouirk

❶ Make card from Maraschino cardstock.

❷ Sand edges of hearts and monogram. Adhere monogram to card.

❸ Spell "Happy anniversary" with rub-ons on card.

❹ Affix dots and "for you" circle to card.

❺ Print "To my hubby…" on tag. Attach thread and tie on large heart.

❻ Adhere hearts to card front.

Finished size: 4¼" x 5½"

SUPPLIES Cardstock: (Maraschino) *Bazzill Basics Paper* **Accents:** (chipboard hearts) *Heidi Swapp;* (mini tag with heart) *Making Memories;* (monogram) *KI Memories* **Rub-ons:** (Classic alphabet, pink dots) *KI Memories;* (script alphabet) *Deja Views;* (for you circle) *Creative Imaginations* **Fibers:** (white thread) **Font:** (Century Gothic) *Microsoft* **Other:** (sandpaper)

✦5✦ STEPS Silhouette Anniversary Party Designer: Jessica Witty

INVITATION *Adhere all accents with foam tape.* ❶ Cut patterned paper slightly smaller than card front; round corners, distress edges, and adhere. ❷ Thread tag on ribbon and tie around card. Adhere tag. ❸ Cut panel from patterned paper. Distress edges, roll corners, and adhere. ❹ Print sentiment on cardstock; trim, bend, and roll corners. Adhere. ❺ Punch heart from chipboard. Cover with patterned paper, sand edges, and apply glitter. Adhere.

PLACE CARDS *Adhere all accents with foam tape.* ❶ Cut card to finished size. ❷ Cut patterned paper slightly smaller than card front; round corners, distress edges, and adhere. ❸ Print guest name on cardstock; trim, bend, and roll corners. Adhere. ❹ Punch heart from chipboard. Cover with patterned paper, sand edges, and apply glitter. Adhere.

VASE WRAP *Adhere all accents with foam tape.* ❶ Cut patterned paper to fit around vase; distress edges and adhere. ❷ Adhere bird scalloped circle. ❸ Print sentiment on cardstock; trim, bend, and roll corners. Adhere. ❹ Punch heart from chipboard. Cover with patterned paper, sand edges, and apply glitter. Adhere. ❺ Tie ribbon.

Finished sizes: invitation 5½" x 4¼", place cards 2¾" x 2", vase wrap 15" x 4½"

SUPPLIES: *Cardstock:* (white) *Patterned paper:* (Wallpaper, Valentines, Heart Filigree from First Blush collection) Paper Salon *Accent:* (clear glitter) Stampin' Up! *Stickers:* (bird scalloped circle, tag) Paper Salon *Fibers:* (silver organza ribbon) Michaels *Font:* (Stanzie JF) www.myfonts.com *Adhesive:* (decoupage) Plaid; (foam tape) *Tools:* (corner rounder, heart punches) EK Success *Other:* (pink shimmer scalloped cards) Paper Salon; (glass vase) Michaels; (chipboard)

5 | I Will Cherish

Designer: Sherry Wright

❶ Make card from cardstock; ink edges.

❷ Trim piece of die cut paper; ink edges and adhere.

❸ Apply rub-on.

❹ Ink edges of chipboard button. Adhere flower and chipboard heart; adhere to card. Insert stick pin.

Finished size: 5" x 6"

SUPPLIES: *Cardstock:* (aqua) Prism *Specialty paper:* (Disco Ball die cut from Pop Culture collection) KI Memories *Chalk ink:* (red) Clearsnap *Accents:* (red heart stick pin) Fancy Pants Designs; (aqua flower) Prima; (red chipboard heart) Heidi Swapp; (white chipboard button) Jenni Bowlin Studio *Rub-on:* (sentiment) Fancy Pants Designs

5 | Love Birds

Designer: Cindy Tobey

❶ Make card from patterned paper.

❷ Trim card front edge in wave. Mat with cardstock and trim with decorative-edge scissors; ink edge.

❸ Spell "Love birds" with stickers.

❹ Paint chipboard heart; adhere. Adhere birds and buttons.

Finished size: 4¼" x 5½"

SUPPLIES: *Cardstock:* (white) Bazzill Basics Paper *Patterned paper:* (My Sweetie from Floral Chic collection) Fancy Pants Designs *Pigment ink:* (Baby Blue) Clearsnap *Paint:* (Banana) Making Memories *Accents:* (chipboard heart, felt birds) Fancy Pants Designs; (black buttons) Blumenthal Lansing *Stickers:* (Getty alphabet) American Crafts; (Franklin Gothic alphabet) The Paper Studio *Tool:* (decorative-edge scissors) Provo Craft

⁵ Love Bird

Designer: Brandy Jesperson

❶ Make card from cardstock.

❷ Adhere patterned paper.

❸ Apply rub-on to journaling tag; adhere. Adhere rectangle, bird, and rhinestone.

❹ Cut slit in top fold of card. Thread ribbon and tie bow. Tie on bird cage tag with ribbon.

Finished size: 5½" x 4"

You & Me

Designer: Debbie Olson

Sand all patterned paper edges.

❶ Make card from cardstock; round bottom corners.

❷ Cut patterned paper slightly smaller than card front; adhere.

❸ Cut rectangle of patterned paper; stitch edges. Cut patterned paper, curl up edges slightly, and adhere. *Note: Trim so sentiment shows clearly.*

❹ Die-cut and emboss label from cardstock; mat with die-cut cardstock label.

❺ Stamp image; color with markers. Adhere with foam tape.

❻ Tie ribbon bow; adhere. Thread button and adhere.

Finished size: 4¼" x 5¼"

SUPPLIES: *Cardstock:* (brown) *Patterned paper:* (Forget My Not, Petticoat from Love Birds collection) SEI *Accents:* (pink rectangle, white bird) American Crafts; (bird cage, cream journaling tags) SEI; (clear rhinestone) *Rub-on:* (happy anniversary) American Crafts *Fibers:* (brown dotted ribbon) American Crafts; (blue ribbon) Michaels

SUPPLIES: *Cardstock:* (white, black) *Patterned paper:* (Berries, lined from Hello Sunshine pad) Cosmo Cricket *Rubber stamp:* (birds from The Birds & The Bees set) Cornish Heritage Farms *Dye ink:* (Tuxedo Black) Tsukineko *Color medium:* (markers) Copic Markers *Accent:* (red button) Autumn Leaves *Fibers:* (blue ribbon) Papertrey Ink *Adhesive:* (foam tape) *Dies:* (nested labels) Spellbinders *Tools:* (die cut/embossing machine) Spellbinders; (corner rounder punch) Marvy Uchida

INSIDE

Love Letter

Designer: Audrey Neal

CARD

❶ Cut two 12" x 3⅛" strips of Cardinal cardstock; score every 3", alternating sides. ❷ Cut letters, following pattern on p. 280. ❸ Write "You!" on tag; attach to card with brad. ❹ Cut four 3" x 2⅞" rectangles of Brighton Love Letter paper; adhere to second strip of Cardinal. ❺ Adhere strips together. ❻ Ink edges of letters with white paint pen. ❼ Accordion-fold card.

CARD COVER

❶ Cut Cardinal cardstock to 5⅞" x 3¼". ❷ Round corners and score 1" and 1⅜" from each side. Crease and fold edges toward center. ❸ Make band, following pattern on p. 280. Score 1½" and 1⅞" from each side. Adhere to Cardinal and fold along same creases. ❹ Punch hole in rounded ends of patterned paper; attach eyelets. ❺ Thread ribbon through eyelets and tie closed. ❻ Insert folded card.

Finished sizes: card 12" x 3⅛", card cover 3" x 3⅛" x ¼"

SUPPLIES: **Cardstock:** (Cardinal) *Bazzill Basics Paper* **Patterned paper:** (Brighton Love Letter) *Scenic Route Paper Co.* **Color media:** (white paint pen) *Hunt Corporation;* (black pen) *EK Success* **Accents:** (Cameo Coral eyelet) *Stampin' Up!;* (pink brad) *The Paper Studio;* (white mini tag) *DMD, Inc.* **Fibers:** (red gingham ribbon) *Offray* **Tools:** (corner rounder punch) *Creative Memories*

The Real Thing

Designer: Michelle Tardie

❶ Make card from Honeycomb cardstock.

❷ Cut strip of Small Multi Stripe paper; adhere to card.

❸ Attach brads to love sentiment; adhere to card with foam squares.

Finished size: 3½" x 3"

SUPPLIES: **Cardstock:** (Honeycomb) *Bazzill Basics Paper* **Patterned paper:** (Small Multi Stripe from Mad About Plaid collection) *Sweetwater* **Accent:** (love sentiment) *Sweetwater;* (earth tone brads) *Junkitz* **Adhesive:** (foam squares)

Us, for Keeps

Designer: Julie Medeiros

1 Make card from white cardstock.

2 Cut Green Blue Floral paper to fit card front; adhere.

3 Cut strip and square of light green cardstock; stitch edges.

4 Tie ribbons around strip and adhere to card.

5 Cut square of blue cardstock; spell "Us" with rub-ons. Affix "For keeps" rub-on.

6 Mat with stitched light green square; adhere to card.

Finished size: 3¾" x 8½"

First Year of Marriage

Designer: Nichole Heady

1 Make card from Old Olive cardstock.

2 Cut Adventure Stripe Teal paper slightly smaller than card front. Adhere reverse side up to card.

3 Cut strip of Adventure Stripe Teal. Tear one edge and adhere to card.

4 Stamp sofa with Basic Black on Whisper White cardstock. Color image with Old Olive reinker.

5 Stamp sofa twice on Adventure Stripe Teal with Basic Black. Cut out pillow images and add dots to heart pillow with gel pen. Adhere pillow images to sofa.

6 Stitch edges of stamped Whisper White; adhere to card.

7 Print "Happy anniversary" in circular text on Old Olive. Adhere to clear button and trim edges.

8 Cover button top with dimensional glaze. Adhere charm to center; let dry. Adhere to card.

Finished size: 4⅝" x 4½"

SUPPLIES: **Cardstock:** (blue, light green, white) **Patterned paper:** (Green Blue Floral) *Anna Griffin* **Rub-ons:** (French Quarter alphabet) *Heidi Swapp;* (for keeps) *Making Memories* **Fibers:** (light green grosgrain ribbon, light green satin ribbon) *Offray;* (white thread)

SUPPLIES: *All supplies from Stampin' Up! unless otherwise noted.* **Cardstock:** (Old Olive, Whisper White) **Patterned paper:** (Adventure Stripe Teal) *My Mind's Eye* **Rubber stamp:** (sofa from Please Be Seated set) *Stampin' Up!* **Dye ink:** (Basic Black, Old Olive reinker) **Color medium:** (white gel pen) *Sanford* **Accents:** (clear button); (number charm) *Making Memories* **Fibers:** (white thread) no source **Font:** (SU Quick) **Tools:** (water brush) **Other:** (dimensional glaze)

R♥mantic C♥medy

Celebrate the moments that bring **laughter** into your relationship.

As funny as it sounds, romance isn't always romantic. While romantic stories often make you say, "awwhh," sometimes romance can also be comedic. (It's just like many favorite chick flicks.) My favorite scrapbook pages are the ones that give me butterflies, make me blush, or even worse, make me laugh out loud in a room full of people who can't possibly understand why I'm rolling on the floor.

Take time to scrapbook the funny and humorous aspects of your relationship, even if they're more comedy than romance. There's bound to be a funny moment from the past month that could have been on your favorite sitcom. Look at the funny, romantic moments on the following pages, and then set aside time to record some of the romantic-comedy moments from your life.

meet market

All relationships have a beginning, and each is unique. Even if you feel your story may seem ordinary, with a little review to think about the details you're sure to see the extraordinary moments worth remembering at the beginning of your relationship. Here are a couple of not-so-everyday beginnings to help you start brainstorming.

April 30, 2005 was the day that changed our lives forever. I had moved home from my college apartment to my parents house that day. Adam had moved to Highland, Utah to his brother Sean, & sister-in-law Sara's house from his college apartment for the summer. I decided to go with my parents to dinner for my nephew Jacob's birthday. Jacob wanted pancakes for his birthday dinner, so the decision was made to go to IHOP.

Adam went with Sara's family to dinner & after finding out that there was a one hour wait to be seated at the Italian restaurant near by, they asked Sara's grandfather what he

would like to eat for dinner. He answered, "pancakes".

Although pancakes was not the dinner everyone had in mind, it sure ended up becoming a life altering decision. Adam was sitting down with his party when my family walked in. Immediately I saw him and found him very attractive. The waiter sat our family at a table parallel to his. Little did I know that Adam was checking me out too!

Through the course of the dinner I was talking extra loud, trying to let on that I was single and very available! Meanwhile, Adam and his brother were ease dropping & scheming to try to find a cool way to

ask me on a date. There was mention of buying my dinner, or an orange juice ... but when it came down to it, Sara's father stood up, walked over to my dad and said, "You don't know me, but I sure would like to buy your families' dinner, if your daughter would be willing to go out with this young man".

Adam was red. I was flattered and both of us were very embarrassed! Either way you have it, Adam got my phone number & called me two days later to ask me on a date.

We never thought that one night at IHOP would turn into an engagement six weeks later, and a very romantic meeting story!

"My husband and I are known as the 'IHOP' couple (see the journaling on my layout). I'm **putting a copy of this layout in each of our children's scrapbooks** so they'll be able to pass along the romantic and funny story of how their parents met."

—Mandy Douglass

Love at First Bite by Mandy Douglass. **Supplies** Cardstock: American Crafts; *Patterned paper:* SEI; *Letter stickers:* American Crafts; *Heart:* Fiskars Americas; *Flower:* QuicKutz; *Arrow and brad:* American Crafts; *Fonts:* Scriptina (happy) and Swiss 721 ("at first bite," "come hungry . . . leave," and journaling); *Adhesive:* Scrapbook Adhesives by 3L.

"Three girls plus a dad. One daughter plus a mom. It was **more crazy than romantic in the beginning,** but we learned to take it as it came. We wouldn't have it any other way."

—Joannie McBride

When This Lady Met This Fellow by Joannie McBride. **Supplies** *Cardstock:* Core'dinations; *Patterned paper:* My Mind's Eye; *Felt scallop circle:* Fancy Pants Designs; *Flowers:* Bazzill Basics Paper (orange paper), Eyelet Outlet (green paper), Fancy Pants Designs (crochet) and Petaloo (orange felt); *Stitching template:* Bazzill Basics Paper; *Circle accents and rhinestone brads:* American Crafts; *Ribbon, epoxy flower and epoxy button:* Making Memories; *Font:* Brady Bunch; *Adhesive:* Glue Dots International and Therm O Web; *Other:* Fabric, yarn, staples and thread.

PROPOSAL and ENGAGEMENT

One of the best parts of a courtship relationship is dreaming of the perfect engagement. We all hoped Prince Charming would bend down on one knee with a glass slipper, and then we would ride away with him into the sunset. But that's someone else's story. We all have our own stories, and they're worth telling in our own ways.

"Cory tried so hard to make the evening of our engagement the perfect night, and that's exactly what it turned out to be. It may not have been what he envisioned, but it ended up being perfect for us—**our own unique (and rather comical) story**. Because of the happenings, I wanted to make my journaling stand out in a unique way as well. I had each journaling spot appear as a reflection off the facets of the diamond."

—Megan Hoeppner

A Multifaceted Event by Megan Hoeppner. **Supplies** Cardstock: Die Cuts With a View and Stampin' Up!; Patterned paper: me & my BIG ideas; Stickers: Bella Blvd and October Afternoon; Letter stickers: KI Memories; Die-cutting machine and journaling-spot die: Stampin' Up!; Glitter: Doodlebug Design; Pens: American Crafts (black) and EK Success (silver); Font: Arial Narrow; Adhesive: Fiskars Americas and We R Memory Keepers; Other: Embroidery floss.

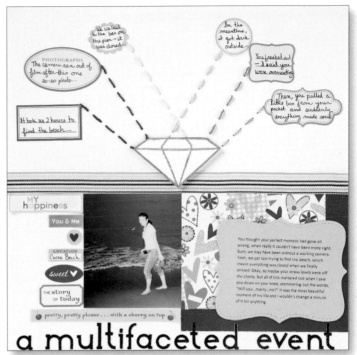

TERMS OF ENDEARMENT

People often refer to the "language of love," but I like to think that there are many languages of love—because everyone expresses theirs differently. Some show quiet affection, others shower their loved ones with attention and yet others give gifts. What expressions of love or terms of endearment show a comedic side of your relationship?

"No one would know that my husband is so animated, but those **small looks show his love for me**. With this layout, I tried to capture all the different looks my husband sends my way. They're all so special, and they all say 'I love you.'" —Mandy Douglass

Expressions of Love by Mandy Douglass. **Supplies** Cardstock, rubons, letter stickers and felt heart: American Crafts; Patterned paper: SEI; Heart pin: Heidi Grace Designs, Fiskars Americas; Font: Gotham; Adhesive: Glue Dots International and Scrapbook Adhesives by 3L.

SO HAPPY TOGETHER

Many factors are important in making a relationship work: love, kindness, unselfishness, commonalities and fun! Highlight some of the everyday moments that keep your relationship strong.

"**Laughter has definitely played a key role** in our success. It's not just about having the same brand of humor, but being able to laugh at and let go of the little things that don't really matter."

—Ria Mojica

Laugh All the Way by Ria Mojica. **Supplies** *Cardstock:* Die Cuts With a View; *Patterned paper:* Prima; *Velvet word and metal clip:* Making Memories; *Ink:* Clearsnap; *Letter stickers:* Scenic Route; *Circle clip:* Creative Imaginations; *Pens:* Dymo and Uni-ball Signo, Newell Rubbermaid.

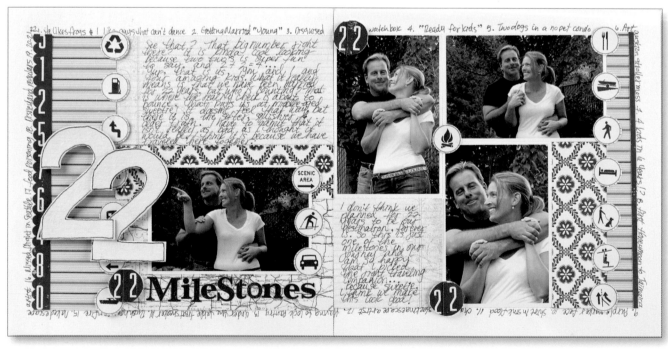

22 Milestones by *Becky Olsen.* **Supplies** *Cardstock:* Bazzill Basics Paper; *Patterned paper:* My Mind's Eye and October Afternoon.

How fun! I love that Becky Olsen chose to use "22" as a main accent to represent both **the years she's been married** and as the math that makes up her family. And I like that both Becky and Ria Mojica chose to use their own handwriting along with fonts.

JOURNALING TIP
Becky created a text border near the outside edges of her layout by recording a humorous moment for each year of her marriage.

OPPOSITES ATTract

Getting to know everything about each other is what puts a spark in every new relationship. Just when you think you know it all, something new springs up—especially when opposites attract. Think about the comedic moments that have resulted from your differences.

Opposites Attract *by Maggie Holmes.* **Supplies** *Cardstock:* Bazzill Basics Paper; *Patterned paper:* BasicGrey (floral, red and yellow) and Studio Calico (green and blue); *Stamps:* Studio Calico; *Stickers:* Making Memories (brown hearts) and Sassafras (flower and pink heart); *Brads:* Making Memories (pink and red) and Sassafras (orange); *Letter stickers:* BasicGrey (navy) and Heidi Swapp for Advantus (teal); *Flower:* Prima; *Pen:* Sharpie, Newell Rubbermaid; *Ink:* StazOn, Tsukineko; *Scissors:* Fiskars Americas; *Adhesive:* Kokuyo; *Color spray:* Maya Road; *Photoshop actions:* MaggieHolmes.Typepad.com.

"My husband and I are **exact opposites in so many ways**. We often laugh about it, because we pretty much know if he loves it, I'll hate it—and vice versa." — Maggie Holmes

DESIGN TIP

To showcase the way opposites attract and also complement each other, Maggie Holmes stamped a female silhouette and a male silhouette on her page. She used the designs to describe the differences between her and her husband.

Known and Unknown

Make sure you take the time to scrapbook details about your relationship that others may not know but that still mean a lot to you. Consider

• Favorite escapes
• Inside jokes
• Things that make you smile at each other

The handwritten journaling reads:

Once upon a time

You may not have thought much of anything when you wrote on Linda's Facebook wall, "tell James to go to Zachary's with us"... but you're about to find out that that one move is going to have more significance than you originally thought. You're going to find out that there's a reason James asked you to be your pool partner – even though you're terrible at pool. You are going to be given high fives when you miraculously make a shot, and be told "oh, that wasn't so bad" when you miss badly. James will give you little nudges throughout the night – and yes they do mean something. No use in debating it later. You will go to bed very happy and giddy that night. You aren't just imagining things. A month later, you'll be back up north, and he will kiss you. He will start calling you every day soon after. A few months later, you will officially be a couple. This is the start of a new adventure. Embrace it.

note to self

to the girl in the picture ♥, yourself, a year later

A DAY TO REMEMBER.

fall in love

Answer just what your heart prompts you

WRITE YOURSELF A LETTER

Forget your diary or Dearest Darling, because when it comes to addressing your next note I want you to write it to yourself. Caroline Ikeji wrote herself a love letter, but not in the I-love-me-to-pieces sense. Instead, it's in the here's-how-I-met-my-boyfriend sense. Her note, written a year after their sparks first flew, describes the first lovey-dovey moments in a way only hindsight can convey. Relive a moment in this fashion. The different perspective will probably bring about details for your journaling that may otherwise have gone unnoticed. Don't worry, your diary will understand your absence.

CONFUCIUS SAYS

Attaching a message from a fortune cookie to your layout will lead to a long, happy scrapbooking life!

Note to Self by Caroline Ikeji. **Supplies** *Cardstock:* Die Cuts With a View; *Patterned paper:* Creative Imaginations (orange), Making Memories (pink) and Studio Calico (red); *Chipboard accents:* Maya Road; *Die cuts, stickers and pins:* Making Memories; *Gems:* Kaisercraft; *Rub-ons:* Heidi Grace Designs; *Calendar accent:* Little Yellow Bicycle; *Stamps:* Studio Calico; *Adhesive:* Fiskars Americas; *Other:* Notebook paper.

matchmaker, matchmaker

FIND TRUE *scrapbooking harmony* USING 6 COMMON RULES OF DATING.

From the title of this feature, there's a good chance you have the lyrics from *Fiddler on the Roof* running through your head: "Matchmaker, Matchmaker, make me a match. Find me a find. Catch me a catch." It's a memorable little ditty and a wish so many of us have made at one time in our lives.

Try applying common relationship rules to scrapbooking to achieve creative bliss. After all, scrapbooking harmony is important whether you've already danced the "Funky Chicken" on your 50th wedding anniversary or you're still "on the market" looking for your perfect match. Whatever your marital status, read on for some tips for creative success.

Share the same vision for the future.

Tangible Love
by Kim Watson.
Supplies *Cardstock:* American Crafts and WorldWin; *Patterned paper:* Pink Paislee (gingham and pink) and SEI (orange); *Ribbon:* American Crafts and Making Memories; *Rub-ons:* Pink Paislee; *Buttons, die-cutting machine and letter and shape dies:* Making Memories; *Border punch:* Fiskars Americas; *Brads and pen:* American Crafts; *Adhesive:* Scrapbook Adhesives by 3L and Tombow; *Software:* Adobe CS3; *Other:* Crepe paper and thread.

Just as relationships thrive when partners have similar life goals, so can designs on scrapbook pages. Starting out on the same foot, or at least on a similar one, can mean the difference between success and breakup. Find common design ground and watch as scrapbooking magic is made! Think in terms of color schemes, product choice and font use—just make sure that *all* the products on your layout create the same mood and feel.

In Kim Watson's creative process, she purposefully went with accents that complement her theme. Hearts are a major focal point on the layout, which makes sense considering her layout is about love.

Birthday Party #10 *by Laura Vegas.* **Supplies** *Cardstock:* American Crafts (white) and Bazzill Basics Paper (red); *Patterned paper:* BasicGrey (balloon and yellow) and KI Memories (blue and green); *Ribbon:* Jillibean Soup; *Letter stickers:* Doodlebug Design (black) and Making Memories (color); *Number stickers:* Making Memories; *Buttons:* Autumn Leaves; *Font:* Prissy Frat Boy; *Adhesive:* Herma Tabs, EK Success; Zots, Therm O Web; *Other:* Staples and scallop border punch.

Themed products are a perfect place to start when focusing on a common vision. For example, bright papers, stickers and accents like the ones Laura Vegas used on the layout above are a perfect choice for telling the story of a child's birthday party. They provide a vivid reflection of her child's age and the moment she's celebrating!

Look for common interests.

June 8, 2009. After hiking around Bear Lake, we took Trail Ridge Road. It is the highest continuous motorway in the United States, with more than eight miles lying above 11,000' and a maximum elevation of 12,183'. At the Alpine Visitor Center (at, I think, 11,798 ft.), we took the path/steps up. Yes. It was a bit of a hike given the cold weather and altitude. At least I wasn't carrying Micah, though. (Nathan got that privilege, lol!) We felt like such adventurers, battling the elements to say we'd made it to the top. At the top, though, we had only about a minute to admire the view before we were pelted with little popcorn snow things that hurt. Fortunately, TJ had the presence of mind to take a picture before we scurried back down. And, in true Colorado style, the pelting stopped by the time we got back to the van. :)

Just as big-picture goals are important, so are everyday interests. Achieve scrapbooking success by selecting a design approach that shares something in common with your story.

Wanting her layout to reflect a newspaper story, Amanda Probst designed her layout in a grid. She didn't stop her unity with the design theme, either—every detail on her layout is intentional—from the color scheme (black, white and red all over) to her font choice (basic newsprint). She went the *Extra, Extra* mile on this one!

At 12,005 Feet *by Amanda Probst. Large photo by TJ Mullinax.* **Supplies** *Cardstock:* Prism Papers; *Letter stickers:* American Crafts; *Number stickers:* Gaffer Tape, 7gypsies; *Chipboard:* Scenic Route; *Font:* Courier; *Adhesive:* Scrapbook Adhesives by 3L.

Speak the same language.

make believe

Imagination is more important than knowledge. Knowledge is limited. *Imagination encircles the world.*
ALBERT EINSTEIN

At 8 months, you began holding objects (not just phones) to your ear and saying "hello." Now, at 16 months, you enjoy all kinds of imaginative activities: dancing around in your tutu, feeding your baby doll, whipping up invisible meals for us to share, helping me vacuum and dust the house, playing with your plastic animals, riding around on your little car, testing my keys on every door, and much more. It's so exciting to watch your imagination grow as you explore the world through make believe.

You say "tomato," I say "tomăto." Before you call the whole thing off, know that scrapbooking unity involves using words and quotes that support your theme too. If you want to include a quote on your layout, then the trick is using a quote that furthers your story and supports your images, rather than just throwing one on for the sake of throwing.

Rachel Gainer used a quote from Albert Einstein on a layout describing her daughter's playful discovery. At first it may seem odd that she used a famous physicist's words on such a layout, but when you read that it's all about imagination, it makes perfect sense and wonderfully supports her overall story.

Make Believe *by Rachel Gainer.*
Supplies *Cardstock:* Bazzill Basics Paper; *Patterned paper:* BasicGrey and Cosmo Cricket; *Brad:* American Crafts; *Border punch:* Fiskars Americas; *Fonts:* Lauren Script (quote and title) and Garamond (journaling and "Albert Einstein"); *Adhesive:* Tombow; *Other:* Flowers.

find a quote

Why spend time coming up with a creative title or statement for a page when there's a world of free quote ideas online? Here are a few websites to turn to when looking for your next inspiring message:

- FreeFamousQuotes.net
- Scrapbook.com/quotes.php
- ScrapbookingQuotes.net
- PaperCraftsMag.com/Sentiments/Index.html

DATING RULE #4

Know your deal-breakers.

Musical Chairs by Megan Hoeppner. **Supplies** Patterned paper: me & my BIG ideas and Sassafras; Journaling spots: American Crafts, Martha Stewart Crafts and me & my BIG ideas; Buttons and chipboard: Sassafras; Chair rub-ons: Glitz Designs; Corner-rounder punch: Fiskars Americas; Adhesive: Scrapbook Adhesives by 3L; Other: Pen and thread.

If living on the beach is a must, you probably shouldn't look for a mate at the local Hydrophobics Anonymous meeting. We all have things we can't live without, both in life and in scrapbooking. Pre-planning for those creative must-haves will make your life easier and your pages satisfying.

I'm not exactly captivated by my handwriting, but I like the personal touch handwritten journaling adds to a layout. It can take up more space than typed journaling, however, so I'm always careful to reserve plenty of room for my written notes. By planning ahead for that extra journaling space, I ensure my layout will showcase my deal-breaker for page designs.

Celebrating 2 by Susan Weinroth. **Supplies** Cardstock: American Crafts (aqua, gray and white), Bazzill Basics Paper (blue) and Die Cuts With a View (red); Patterned paper, brads and chipboard letters: American Crafts; Die-cutting machine and number die: Cricut, Provo Craft; Circle punch, triangle punch, circle template and adhesive: Fiskars Americas; Font: Bodoni XT; Other: Thread.

Making room for numerous photos is a deal-breaker for Susan Weinroth. On this layout about her son's birthday, she wanted to accommodate eight photos. (Who can blame her with images this cute?) Knowing this goal going into her design process, Susan purposefully created a layout with plenty of open space across the center for all her adorable images.

Opposites attract.

My Superpower *by Jen Jockisch.* **Supplies** *Cardstock:* American Crafts; *Patterned paper:* 7gypsies (cream), American Crafts (green stripe and teal), Prima (green dot, pink and yellow) and Sassafras (orange and peach); *Ribbon:* American Crafts and Prima; *Letter stickers:* American Crafts and Making Memories; *Buttons:* American Crafts and Bazzill Basics Paper; *Gems and leaves:* Prima; *Punches:* EK Success (corner rounder) and Fiskars Americas (border); *Brads and pen:* American Crafts; *Font:* Times New Roman; *Adhesive:* 3M and The Paper Studio; *Other:* Pearls, tags and thread.

Yes, this does slightly contradict rules #1 and #2, but there are times when using opposing elements on a scrapbook page will work to strengthen your design and further your story.

Wait just a minute here: this page has photos of a man and yet it's covered in feminine colors, frilly lace and brilliant flower blooms. Jen Jockisch, what were you thinking? Oh, of course, now it's clear! The title of the layout is "My Superpower is a Woman's Intuition" and this layout is all about the story behind that funny moment. In this case, telling the story in such a girly-girl way only adds to this humorous story. If you're creating a layout about your husband's manly tool room, however, it's probably best to leave your flowers in their storage container.

Free Spirit *by Becky Olsen.* **Supplies** *Cardstock:* Core'dinations (white) and Cornish Heritage Farms; *Patterned paper:* BasicGrey; *Ribbon:* Creative Impressions; *Chipboard:* BasicGrey and Maya Road; *Chipboard letters and pen:* American Crafts; *Brads and rub-ons:* BasicGrey; *Button:* My Mind's Eye; *Gems:* Kaisercraft; *Crackle paint:* Ranger Industries (pink and white); *Adhesive:* Therm O Web and Tombow; *Other:* Crepe paper and thread.

At first glance, the elegant paper Becky Olsen used on her layout feels like it belongs on a wedding layout, but Becky saw symbolism in its empty bird cages and decided it was just the design to illustrate her daughter's free spirit. She says she'd ordinarily never use soft pink and dainty ribbon to describe her beautiful teen, but with this story it was a perfect match!

Look for someone with a compatible disposition.

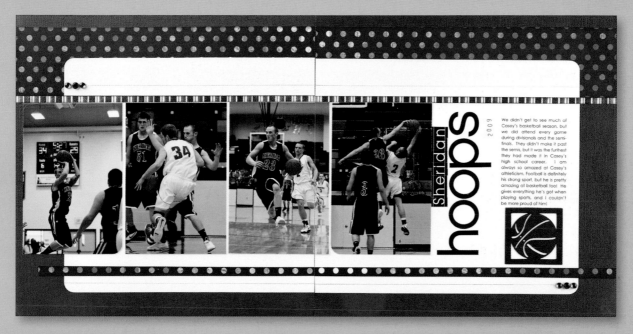

Sheridan Hoops *by Lea Lawson.* **Supplies** *Cardstock:* Bazzill Basics Paper; *Patterned paper:* Glitz Designs; *Stickers:* American Crafts, Jenni Bowlin Studio and Making Memories; *Gems:* Darice and Doodlebug Design; *Corner-rounder punch:* EK Success; *die-cutting machine and basketball die:* Cricut Expression, Provo Craft; *Font:* Century Gothic; *Adhesive:* EK Success and Tombow.

An even temperament brings a calming effect to any relationship, just as a compatible color scheme will balance a scrapbook design. Select colors that work with your photos and the mood of your layout, and true tranquility will result.

Basketball games are action packed and adrenaline pumped, making the bold purple-and-black color combination Lea Lawson used on her layout a logical choice. Plus, these are the school colors seen on the players' jerseys, so her colors support her photos rather than compete for the eye's attention.

create hue harmony

Do you {insert theme} take this {insert color} to have and to hold in creative matrimony for as long as you both shall exist in this scrapbook? Okay, so unless you're scrapbooking at a crop, you're not going to join your colors and themes together in front of a room full of teary-eyed onlookers, but this can be a rather special scrapbooking union. After all, color can drastically alter the mood of a page—and mood is a strong factor for supporting your theme. So in front of you and all of our CK witnesses, we've paired a list of themes with well-suited colors for you to use on your layouts. Any objections?

• Birthday + orange, blue and green = a feeling of happiness and jubilee

• Family + red, blue and white = a feeling of togetherness and strength

• Travel + yellow, teal and pink = a feeling of pure enjoyment and pleasure **ck**

Buttons may be basic, but they're not boring!

These everyday embellishments come in countless colors, shapes, and sizes. They're perfect for making multilayered accents, decorating simple patterns, and creating funky borders. Just stack 'em up, spread 'em out, or dress 'em up—whatever makes you happy! We challenged designer Margaret Scarbrough to dig into her box of buttons and try a few new tricks. Check out her handiwork below. Then turn to your own button collection, and learn firsthand just how fun building with buttons can be.

TIP: To make sure you get complete paper coverage behind your button, cut your patterned paper slightly larger than the button and trim after you adhere.

try this!

CUSTOMIZE CLEAR BUTTONS

Achieve a one-of-a-kind look by layering clear buttons on top of patterned paper. To make this button border, Margaret started with a stack of pink papers. She cut out 14 small circles, ran them through her Xyron machine (patterned side facing the adhesive), and stuck them to the backs of her acrylic buttons. After adding a few rub-ons to the button tops, she arranged the pieces on her layout and adhered them in place.

materials clear buttons (7gypsies) • heart buttons, letter stickers, journaling card, die cut (Making Memories) • patterned papers (KI Memories, SEI, Scrapworks, Sweetwater) • rub-ons (Crate Paper) • letter stamps (Hero Arts) • stamping ink (Ranger) • ribbon (BasicGrey) • ric rac • corner rounder • circle punch • 8½ x 11 spread by Margaret Scarbrough

a lot like Love

scrapbookers share the things that make their hearts go pit-a-pat

EVER BEEN IN LOVE? Then you know that all the clichés about having your head in the clouds or stars in your eyes are not just the stuff of harlequin romance novels. After meeting the love of your life, surely you walked into a wall or two, adrift as you were in your own dream world. And anyone who's held a newborn in her arms knows that love like that doesn't come just from romance. Anything that captures your heart can cause endorphins to zip through your veins. A new camera lens, a first glimpse of the white-sand beaches of Maui, a really good chocolate cupcake—all these things can make you fall in love all over again.

If you really want to get to know someone, find out what makes her heart pound. With that very goal in mind, we asked you to tell us about your love affairs—big or small. And from triathlons to television, you answered! Read on for a peek into the (G-rated) love lives of scrapbookers just like you.

love is blind

Love is blind, and according to our readers, it may be deaf and tastebud-challenged as well! There's no predicting what's going to capture your emotions, and there's no fighting it either. These readers have learned to embrace their hearts' desires, as wacky as they may be.

Go ahead, laugh! Grace loves sappy songs, and she's proud of it. "This is one of my favorite pages, not so much because of the design or the things I used on it, but because I documented something my kids would never have known about me unless I directly shared it with them," she says.

materials patterned paper (Bo-Bunny) • ribbon (American Crafts) • letter stickers (Making Memories, me & my BIG ideas, Die Cuts With a View) • flower (Prima) • button • chipboard heart • Goudy Old Style font • 8½ x 11 page by Grace Tolman, Norwalk, CA

Yeah I admit it; I'm a sappy love song lover, the sappier the better! I'm drawn by the words, the smooth melody and usually dream that I can hit those high notes the singers do. I've gone through a lot of "heartbreaks" by listening to these songs and although people think it's corny, I don't care; I would still prefer putting on my Mariah Carey song any day. June 2008

ALWAYS LOVING POPCORN & PICKLE ♥ SAME TIME EVERY DAY I CRAVE MY FAVORITE SNACK ♥ CONSTANT THROUGH THE YEARS

obsession

Her taste for popcorn and pickles may raise a few eyebrows, but that's fine with Monica. "As silly as this obsession is, it is a small part of what defines me. It's really clicked lately that my quirks are exactly what make me loved by my family, and I'm starting to embrace and document them."

materials Photoshop (Adobe) • letter masks (Heidi Swapp) • chipboard arrow (American Crafts) • acrylic paint • *12 x 12 page by Monica McNeill, Dallas, TX*

HIDDEN JOURNALING CARD (SLIDES OUT FROM BEHIND PHOTO)

ALWAYS LOVING POPCORN & PICKLE ♥ SAME TIME EVERY DAY I CRAVE MY FAVORITE SNACK ♥ CONSTANT THROUGH THE YEARS

THERE ARE SOME OBSESSIONS THAT CAN BE HIDDEN AND INDULGED IN PRIVATE. HOWEVER, A HANKERING FOR PICKLES AND POPCORN EVERY SINGLE DAY IS NOT ONE SUCH OBSESSION.

MOST OF THE OUTSIDE WORLD IS ABLE TO TOLERATE MY LOVE OF POPCORN. I'VE BECOME ACCUSTOMED TO THE QUESTION "WHAT IS THAT SMELL?" EVEN WHEN I HAVE **NOT** IN FACT BURNED THE POPCORN. BEING ASKED THE QUESTION ALMOST DAILY LEADS ME TO BELIEVE THAT THEY DO KNOW WHAT "THAT SMELL" IS BUT INSTEAD ARE ASKING IN HOPES OF AN OFFERING TO SHARE MY COVETED SNACK. NOT ALL POPCORN IS CREATED EQUAL. GROWING UP IT WAS A REAL TREAT TO SEE MOM BRING OUT THE STEEL LOOKING PAN, WATCH HER ADD OIL AND KERNELS AND HEAR THE POPPING. THE SPRINKLING OF SALT OVER THE PIPING HOT POPCORN WITH A HINT OF OIL WOULD SEND ME OVER THE EDGE. THAT IS A GUILTY PLEASURE. BUT WITH THE GOOD COMES THE BAD. I CANNOT EAT MOVIE THEATRE, TARGET OR SPORTING POPCORN WITHOUT RUNNING THE RISK OF GETTING SICK. FOR SOME REASON IT JUST DOESN'T SIT WELL. BUT STILL I INDULGE MUCH TO MY HUSBAND'S CHAGRIN. PERHAPS IT IS BECAUSE MOST DAYS I INDULGE IN THE RUN OF MILL 98% FAT FREE POPCORN AND THE RICHNESS OF THE BUTTER IS JUST TOO MUCH FOR MY POPCORN SATURATED DIGESTIVE SYSTEM. I LOVE POPCORN.

NOW MY LOVE OF PICKLES IS OFTEN A MISUNDERSTOOD VICE AND I HAVE BEGUN TO HIDE IT. FOR OTHERS THE THOUGHT OF ME GOBBLING DOWN AN ENTIRE PICKLE IS JUST TOO MUCH TO EVEN THINK ABOUT. PEOPLE SAY IT SMELLS BUT I HAVE NO IDEA WHAT THEY ARE TALKING ABOUT. FOR ME THE MERE THOUGHT OR GLIMPSE OF A BIG PICKLE MAKES ME SALIVATE. MY FAVORITE PICKLES ARE WHAT I CALL THE "GAS STATION PICKLES". THESE ARE THE ONES IN THE HUGE JAR THAT HAVE TO HAVE BEEN SITTING THERE FOR MONTHS SINCE THERE ISN'T NORMALLY A HUGE RUSH ON PICKLES. PERHAPS IT IS THEIR EXTENDED PICKLING PERIOD THAT MAKES THEM SO DELICIOUS. A CLOSE RUNNER UP IS THE "PICKLE IN A BAG". WHICH I BELIEVE HAS THE HIGHEST GROSS OUT FACTOR FOR OTHERS. SEEM PRETTY INNOCUOUS RIGHT? WELL, I LIKE TO DRINK THE JUICE. I KNOW A BIT MUCH BUT WHAT CAN I SAY? AT HOME, WE KEEP THE PICKLES IN A HUGE JAR STOCKED. WHEN I WAS PREGNANT PEOPLE WHO DID NOT KNOW MY HABITS VERY WELL AND ASSUMED MY PICKLE OBSESSION WAS THE BABY BUT THOSE WHO DID KNOW ME WOULD QUICKLY CORRECT THEM AND REVEAL THAT I AM JUST A PICKLE FEIGN. DID YOU SEE THAT MAN IN LOUISVILLE, KY IN 2004 THAT WOULD HAVE ABOUT 7 PICKLES IN A BAG IN HIS BASKET? YEAH - MY HUSBAND PLEASING HIS PREGNANT WIFE. OR THE CAR ON A ROAD TRIP THAT KEEPS STOPPING AT GAS STATIONS? YEAH - MY HUSBAND PULLING OVER AND LETTING ME SEE IF THEY CARRY MY COVETED PICKLE IN A JAR. I UNDERSTAND THAT THIS IS ALL A BIT STRANGE BUT I LOVE MY PICKLES.

NOTEWORTHY

i get

weak

Even before Sage was born, I've had a huge weakness for little girls' clothes. Val and I would shop together & wander into the girls' section at BabyGap, hold up outfits to show each other and say things like: "Awww! This is so cute!" Then, we'd reluctantly return to the boys' section to shop. Now, with my very own little girl, it's great to have the excuse to look in the girls' section & swoon. I know I have to be realistic and not spend to my heart's content, however. But it is so very fun to splurge each season on a few cute outfits for my best girl to wear. (Photo & journaling: June '08)

Love can come in all shapes and sizes, but for Leigh, it exists especially in the form of tiny, pink outfits on adorable, wee hangers! Leigh is powerless in the face of such delights, as her daughter's closet can attest.

materials patterned papers (My Mind's Eye, Making Memories) • letter stickers (Making Memories) • chipboard letters (Bo-Bunny) • stamp (Catslife Press) • buttons (SEI) • 8½ x 11 page by Leigh Penner, Morden, MB, Canada

love is an escape

Love can transport us to another world. What better way to take a break from reality than by escaping for a few minutes or hours to a more exciting—or more relaxing—life?

at the park with

{harry potter}

The way I see it, it's not actually neglect. Sure, we pretty much ignore our kids for two or three days when a new Harry Potter book comes out, but we ignore them at fun places, like the park. So that's ok, right?

Scott and I love Harry Potter. Years ago in Memphis, we started checking out the books on tape and listening to them in the car while we drove around the city, trying to calm crying babies. Scott read book 4 out loud to me while I made cookies to give as Christmas gifts for our neighbors. As each subsequent book has been released, we've taken turns reading it aloud to each other, spending the better part of three days immersed in J.K.'s world. The final book was released on a Friday night, and Saturday morning found us at the park, hoping the kids would play for a few hours so we could read as much as possible. That weekend we read while they watched movies, we read while they ate snacks, we read after they went to bed. We hated to see the book going by so fast, but we hated even more when we had to stop reading in order to take care of daily life. We loved being able to share the stories with each other and we can't wait until the kids are old enough that we can share the series again as a family. 8.08.

Autumn says that the best part about her obsession with Harry Potter is sharing it with her husband. "We don't have that many common interests, so I was excited when we watched the first movie together and he decided he wanted to read the books as well," she says. "I've been trying to incorporate more of the two of us into my scrapbooks, since they are so heavily dominated by pages about my kids."

materials lace paper (KI Memories) • ric rac (May Arts) • letter stickers (American Crafts) • Optima font • 8½ x 11
spread by Autumn Baldwin, Spanish Fork, UT

Once UPON a bath...

...there was a girl who, raised in a family on a budget, never knew the joys of a truly indulgent bath experience. Years of frugality had kept her from the bliss one can only achieve in the embrace of a tubful of moisturizing, aromatic bubbles. Calgon may take some people away, but this girl gets swept off her feet by cinnamon buns and lemon meringue pie. Truly... ...a match made in heaven!

Forget Paris! Stefanie says that, to escape the daily grind, she doesn't need to go any farther than her own bathroom. "I'm not a high-maintenance girl, but pampering bath products are very much an obsession of mine," she explains. She says she wanted to capture her attachment to her bath for some time, and this challenge was the perfect way to do it.

digital tools Photoshop (Adobe) • ribbons from "Afterglow" collection by Keri Schueller; lace from "Bouncing Baby Girl" dynamic brush collection by Erica Hite; frame from "Sweet Whispers" collection by Angie Briggs; flowers from pressed petals embellishment template by Brandy Hackman; paper from "Scalloperoo" kit by Ursula Schneider; fancy metals and inked edges by Cheryl Barber; alphabet from "All About Marriage" kit by Thao Cosgrove (scrapgirls.com) • Renaissance and Rockford fonts • 8 x 8 page by Stefanie Harris, Enterprise, AL

love is all-consuming

When you love to do something, you find a way to fit it into your day, no matter how packed your schedule is. In fact, take a look at where you spend your time—most likely, that's where your heart is.

I scrap almost every single day. It is how I spend my evenings winding down after the boys go to bed. And here is where I scrap....upstairs in the guest room. I love every single bit of my space!

Yes i Scrap!

If you're reading this magazine (or even just looking at the pretty pictures), we'll bet you share Michelle's obsession. According to her, there's no better way to spend an hour or two than with paper, glue, embellishments, photos, and a few treasured memories. Michelle, we couldn't agree more!

materials patterned papers, rub-ons (American Crafts) • Arial font • 12 x 12 spread *by Michelle St. Clair, Fuquay-Varina, NC*

re
news

That's me: a frustrated designer, a HGTV design star aspirant. And I can do it, too. Really. I've survived a major bath remodel that's now spread to the living room & basement. I have resurfaced walls, agonized over colors, and painted. Just last week I ripped paneling off walls. I can replace electrical outlets! It's exhilarating making the rooms in this house work instead of just making do, as we had to for three years. Now there's a magazine-quality master bath, renovated living/dining room, a functional & chic scrap area, and a soon-to-be revitalized family room/ play area. Now, everyday I walk through my house smiling. Now it really feels like home.

Hmm … just have to find a job with a big salary because I've got some ideas for that old kitchen …

create

Sometimes love sneaks up on you, as it did with Deborah. She was aware that her "new" 40-year-old house would need a coat of paint and an upgrade or two, but before she knew it, house renovation became her primary pastime—and she's moved far beyond paint and fixtures. "I thought my efforts would make a perfect topic to scrap, since it's been quite time-consuming. One project always leads to another, either by choice or because I find 'surprises,' " she says.

materials patterned papers (SEI, KI Memories, Scenic Route, Hot Off The Press) • metal embellishment (Making Memories) • letter rub-ons (American Crafts) • sticker strips (7gypsies) • 8½ x 11 page by Deborah Mahnken, Springfield, VA

love broadens horizons

Fall in love with a NASCAR fan, and you just might find yourself screaming at the Talladega Superspeedway. Fall in love with a cowboy, and get ready to sport a pair of boots. Love has a way of taking us outside of our ordinary boundaries and showing us something more, and the possibilities inside of us and the world around us begin to unfold.

"I am passionate about food (and the scale shows it!)," says Emilie. But the joy this hobby brings her far outweighs the potential drawbacks. Her love of all things edible has expanded her culinary horizons and given her a way to connect with others—particularly her husband, who gets as excited about a well-cooked meal as she does.

materials patterned papers (Scenic Route, SEI) • square punch (Marvy Uchida) • foam letters (Adornit) • Cricut die-cut letters (Provo Craft) • Arial font • 8½ x 11 page by Emilie Ahern, New Castle, DE

I own more than 50 cookbooks

I know what crème fraiche is

I have tasted duck, ostrich and shark meat

I own a Culinary Torch and I'm not afraid to use it

I record and re-watch the Food Network

I have baked and decorated an 8 layer cake

I have eaten at Peruvian, Argentine, Korean and Mediterranean restaurants in the past six months.

I could sit down to a place setting with 20 different pieces and know exactly which fork to use.

I know the difference between a mornay and a béchamel sauce

I can tell what a dish will taste like just by reading the recipe

I plan vacations around possible food experiences

I think Gordon Ramsey is sexy

i am a foodie.

When Courtney took her place at the starting line of her first triathlon, she had no idea she'd fall in love with the sport. "I love pushing myself to go where I never thought possible," she says. "That exhilarating feeling is why I keep racing. I realized who I am and what I can become." And isn't that what love is all about?

digital tools Photoshop (Adobe) • paper and brushes from "Pen and Ink" kit by Rhonna Farrer; bubble wrap stamp by Erika Hernandez; tag from "Sweet Spot" kit by Cherrie Mask (twopeasinabucket.com) • Script MT Bold and Ghostwriter fonts • 12 x 12 page by Courtney Koenig, Arlington, TX

My True Love

Crafting is the most fun when you're using a treasured item or technique. Our designers used their favorite products and methods to create some impressive items. Give them a try and you might find some true loves of your own.

5 STEPS — Love Rhinestones Card

Designer: Diane DiTullio, courtesy of Creative Imaginations

❶ Make card from cardstock; affix border strips stickers.

❷ Ink edges of circle stickers; affix.

❸ Cut thin strip of cardstock; adhere inside top of circle.

❹ Adhere flower and rhinestones.

❺ Adhere I love you sticker with foam tape.

Finished size: 5" x 5½"

While I like so many paper crafting products, bling is my one true love. I love the added twinkle and glamour that rhinestones bring to a card or other craft. It's one little detail that can add so much.

5 STEPS — B Mine Gift Bag

Designer: Alisa Bangerter

❶ Cut cardstock slightly smaller than gift bag; adhere.

❷ Cut smaller cardstock piece; stitch heart, using different thread colors and stitch types. Chalk edges and adhere.

❸ Apply rub-on to cardstock. Trim, chalk edges, and mat with cardstock. Adhere with foam tape.

❹ Thread string through buttons; adhere.

❺ Tie ribbon on handle.

Finished size: 5¼" x 8½"

Stitching on paper is a great way to add a nice finishing touch—with or without thread. Sewing is also a great way to attach items such as vellum, transparency pieces, and ribbon. Stitching without thread is a quick way to create a border. Stitches can also be the focal point of a craft.

SUPPLIES: *Cardstock:* (black) Bazzill Basics Paper *Chalk ink:* (Charcoal) Clearsnap *Accents:* (black rhinestones) Doodlebug Design; (pink flower) *Stickers:* (border strips, circles, I love you) Creative Imaginations *Adhesive:* (foam tape)

SUPPLIES: *Cardstock:* (pink, white) *Color medium:* (pink chalk) Craf-T Products *Accents:* (pink buttons) *Rub-on:* (b mine) Scrapworks *Fibers:* (pink stitched ribbon) Michaels; (white string) *Adhesive:* (foam tape) Making Memories *Other:* (pink gift bag) DMD, Inc.

Kindred Spirits Frame

Designer: Susan Neal

1. Stamp frame with Polka Dots Backgrounder.
2. Ink edges with both colors.
3. Stamp kindred spirits; stamp Bohemian Background on corners. Accent with glitter glue.
4. Stamp butterfly twice each on frame and cardstock. Cut out cardstock butterflies; fold in half and slightly curl wings. Adhere to butterflies on frame. Accent with glitter glue and adhere bugle beads to center.

Finished size: 6" x 7½"

Rubber stamps and ink are my one true love in paper crafting product because they offer endless creative possibilites!

Best Friends Card

Designer: Kim Hughes

1. Make card from cardstock; trim all but ¾" from front flap.
2. Trim transparency sheet and adhere in front of flap. Adhere cardstock strip in front of flap. Tie ribbon around flap.
3. Apply best friends rub-on.
4. Apply green flourish rub-on to separate piece of transparency sheet. Punch out, apply butterfly rub-on, and pin to ribbon.

Finished size: 6" x 4"

Transparency sheets give any craft a unique look. Using them challenges my creativity and helps me come up with great design ideas.

SUPPLIES: *Cardstock:* (white) *Rubber stamp:* (Polka Dots Backgrounder) Cornish Heritage Farms; (Bohemian Background) Inkadinkado *Clear stamps:* (kindred spirits from Hearts & Love set, butterfly from Garden Words set) Inkadinkado *Chalk ink:* (Chestnut Roan, Yellow Cadmium) Clearsnap *Accents:* (gold glitter glue) Ranger Industries; (gold bugle beads) *Other:* (chipboard frame, photo)

SUPPLIES: *Cardstock:* (white) Bazzill Basics Paper *Transparency sheet:* (Compass) K&Company *Accent:* (green safety pin) Creative Impressions *Rub-ons:* (best friends) My Mind's Eye; (green flourish) Crate Paper; (butterfly) Urban Lily *Fibers:* (patterned ribbon) Fancy Pants Designs *Tool:* (1¼" circle punch) EK Success

Ribbon Shadow Box

Designer: Nichole Heady

❶ Cut six chipboard squares to fit behind shadow box sections; cover with ribbon. Adhere to back of shadow box.

❷ Cut three stencil plastic squares to cover sections. Apply rub-ons and adhere.

❸ Create accents, as shown in photo; adhere with foam tape.

Finished size: 12¾" square

My true love is ribbon. Thin, wide, sheer, or satin. I love the hundreds of colors, patterns, and textures available. Because of the wide array I have added to my collection over the years, ribbon often serves as the starting point of my projects. I find it truly inspiring!

SUPPLIES: *Cardstock:* (orange, lavender) *Accents:* (heart die cut) My Mind's Eye; (red stick pin) Boxer Scrapbook Productions; (smile metal tab, purple clip) Making Memories; (genuine silver button) We R Memory Keepers; (white daisies) Heidi Swapp; (polka dot chipboard number) EK Success; (blue slide frame) Magic Scraps *Rub-ons:* (Jack Jr, Ricky alphabets) American Crafts *Fibers:* (assorted ribbon) *Adhesive:* (foam tape) The Paper Studio *Tool:* (scalloped circle punch) Marvy Uchida *Other:* (shadow box) Target; (stencil plastic sheet) Plaid; (chipboard, photos)

Winged Heart Card

Designer: Terri Davenport

❶ Make card from patterned paper; ink edges.

❷ Print image on cardstock and each patterned paper. Trim cardstock piece. Ink edges, mat with cardstock, and adhere.

❸ Cut remaining images from patterned paper. Ink crown. Adhere to cardstock piece.

❹ Affix "O" and "X" stickers.

Finished size: 5" square

Digital brushes have many of the same advantages as stamps minus the inky fingers and not-quite-right impressions. Although I've always been a rubber stamp fan, I enjoy digital brushes because they allow me to adjust the size of an image. Best of all, if I make a mistake, I can just hit the undo button!

Love U Forever Card

Designer: Anabelle O'Malley

❶ Make card from cardstock.

❷ Cut cardstock; round outside edges. Adhere.

❸ Cut patterned paper; round outside edges. Adhere.

❹ Trim felt flowers; adhere.

❺ Trim cardstock strip with decorative-edge scissors; attach brads and adhere. *Note: Ink edges of love tag and attach with brad.*

❻ Attach brad to felt flower; adhere.

❼ Ink edges of forever tag and tie to felt letter with twine. Adhere with foam tape.

Finished size: 4½" x 5½"

My current fetish is felt! I love all forms of felt accents—they add a nice texture to cards. I also enjoy stitching and accenting them with rhinestones and brads.

SUPPLIES: *Cardstock:* (black) Bazzill Basics Paper; (white) *Patterned paper:* (Sweetland Street from Rockland collection) Scenic Route; (Summers Day, The Rose from Shakespeare collection) Imagination Project *Dye ink:* (gold) Scrappy Cat Creations *Solvent ink:* (Jet Black) Tsukineko *Stickers:* (Mini alphabet) EK Success *Software:* (photo editing) *Other:* (winged heart image) www.designerdigitals.com

SUPPLIES: *Cardstock:* (black) Prism; (cream) Bazzill Basics Paper *Patterned paper:* (Black Polka Scalloped from Antique Cream collection) Creative Imaginations *Dye ink:* (Lipstick) Paper Salon *Accents:* (red felt flowers, brads) Queen & Co.; (felt letter) KI Memories; (forever, love tags) Making Memories *Fibers:* (twine) *Adhesive:* (foam tape) Stampin' Up! *Tools:* (decorative-edge scissors) Fiskars; (corner rounder punch)

Heartfelt Gifts & Accessories

⟨5 STEPS⟩ You Are Loved Mouse Pad

Designer: Kim Hughes

1. Cut patterned paper to fit mouse pad; round corners and sand edges.
2. Draw flourishes.
3. Apply rub-on.
4. Adhere paper to mouse pad.

Finished size: 8" square

SUPPLIES: *Patterned paper:* (Baywood Lane from Laurel collection) Scenic Route *Color medium:* (colored pencils) Around the Block *Rub-on:* (sentiment) Urban Lily *Tool:* (corner rounder punch) EK Success *Other:* (mouse pad)

(5 STEPS) Sugar & Spice Box

Designer: Beatriz Jennings

❶ Paint box; let dry. Distress edges.

❷ Trim patterned paper to fit box lid. Stitch and ink edges; adhere.

❸ Trim and adhere patterned paper strip to lip of lid.

❹ Tie ribbon around lid. Attach button and flower.

❺ Trim strip of patterned paper with decorative-edge scissors; adhere. Apply sentiment rub-on and sand edges.

Finished size: 3½" x 2½" x 1½"

(5 STEPS) Cross-stitch Tin

Designer: Melanie Douthit

❶ Paint tin; let dry.

❷ Trim patterned paper to fit sides of lid and tin. Ink edges and adhere.

❸ Tie on ribbon.

❹ Stitch button to butterflies; adhere.

Finished size: 2½" x 2½" x 1¾"

SUPPLIES: *Patterned paper:* (Susan, Lindsay) Melissa Frances; (pink ruler) *Dye ink:* (Old Paper) Ranger Industries *Paint:* (cream) *Accents:* (green flower, white button) *Rub-ons:* (sentiment) Melissa Frances *Fibers:* (cream twill ribbon) *Tools:* (decorative-edge scissors) Provo Craft *Other:* (paper mache box)

SUPPLIES: *Patterned paper:* (Megan, Ella from Honey Pie collection) Cosmo Cricket *Chalk ink:* (Chestnut Roan) Clearsnap *Paint:* (Parchment) Delta *Accents:* (pink button) Autumn Leaves; (butterfly die cuts) Cosmo Cricket *Fibers:* (cranberry ribbon) Piggy Tales *Other:* (metal tin)

Antique Sentiments Card Set

Designer: Danni Reid

GIFT BAG

❶ Fold down top of bag; punch two holes.
❷ Thread twill and jute through holes; attach tag and tie bow. ❸ Cut circles of patterned paper in descending sizes; layer together with foam tape. *Note: Bend edges of circles randomly for dimension.*
❹ Cut out bird from patterned paper; adhere with foam tape. Adhere circle accent to tag.

CUTIE CARD

❶ Make card from cardstock. ❷ Cut cardstock slightly smaller than card front; emboss and adhere. ❸ Adhere chipboard shapes. ❹ Punch butterfly from bag paper; adhere rhinestone and adhere to card. ❺ Apply rub-on.

HAPPY DAY & LOVE YOU CARDS

❶ Repeat steps 1-3 from Cutie Card.
❷ Cut circles from bag paper in descending sizes; layer together with foam tape. *Note: Bend edges of circles randomly for dimension.*
❸ Attach epoxy brad; adhere accent to card. ❹ Apply rub-on and Adhere seed pearl. *Note: Only adhere seed pearl to Happy Day Card.*

BEST FRIEND CARD

❶ Repeat steps 1-3 from Cutie Card .
❷ Punch butterfly from bag paper; adhere seed pearl and adhere to card.
❸ Apply rub-on.

HUGS CARD

❶ Repeat steps 1-3 from Cutie Card.
❷ Trace butterfly twice on bag paper; cut out. ❸ Slightly crumple butterfly; adhere to other butterfly. Attach epoxy brad; adhere entire piece to card. ❹ Apply rub-on.

Finished sizes: gift bag 8½" x 9", cards 4" x 6"

SUPPLIES: *Cardstock:* (white) Bazzill Basics Paper *Patterned paper:* (floral from Urban Prairie 6x6 pad) BasicGrey *Accents:* (chipboard flowers, bird) BasicGrey; (seed pearls) K&Company; (green rhinestone) Kaisercraft; (epoxy brads) Chatterbox; (acrylic tag) Maya Road *Rub-ons:* (cutie) Sandylion; (hugs, love you, happy day, best friend) *Fibers:* (white twill ribbon) Martha Stewart Crafts; (jute) *Adhesive:* (foam tape) *Templates:* (large butterfly chipboard) Scenic Route; (Swiss Dots embossing) Provo Craft *Tool:* (butterfly punch) Martha Stewart Crafts *Other:* (printed paper bags)

Pretty in Pink Box Album

BOX:
Cover box, lid, and inside with patterned paper.
Tie ribbon around box lid.

ALBUM:
Paint album; let dry. Adhere patterned paper and chipboard monogram to album cover. Create name label. Affix label and memories sticker. Tie rickrack around cover. Adhere patterned paper and accents to remaining pages of album.

Finished sizes: box 6" x 6" x 3", album 5" square

SUPPLIES: *Patterned paper:* (Stripe from Gracen collection, Pink Floral, Pink Polka Dot) Making Memories *Paint:* (Manila) Making Memories *Accents:* (chipboard monogram) Pressed Petals; (blue tab) *Sticker:* (memories) Heidi Swapp *Fibers:* (pink rickrack, green polka dot ribbon) *Tool:* (label maker) Dymo

The Sweet Things in Life Journal

COVER:

Journal front with patterned paper; adhere borders. Adhere remaining patterned paper and accents. Print section headers on cardstock; cut out, place in tabs, and affix tabs to pages.

Finished size: 7½" x 9¾"

BONUS IDEA

Divide your journal by months of the year and write down happenings and thoughts from each month. Include lists of things you're thankful for, fun things you did, or activities that you're looking forward to doing.

SUPPLIES: *Cardstock:* (kraft) *Patterned paper:* (Stripe, Red Dot, Rose Print from Gracen collection) Making Memories *Accents:* (scalloped floral borders) My Mind's Eye; (the sweet things frame, red flower, kraft heart) Cosmo Cricket *Font:* (your choice) *Other:* (tab dividers, composition notebook)

Wedding Wall Hanging

Designer: Kim Kesti

1. Double-mat two photos with patterned paper and cardstock; adhere to specialty paper.

2. Affix bead strips.

3. Trim photos to fit behind frame stickers; affix. Mat with cardstock and adhere with foam tape.

4. Spell "True love" and couple's initials with stickers.

5. Punch top and tie on ribbon.

Finished size: 12" square

SUPPLIES: *Cardstock:* (Lily White) Bazzill Basics Paper *Patterned paper:* (Aviary Garden, Dragon Flower from Cosette collection) GCD Studios *Specialty paper:* (Houndstooth 1 die cut from Sheer Delights collection) KI Memories *Stickers:* (bead strips) Glitz Design; (black frames, Poolside alphabet) American Crafts *Fibers:* (aqua ribbon) Offray *Adhesive:* (foam tape) *Other:* (photos)

Wedding Pillows

Designer: Beatriz Jennings

4EVER PILLOW

❶ Cut pillow from fabric, following pattern on p. 90. Stitch with right sides together, leaving hole at top; turn. ❷ Apply 4ever rub-on. Fill with fiberfill and stitch closed. ❸ Tie on ribbon. Adhere chipboard heart. Thread button with string and adhere.

Finished size: 5" x 4¾" x 1½"

ENDLESS PILLOW

❶ Cut pillow from fabric, following pattern on p. 90. Stitch with right sides together, leaving hole at top; turn. ❷ Apply endless rub-on. Fill with fiberfill and stitch closed. ❸ Tie on ribbon. Adhere chipboard flower. Thread button with string and adhere.

I LOVE YOU PILLOW

❶ Cut pillow from fabric, following pattern on p. 90. Stitch with right sides together, leaving hole at top; turn. ❷ Apply I love you rub-on. Fill with fiberfill and stitch closed. ❸ Tie on ribbon. Adhere flower. Thread button with string and adhere.

SUPPLIES: *Accents:* (glitter chipboard heart, flower) Melissa Frances; (cream flower; clear, cream, silver buttons) *Rub-ons:* (4ever and always, endless, I love you) Melissa Frances *Fibers:* (white, cream ribbon; cream string) *Other:* (white floral, tiny floral, red stripe fabric; polyester fiberfill)

Day to Remember Card & Box

Designer: Lisa Nichols

CARD

① Make card from cardstock. Trim cardstock slightly smaller than card front; adhere. **②** Trim square of patterned paper. Mat with cardstock. Trim strip of cardstock; adhere. Adhere ribbon around piece; adhere with foam tape. **③** Stamp sentiment on cardstock; punch and mat with cardstock. Punch scalloped circle from cardstock, pierce edges, and adhere stamped circle. Punch smaller circle and flower from cardstock; attach with brad. **④** Adhere to strip of cardstock with foam tape; adhere to card.

BOX

① Trim pattered paper to fit box and lid; adhere. **②** Adhere ribbon around lid. **③** Cut two strips of cardstock; adhere. **④** Attach brads to flowers; adhere. **⑤** Print sentiment on cardstock. Punch and mat with larger oval. Adhere with foam tape.

Finished sizes: box 4½" x 3½" x 2½"; card 5¼" square

SUPPLIES: *Cardstock:* (Very Vanilla, black) Stampin' Up! *Patterned paper:* (black and cream scrolls) Paper Studio *Rubber stamps:* (a day to remember from Sweet Celebrations set) Stampin' Up! *Dye ink:* (black) Stampin' Up! *Accents:* (pewter brad, decorative brads) Making Memories; (white flowers) Bazzill Basics Paper *Fibers:* (black polka dot ribbon) *Font:* (Times New Roman) Microsoft *Adhesive:* (foam tape) *Template:* (circle) Provo Craft *Tools:* (scalloped circle punch) Marvy Uchida; (¾" circle punch, flower punch, large oval punch, small oval punch) Stampin' Up!

Bliss Canister

Designer: Sharon L. Johnson

❶ Trim cardstock to fit around canister. Score vertical line every ½". Adhere around tin. **❷** Adhere ribbon around bottom of tin and lid. **❸** Stamp "Bliss" on cardstock. Die-cut/emboss into oval; die-cut/emboss ovals and scalloped oval from cardstock. Layer and adhere to stamped oval. Adhere rhinestones. Punch holes in stamped piece. Thread ribbon and tie ribbon around can.

❹ Attach flowers to pin; attach to ribbon. **❺** Stamp sentiment and butterfly on cardstock; color. Die-cut/emboss into circle; die-cut/emboss circles and scalloped circle from cardstock; adhere circles together and to lid. Adhere rhinestones. **❻** Tie flowers to ribbon; adhere. **❼** Adhere lace around can. Adhere rhinestones.

Finished size: 3½" diameter x 7½" height

SUPPLIES: *Cardstock:* (white, black) Stampin' Up!; (light blue) Prism *Rubber stamps:* (butterfly sentiment from Harmony Classic Circle III set; Special Occasions alphabet; Times New Roman alphabet) JustRite *Dye ink:* (black) *Color medium:* (blue, yellow markers) *Accents:* (cream satin flowers) Offray; (pearl head stick pin) Stampin' Up!; (black rhinestones) Kaisercraft *Fibers:* (black velvet ribbon) May Arts; (cream ribbon, cream lace) Jo-Ann Stores *Adhesive:* (foam tape) *Dies:* (embossed ovals, circles; scalloped oval, circle) Spellbinders *Tool:* (die cut machine) Spellbinders *Other:* (tin canister)

A

{ Marriage }

[MARIJ] 1. UNION BETWEEN A MAN AND A WOMAN
2. COMBINATION OF TWO OR MORE ELEMENTS
3. ULTIMATE COMMITMENT

FOR RICHER, FOR POORER, IN SICKNESS & IN HEALTH, FROM THIS DAY FORWA

I WILL MARRY MY FRIEND, THE ONE I LAUGH WITH, LIVE FOR, DREAM WITH

WITH THIS RING, I THEE WED YOU ARE MINE I AM YOURS TOGETHER YOU & ME

enjoy

BONUS IDEA

Include a matching blank recipe card in each invitation. Let the guests know to write down their favorite recipes on the cards and bring them to the shower for the bride-to-be.

RECIPE HOLDER

Red Floral Bridal Shower

INVITATION:

Make invitation from cardstock; mat patterned paper with cardstock and adhere. Cut bands from patterned paper and cardstock; fold around card and adhere ends. Tie ribbon around band.

ALBUM:

Trim edge of album cover. Trim edges of consecutive pages so each protrudes slightly when album is closed. Decorate cover and album pages with patterned paper, cardstock, ribbon, and stickers.

RECIPE HOLDER:

Cover folder cover with patterned paper; sand edges. Affix sticker. Use remaining patterned paper to mat recipe cards and place inside file folder.

Finished sizes: invitation 5" x 7", album 5" x 7", recipe holder 7" x 5" x 1½"

SUPPLIES: *Cardstock:* (Kraft, Pomegranate) Bazzill Basics Paper *Patterned paper:* (Rose Print, Red Polka Dot, Little Flower, White Polka Dot from Gracen collection) Making Memories *Stickers:* (wedding sentiments) 7gypsies; (enjoy) Heidi Swapp; (monogram A) *Fibers:* (cream organza, green satin ribbon) May Arts *Other:* (kraft album, expandable file folder)

Love Story Box

Ink or sand edges of paper and accents as desired. **PAINT** lip of box lid. Adhere patterned paper inside box; paint inside of box, dry-brushing paint over paper. Cover box and lid with patterned paper. Adhere labels and flourishes; ink heart and adhere with foam dot. Adhere love label. Embellish album with patterned paper, fibers, stickers, and accents. Create interactive pieces that lift and open with various messages inside.

Finished size: box 9" x 5" x 1½", album 8" x 4"

SUPPLIES: *Patterned paper:* (assorted from Romantica collection) Prima *Chalk ink:* (Sahara Sand, black, red) Clearsnap *Paint:* (Chocolate) Making Memories *Accents:* (love sentiments, bracket die cuts) Prima; (chipboard hearts, frames; love fabric label; flourish, decorative labels; brown photo corner die cuts) *Stickers:* (lined alphabet circle epoxy, black decorative circles) *Fibers:* (brown twill ribbon) *Adhesive:* (foam dots) *Other:* (chipboard accordion album and box) Heart & Home

INSIDE

Red Rose Love Album

ADHERE patterned paper rectangle and strip. *Note: Tear and sand edges of strip.* Mat sticker with patterned paper; sand edges and adhere. Adhere rose; adhere heart with foam tape. Double-mat photo; adhere inside album. Write journaling, add highlights with markers, and affix stickers. Apply rub-on to opposite page.

Finished size: 8" square

SUPPLIES: *Patterned paper:* (Leopard Print) Me & My Big Ideas; (cream/red polka dot, green polka dot, brown dots, blue distressed) *Color medium:* (black, gray, pink markers) *Accents:* (glitter chipboard heart) Heart & Home; (red velvet rose) Making Memories *Rub-on:* (I love you) Deja Views *Stickers:* (love label, gold glitter alphabet) Making Memories *Adhesive:* (foam tape) *Other:* (black album) Bazzill Basics Paper; (photo)

From My Heart Gift Card Holder

CUT 3¼" x 7½" rectangle of tan felt; fold in half. Fold up bottom 2½" to create pocket; stitch sides and around top and edges of pocket. Trace chipboard heart on red felt and cut out. Stitch to front of pocket and place gift card in pocket.

Finished size: 3¼" x 3¾"

SUPPLIES: *Accent:* (chipboard heart) *Fibers:* (brown floss) *Tool:* (embroidery needle) *Other:* (gift card; red, tan felt)

Little Book of Love
Designer: Stephanie Ackerman

Little Book of Love
Designer *Stephanie Ackerman* **Supplies:**
Patterned paper: (star from Black Line collection, red from Vintage Red Line collection) Jenni Bowlin Studio *Accents:* (cream buttons) *Rub-ons:* (flourishes, sentiment) Creative Imaginations *Fibers:* (black gingham ribbon) *Other:* (chipboard book) 7 gypsies; (photo) Finished size: 5" x 2½"

*Don't let another day go by
without telling that special
person how much you love
them. It's such a simple thing
to do, yet it makes such a
wonderful difference!*

We stick together. we look out for each other on each other. we depend have fun we give lots of other. we we me an the world Love we are Thankful to each other. for each other.

DESIGNER TIP
Pick a poem or quote that reflects the sentiment of the picture.

We Stick Together Frame

WRITE sentiment and create border around frame's window. Color key words and border with watercolors. Insert photo.

Finished size: 9" x 11"

This little frame was born in the wee hours of the night, with just a few markers and a fabulous quote. It's funny how creativity and inspiration come at times when you least expect it—and some of the most meaningful projects are the result.

—Stephanie

SUPPLIES: *Color media:* (watercolors, black pen) *Other:* (white frame, photo)

Life, Love, & Understanding Frame

WRITE or print quote on cardstock; color with watercolors. Triple-mat with cardstock; stitch border. Adhere patterned paper around edges of frame background. Adhere quote to background. *Note: Use foam squares or cardboard to raise quote so it touches glass.*

Finished size: 9" x 11"

SUPPLIES: *Cardstock:* (kraft, light blue, red, white) *Patterned paper:* (large stripe) *Color media:* (watercolors, black pen) *Other:* (shadow box frame)

Sentiments & Patterns

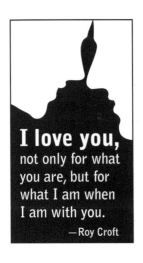

I love you, not only for what you are, but for what I am when I am with you.

—Roy Croft

"When you are in love you can't sleep because reality is better than your dreams."

—Dr. Seuss

Be Mine

"A kiss is a lovely trick, designed by nature, to stop words when speech becomes superfluous."

—Ingrid Bergman

XOXO

two lives, two ♡s joined together in friendship, united forever in love. —anonymous ♡

Happy Valentine's Day

Finish What You Started

Use these seasonal quotes to help you create a sentiment perfectly customized for any recipient.

Front of Card	Inside Card
"A kiss is a lovely trick, designed by nature, to stop words when speech becomes superfluous." —*Ingrid Bergman*	You can stop my words anytime!
"When you are in love you can't fall asleep because reality is better than your dreams." —*Dr. Seuss*	Thanks for making all my dreams become a reality. I love you!

Real love stories never have endings.

–RICHARD BACH

A happy marriage has in it all the pleasures of friendship, all the enjoyments of sense and reason, and indeed, all the sweets of life.

– JOSEPH ADDISON

May there always be work for your hands to do.

May your purse always hold a coin or two.

May the sun always shine on your windowpane.

May a rainbow be certain to follow each rain.

May the hand of a friend always be near to you.

May God fill your heart with gladness to cheer you.

–IRISH BLESSING

Kisses are the messengers of love.

–DANISH PROVERB

Love can make you do things that you never thought possible. –Phil Collins

I love thee, I love but thee
With a love that shall not die
Till the sun grows cold
And the stars grow old.

– WILLIAM SHAKESPEARE

Once in awhile, right in the middle of an ordinary life, love gives us a fairy tale.

Love is the master key that opens the gates of happiness. –Oliver Wendell Holmes

Grief can take care of itself, but to get the full value of joy you must have somebody to divide it with. –MARK TWAIN

There is no more lovely, friendly, and charming relationship, communion or company than a good marriage. –MARTIN LUTHER

A successful marriage requires falling in love many times, always with the same person. –MIGNON MCLAUGHLIN

There are a lot of fish in the sea, but you're the only one for me!

SO, FALL ASLEEP LOVE, LOVED BY ME....
FOR I KNOW LOVE, I AM LOVED BY THEE.

–ROBERT BROWNING

Your love puts a twinkle in my eye and a smile in my heart.

We might not have it all together, but together we have it all.

I am, in every thought of my heart, yours. –WOODROW WILSON

Flowers
and butterflies
drift in color,
illuminating spring.

"How does one become a butterfly?" she asked.
"You must want to fly so much
that you are willing to give up being a caterpillar."
—Trina Paulus

Anyone can be passionate,
but it takes real lovers to be silly.
—Rose Franken

When you meet someone
who can cook
and do housework,
don't hesitate a minute
—marry him.
—Unknown

Use these heartfelt and humorous quotes to help you create a sentiment perfectly customized
for any occasion or recipient.

Front of Card	Inside Card
When you meet someone who can cook and do housework, don't hesitate a minute—marry him.	Congratulations on finding the perfect guy!
Anyone can be passionate but it takes real lovers to be silly.	Thanks for being silly!

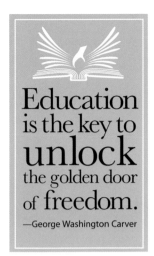

Education is the key to **unlock** the golden door of **freedom.**

—George Washington Carver

The key to wisdom is knowing all the right questions.

—John A. Simone, Sr.

If you find it in your heart to care for someone else, you will have succeeded.

—Maya Angelou

BE MINE

Be My Valentine

When the heart speaks, the mind finds it indecent to object.

—Milan Kundera

Success is not the key to happiness. Happiness is the key to success. If you love what you are doing, you will be successful.

—Herman Cain

☺ Valentine's Day

One of the keys to happiness is a bad memory

—Rita Mae Brown

LOVE YA

BE MINE

I believe that every human has a finite number of heartbeats. I don't intend to waste any of mine running around doing exercises.

—*Buzz Aldrin*

Everyone should carefully observe which way his heart draws him, and then choose that way with all his strength.

—*Hasidic saying*

Once you have them by the funny bone, their hearts and minds will follow.

—*Robert Wieder*

Empty pockets never held anyone back. Only empty heads and empty hearts can do that.

—*Norman Vincent Peale*

The key to your universe is that you can choose.

—*Carl Frederick Frieseke*

Finish What You Started

No matter the theme, you can customize quotes to fit the occasion. Send love and greetings to friends and family with these sayings that evoke the familiarity of home.

Quote	Inside of Card
Education is the key to unlock the golden door of freedom.	Congratulations on your acceptance to college!
One of the keys to happiness is a bad memory.	There's no need to apologize. It's forgotten already.
When the heart speaks, the mind finds it indecent to object.	I'm proud of you for following your heart. I know you'll be successful!

Trip over love, and you can get up. Fall in love and you fall forever.

—Unknown

Tell me who admires you and loves you, and I will tell you who you are.

—Charles Augustin Sainte-Beuve

Monogamy is fabulous. It gives you a deep and profound connection with another human being, and you don't have to shave your legs as much.

—Unknown

"I HAVE SEEN HIM IN HAWAIIAN SHIRTS," SHE SAID, "SO THERE IS NOTHING HIDDEN BETWEEN US."

—BRIAN ANDREAS

IF YOU DON'T UNDERSTAND HOW A WOMAN COULD BOTH LOVE HER SISTER DEARLY AND WANT TO WRING HER NECK AT THE SAME TIME, THEN YOU WERE PROBABLY AN ONLY CHILD.

—LINDA SUNSHINE

Your girlfriend's love advice is only as good as the relationship she is currently in.

—Unknown

There are things you do because they feel right & they may make no sense & they may make no money & it may be the real reason we are here: to love each other & to eat each other's cooking & say it was good.

—Brian Andreas

Love is an exploding cigar we willingly smoke.

—Lynda Barry

Have a quote you love that doesn't quite express what you want to say? Tie it to your feelings with a heartfelt addition in your own words. Sometimes a quote can be a clever way to say half a sentiment, but you can really bring your message home by personalizing it for the recipient or the occasion.

TAKE A QUOTE AND ADD YOUR WORDS

Quote:

Soulmates are people who bring out the best in you. They are not perfect but are always perfect for you.

—Unknown

Personalize it by adding, "I love you exactly the way you are."

Quote:

Trip over love, and you can get up. Fall in love and you fall forever.

—Unknown

Personalize it by adding, "I fell for you 10 years ago." (change the number to match your anniversary.

Marriage has **no guarantees.**
If that's what you're looking for,
go **live** with a **car battery.**
—Erma Bombeck

It's easy to **fall in love.** The hard part
is **finding** someone to **catch you.**
—Bertrand Russell

*To love a person is to learn
their song and sing it to them
when they have forgotten.*
—Unknown

*There is no remedy for
love but to love more.*
—Henry David Thoreau

Men and women belong to different
species, and communication between
them is a **science** still in its **infancy.**
—Bill Cosby

All I **really** need is **love,**
but a **little chocolate**
now and then doesn't hurt.
—Lucy Van Pelt from "Peanuts"

Love is a fruit in
season at all times,
and within the reach
of every hand.
—Mother Theresa

FINISH WHAT YOU STARTED

Take your favorite quote and personalize it with your own heartfelt sentiment. The well-known words will come to life in a special way for the recipient.

CARD FRONT	CARD INSIDE
To love a person is to learn their song and sing it to them when they have forgotten.	Thank you for reminding me.
I have learned not to worry about love; but to honor its coming with all my heart.	Congratulations on your engagement. (For older bride, second marriage, etc.)
There is no remedy for love but to love more.	Welcome to your new little one! (Adoption, birth, etc.)

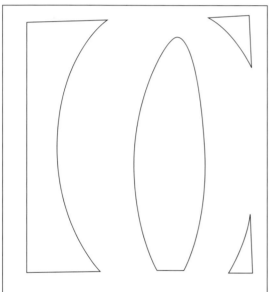

LOVE LETTER
Instructions on p. 226

**Love pattern
Actual Size**
Cut from 12″ x 3⅛″ strip
of Cardinal cardstock

LOVE LETTER
Instructions on p. 226

**Cover band pattern
Actual Size**
Cut from Brighton Love
Letter paper

I'M A SUCKER FOR YOU
Instructions on p. 114

**Heart pattern
Enlarge 150%**
Cut from reverse side of
Little Lady Stripe paper

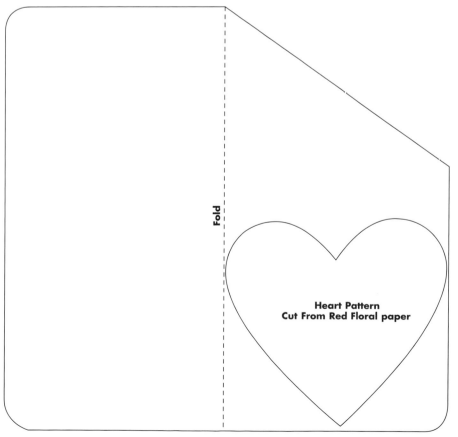

Fold

**VALENTINE
LOVE NOTE**
Instructions on p. 114

**Pocket card pattern
Enlarge 150%**
Cut from black card
stock: score and fold
where indicated.

**Heart Pattern
Cut From Red Floral paper**

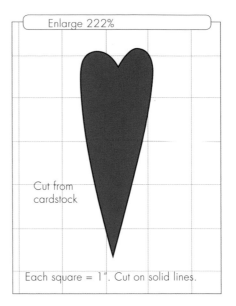

Enlarge 222%

Cut from cardstock

Each square = 1". Cut on solid lines.

GROW WITH LOVE JOURNAL HEART PATTERN
Instructions on p. 14

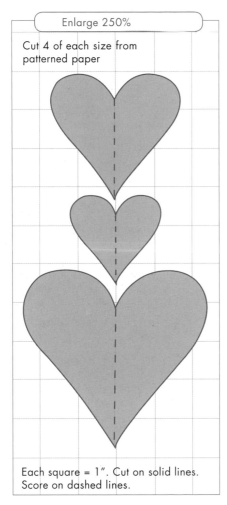

Enlarge 250%

Cut 4 of each size from patterned paper

Each square = 1". Cut on solid lines.
Score on dashed lines.

HEART ORNAMENTS HEART PATTERNS
Instructions on p. 93

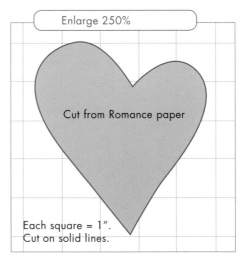

Enlarge 250%

Cut from Romance paper

Each square = 1".
Cut on solid lines.

AUTHENTIC CARD HEART PATTERN
Instructions on p. 88

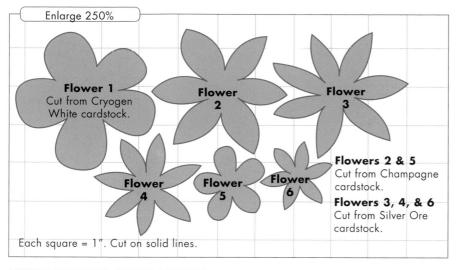

Enlarge 250%

Flower 1
Cut from Cryogen White cardstock.

Flower 2

Flower 3

Flower 4

Flower 5

Flower 6

Flowers 2 & 5
Cut from Champagne cardstock.

Flowers 3, 4, & 6
Cut from Silver Ore cardstock.

Each square = 1". Cut on solid lines.

WEDDED BLISS CARD FLOWER PATTERNS
Instructions on p. 181

Enlarge 250%

Card
Cut on fold from Cryogen White cardstock

Each square = 1". Cut on solid lines.
Fold on dashed line.

WEDDING BELL CARD PATTERN
Instructions on p. 182

WEDDING PILLOWS
Instructions on p. 263

Heart Pillow Pattern
Enlarge 200%
Cut 2 from each fabric
right sides together.

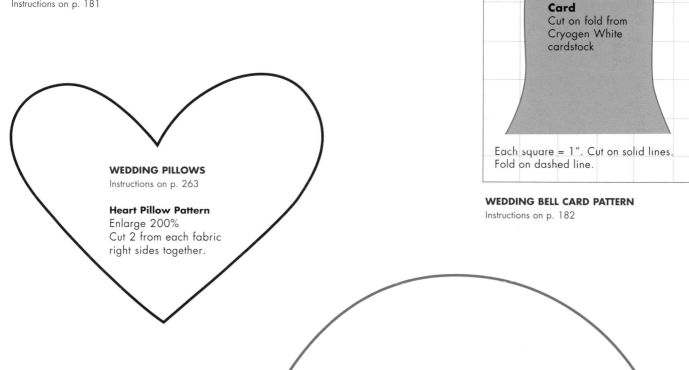

UMBRELLA BRIDAL SHOWER INVITATION
Instructions on p. 171

Umbrella Pattern
Actual Size
Cut 1 from Patio Umbrella patterned paper

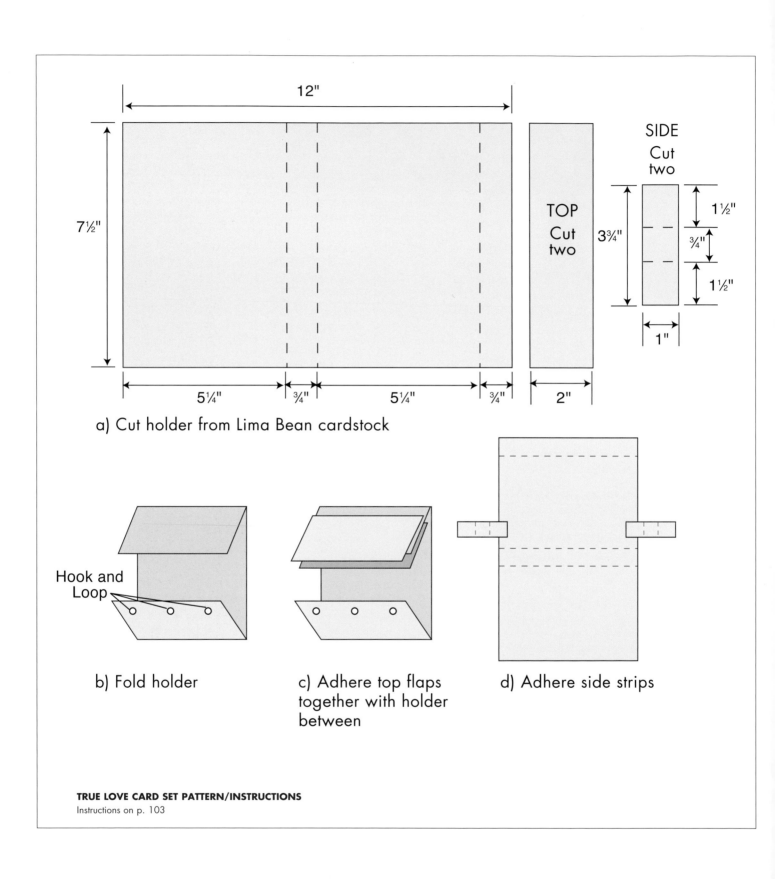

12"

7½"

5¼"   ¾"   5¼"   ¾"

a) Cut holder from Lima Bean cardstock

TOP
Cut
two

2"

SIDE
Cut
two

3¾"

1½"
¾"
1½"

1"

Hook and
Loop

b) Fold holder

c) Adhere top flaps
together with holder
between

d) Adhere side strips

TRUE LOVE CARD SET PATTERN/INSTRUCTIONS
Instructions on p. 103

Index

WEDDING ANNOUNCEMENTS

SCRAPBOOK LAYOUTS

Dating

Family

Friendship

LOVE NOTES

Love through the Years

Obsessions

Valentine's Day

Wedding

TAGS

Hello

Love

Valentine's Day

Wedding